PLAYBOOK

PLAYBOOK

FIVE PLAYS

FOR A NEW THEATRE

THE DEATH OF ODYSSEUS *by Lionel Abel*

THE TICKLISH ACROBAT *by Robert Hivnor*

TWILIGHT CRANE *by Junji Kinoshita*

THE IMMORTAL HUSBAND *by James Merrill*

A LEAK IN THE UNIVERSE *by I. A. Richards*

A NEW DIRECTIONS BOOK

CONTENTS

THE DEATH OF ODYSSEUS

Lionel Abel

for Gertrude

CHARACTERS

ODYSSEUS

TELEMACHUS

DESERTER

CAPTAIN

PENELOPE

SOLDIERS

The palace in Ithaca. A salon, with an opening on the beach, formed by two columns. Below, two armies are in contact, and we hear, from time to time, some of the sounds of war. A stairway to the left, to the right a throne. ODYSSEUS *is discovered, his back to the audience, resting between the columns. He faces the audience.*

ODYSSEUS. You are right. I am Odysseus.

He goes to his throne.

Not as I was when I set sail for home from Troy, nor even as when I arrived, long afterwards, battered from too many triumphs, on my own shores.

He sits back on his throne.

Less hale now, honored and sedentary, I, as you will no doubt remark, have put on weight. But, the fact is, I have no longing now to seek and strive and war as I did once. No, these days, there is even a certain coldness between me and the man I was, bringing off those bold and lucky acts for which I am known.

I am master of Ithaca, the island kingdom I made such unceasing efforts to attain, defeating, in so doing, the wrath of Poseidon, the rage of Polyphemus, the appeals of Calypso, the song of the Sirens, and all of the enchantments of Circe. Here I am, in my own land, come to an age and condition that surely entitle me to run no further hazards; for I have earned, if I say it myself, the right to coast on what I have already done. And "coast" is the very word to use in this connection, I think, since from now on, the way is obviously down.

Yet to what lies before me I bring an undiminished confidence. I know my capacities. Whatever happens will remind me of what I am at that very moment and of what I can then do. Age is not weakness: Weary, I am. Yes.

But this may even prove to be of help. Weakness, after all, lies simply in preferring some other type of strength to the sort one can actually exert. And as with one's own qualities, so with circumstance. The great thing, the capital thing, I have discovered, is this: one has to be in favor of the predicament one happens to be in. Who can do that? Odysseus.

Ladies and gentlemen, you may judge of my assurance by my willingness to be seen by you, and heard, and even overheard. Would I want you to understand what it might be impossible for me to endure? Would I want to tell you what the situation is in which I find myself, if I did not hope to master it? Certainly not.

About the situation. It is, briefly, as follows: An army has landed in Ithaca, bearing no banners, announcing no purpose, led by a daring and vigorous warrior, whose manly exertions I have observed all week with admiration and even—I can admit to it—a certain envy. Against his force my whole army seems to be of little account. For while the invaders do not exceed us in numbers, my men have shown little spirit, and thus far, in any case, have not had the qualities necessary for the defense of their kingdom. We have been driven back, and not step by step either. The invader has been able to secure his beachhead and bring his main force clear to my palace grounds. He must be stopped. No further retreat is possible.

He goes to look out through the columns.

I must have been mistaken about that. We have retreated again. Captain!

Enter CAPTAIN.

Captain, you sometimes answer me truthfully. . . .

CAPTAIN. You do me honor, Sire.

ODYSSEUS, *seated on his throne.* Tell me the truth, then, the whole truth, not just the encouraging part of it. What is wrong with our army?

CAPTAIN. The truth about our army, Sire, has to be the whole truth. . . .

4

He hesitates.

ODYSSEUS. Go on.

CAPTAIN. Everything is wrong with our army.

ODYSSEUS. Everything?

CAPTAIN. The soldiers break training, go off without leave, overstay their furloughs, are insolent to the officers, give way to illnesses, mainly fancied. They are covered with self-inflicted wounds and seize upon any and every pretext to avoid their duties.

ODYSSEUS. I know these conditions. What I want is your opinion as to their cause.

CAPTAIN. You still want the truth?

ODYSSEUS. Come, Captain, don't threaten me with it, tell it to me.

CAPTAIN. The faults of an army, Sire, must always be laid up to its chief.

ODYSSEUS. Well, I am the chief here. But I don't see how the faults of my soldiers can be laid up to me. Everyone knows of my exploits.

CAPTAIN. That's the whole trouble.

ODYSSEUS. Indeed?

CAPTAIN. Everybody knows that you, Odysseus, under all circumstances, never put your whole trust, if I may express the matter thus, in sheer physical courage, but were always attentive to what could be accomplished by wit. And thus you got the better of the brutes to whom you stood opposed. Everybody knows that while the other Greek leaders were bent on saving reputation, you, Odysseus, also had a view to saving your own life.

ODYSSEUS. Do I understand you to mean that my soldiers would be more courageous, if I had been less—adroit?

CAPTAIN. Excepting for your son Telemachus, there is scarcely a man in the Ithacan army, private or officer, who is not convinced—and on the basis of his very great admiration for you, Sire—that for a soldier to be killed in battle is to show lack of intelligence. Each one remembers that

5

while the bravest of the Greeks fell at Troy, you got through the wars and came home safe to your family.

ODYSSEUS, *musing.* Should I have died nobly like Achilles?

CAPTAIN. It would have been much better for the men in the ranks. The army would not be composed as it is, Sire, of stragglers, plain cowards, and as of now, deserters.

ODYSSEUS, *starting up from his throne.* Well, has it come to that? Are there deserters now?

CAPTAIN. Easy, Sire. As a matter of fact, one of them, whom I have arrested, may even interest you.

ODYSSEUS. Why?

CAPTAIN. He claims to have a relative fighting with the enemy.

ODYSSEUS, *exuberant.* Excellent! Perhaps we can find out who these invaders are. Send him to me.

CAPTAIN. He is waiting outside.

He claps his hands. The DESERTER *is brought in by two* SOLDIERS.

He was caught in the rear of our lines.

ODYSSEUS, *to the* DESERTER. You deserted your post?

DESERTER. Yes, Sire.

ODYSSEUS. And what is your explanation for such un-soldierly conduct?

DESERTER. Sire, I do not admit to being a coward.

ODYSSEUS, *softly.* Nobody admits to it.

DESERTER. Sire, a relative of mine is with the enemy. I do not want to meet him in battle.

ODYSSEUS. That's very interesting. Who is this relative?

DESERTER. I don't know, Sire.

ODYSSEUS, *cynically.* I suppose the fellow is a close relation?

DESERTER. That I can't say.

ODYSSEUS. Yet you are afraid to encounter him?

6

DESERTER. Yes, Sire.

ODYSSEUS. He might be only a cousin.

DESERTER. He might be closer to me than that.

ODYSSEUS, *exploding*. But this is preposterous. You don't even know who he is! And by the way, how were you informed of his presence with the enemy?

DESERTER. In a dream, Sire.

ODYSSEUS. In a dream! Look here—I am a reasonable man. But there is nothing in your story.

DESERTER. Sire!

ODYSSEUS. Besides, I hoped to find out something, and you have disappointed me.

DESERTER. Sire!

ODYSSEUS. Now, I won't punish you for that, nor even for your act of desertion. . . .

DESERTER. Sire!

ODYSSEUS. If you return to your post at once. (*Turning his back.*) Dismissed.

DESERTER. Sire?

ODYSSEUS, *turning about*. Haven't you gone yet? Don't you want to live?

DESERTER. I cannot return to action. I do not want to kill or be killed by a member of my family.

ODYSSEUS. And why not, may I ask?

DESERTER. Because this is a great misfortune.

ODYSSEUS. So is life, but we all—I am including you, too —want to put up with it and for as long as possible. Be off with you now. I have other things to think about.

DESERTER. I must refuse, Sire.

ODYSSEUS, *losing his patience*. You must refuse! Then you must be punished. And the punishment is death.

After a moment's reflection.

Well, I promise you this: the man who executes you will not be a member of your family. You understand?

7

DESERTER. Yes, Sire.

ODYSSEUS. We shall see if you are sincere. Captain, keep this man under arrest until noon, and if he does not consent to return to action by then, have him executed.

To the PRISONER.

I think I have treated you with consideration.

DESERTER. You have indeed, Sire.

The PRISONER *is marched out.*

ODYSSEUS, *looking after him, clearly puzzled.* Captain, that man is not afraid of dying. Which means, all men being cowards, that he must be much more afraid of something else. But of what? Could he have been telling the truth?

A voice is heard outside through an amplifier of some sort. The sounds are indistinct. ODYSSEUS *looks out through the columns.*

This whole matter bothers me, but I can't waste time now speculating.

Pause, while he listens to the announcement.

A magnificent warrior. His shoulders remind me of those of Ajax. Who can he be? And what has he said? In any case, he has found favor with my soldiers, for they are filling the air with helmets and hurrahs. I swear, he must have promised an end to the fighting! I must be informed.

Enter TELEMACHUS.

TELEMACHUS. Bad news, father.

ODYSSEUS, *returning to his throne.* I want the news, Telemachus. I can judge for myself whether it is good or bad.

TELEMACHUS. Who could have expected such a stroke from our antagonist? He has brought off a trick of propaganda worthy of Odysseus himself.

ODYSSEUS. His shoulders make me think of Ajax and his tactics remind you of Odysseus. What a paragon! But what was the announcement he made, which was received so favorably by our troops?

8

TELEMACHUS. He proclaimed that it was not his purpose to seize hold of Ithaca, to despoil the kingdom, or to take the life of a single person on this island, other than yours, Odysseus.

ODYSSEUS. He asked for my life? And my soldiers cast it to him, hip, hip, hooray?

TELEMACHUS. He offers to settle his argument with you by single combat, and thus put an end to the general fighting. None but the two chiefs are to face the shock and horror of battle. The armies are to have a spectacle. Of the two leaders, one shall have glory, the other a grave. So you see the great cleverness of it, Odysseus. For if you refuse to meet him and the fighting continues, your soldiers will think they are being sacrificed to your personal safety, and there will be no stopping them from seeking their own. Moreover, you have only until noon to give your answer. And if it is negative, the enemy will attack in force.

ODYSSEUS. And what would happen in that case?

TELEMACHUS. Total victory for the enemy, I should say.

CAPTAIN. And without many losses.

ODYSSEUS, *rising to reflect*. Can I accept this challenge? I am no longer young. . . . But I am still vigorous . . . against an ordinary warrior. . . . Who knows . . . ? But this challenger is most remarkable. But why does he not reveal his identity, and the nature of his quarrel with me? I don't even know his name.

TELEMACHUS. The reason for his quarrel with you, he did not state. But his name he told.

ODYSSEUS. Who is he?

TELEMACHUS. Telegonus, son of Circe. His father, he said, you would know.

ODYSSEUS, *for the first time loses his aplomb, and is reduced to mechanically repeating what Telemachus has told him.* I would know his father!—And he wants to meet me in combat? And I must decide at once? . . . By the way, does your mother know about this?

9

TELEMACHUS. She was outside the palace when the announcement was made.

ODYSSEUS. Then she must be on her way here. I'd rather not see her right now. Go—and keep her out on any pretext.

TELEMACHUS. Yes, father, but it won't be easy.

By the time TELEMACHUS *has mounted one-third of the way up the staircase to the left,* PENELOPE *has entered from right.*

PENELOPE. I am emboldened to inform you by all that has happened, that though you forbade me to do so, I sent to the Oracle for a prophesy of what is to come. Here is the message with the words of the god.

She extends a scroll.

ODYSSEUS. You sent to the Oracle, against my wish?

PENELOPE. I sent to the Oracle, but for your good. Am I forgiven?

ODYSSEUS, *harshly.* No, I do not forgive you.

PENELOPE. Then do not forgive me, but read the message.

ODYSSEUS, *still harsh.* Destroy the message! I do not want to hear the words of the Oracle. When have the Oracles spoken clearly? We ask them in anguish. They answer us ambiguously. And how else could they answer? For to ask what is going to happen to you is like asking who you are. I know who I am. I am Odysseus. I do not want to be informed about the future by the Oracle. I shall know the future when I myself create it. You may destroy the message.

TELEMACHUS. Father, is this wise? The fatal words have been set down. Should you not read them? To refuse would be impiety. Besides, are you not on the point of a very grave decision? I must say, my curiosity is boundless. . . .

ODYSSEUS. So is your mother's. But I think it is more because of her desire to know what has already happened, than what is yet to come. What I did, rather than what may befall.

PENELOPE. Odysseus, you are unjust! I have no desire to discover what you will not freely reveal. Here, take the message, and do not disclose the prophecy. I ask only if it be good or ill.

She again extends the scroll to ODYSSEUS.

ODYSSEUS, *shamed*. Let Telemachus read it.

TELEMACHUS *takes the scroll and unfolds it.* ODYSSEUS *leans back on his throne.*

ODYSSEUS. Well, is it good or ill, Telemachus?

TELEMACHUS, *stricken, having read*. So very ill. . . .

ODYSSEUS. I see that you who urged me to hear it, now would rather I did not. Well, you wanted this. Read the message. What is the word of the Oracle concerning Odysseus?

TELEMACHUS. The word of the Oracle, Odysseus, is that you are to die, this day, at the hands of your own son. . . .

ODYSSEUS, *starting up and stepping back*. No! That cannot be!

He advances threateningly toward TELEMACHUS, *who, however, does not give way.* PENELOPE *steadies herself against a column.*

Unless this is a plot! Have we treason here?

He looks first at TELEMACHUS, *then at* PENELOPE.

You both knew of this?

TELEMACHUS. By all that's sacred, Father, I swear I knew nothing of this.

ODYSSEUS. You swear it! By all that is sacred? But just what is sacred? My life perhaps?

TELEMACHUS. Father, take mine. Though I am innocent of intrigue against you. Do you think I want to live even this day out cursed by such a prophecy? Here!

He swiftly lifts Odysseus' dagger, and holds him off.

Plunge this now into my breast! No! I can best perform this office for you and for myself, also.

ODYSSEUS *immediately leaps forward and with the* CAPTAIN's *aid wrests the dagger from him.*

ODYSSEUS. By all that's wonderful!

He breaks into laughter.

I, too, was taken in. Even I, who warned against the Oracles. Didn't I say that when you listen to them you forget who and what you are? Telemachus, hear me. I say I was wrong to suspect you. As if you could be anything but what you think you are! As if you could hide anything from me. Telemachus! The enemy announced that he was the son of Circe and that I would know his father. I am his father.

PENELOPE. He is your son?

ODYSSEUS. By Circe.

TELEMACHUS. Then. . .

ODYSSEUS. The meaning of the prophecy is thus made clear. Not you, Telemachus, but Telegonus, is the son by whose hand I am supposed to die. . . .

TELEMACHUS, *greatly relieved.* Then you may not accept his challenge. . . .

ODYSSEUS. That is what I think also. So it is well that I heard the words of the Oracle. Well, too, though, that I knew how to interpret them.

Turns toward PENELOPE, *who is absolutely stricken.*

You did help me by sending to the Oracle.

PENELOPE. You have a son.

ODYSSEUS. So it appears. . . .

PENELOPE. A son by Circe. . . .

ODYSSEUS. Of that more later. Now we must be busy.

PENELOPE. Odysseus—

ODYSSEUS. I have not yet given my answer to my challenger. But at least I can now form a plan. I have it! Telemachus, you were ready to take your life just before, in order to assure my safety. Are you ready to risk your life and mine along with it?

TELEMACHUS. Yes!

ODYSSEUS. You shall meet Telegonus in my place.

PENELOPE. No!

ODYSSEUS. And my life will be staked on your success. If he prevails, I promise to surrender my person to him. But he shall not prevail. You shall carry my bow. With it I slew your mother's suitors. And you will gain the day for me. The Oracle shall be proved wrong. My son shall save me from my son.

TELEMACHUS. Are you willing to entrust your life to these arms, untried in war?

ODYSSEUS. I know their capabilities, yes.

TELEMACHUS. Then this, which began as the most desperate, has become the most fortunate day of my life.

ODYSSEUS. The day is not yet over and fortune may take another turn. But I approve your sentiment. And now to action!

PENELOPE. Odysseus!

ODYSSEUS. Captain!

PENELOPE. Telemachus!

ODYSSEUS, *to* CAPTAIN. Announce to the enemy that Telemachus shall fight in place of Odysseus.

CAPTAIN. But . . . ?

ODYSSEUS. And that Odysseus shall yield himself up to the challenger if the latter triumps.

CAPTAIN. Sire!

ODYSSEUS. No! There is nothing to discuss. Have this announced forthwith and bring me the enemy's reply.

CAPTAIN. Yes, Sire.

Exit CAPTAIN.

ODYSSEUS. Telemachus, put on your battle gear, you fight at once.

TELEMACHUS. I shall be ready, father.

Exit TELEMACHUS.

PENELOPE. You have a son by Circe. You never told me of Circe. . . .

ODYSSEUS. You never asked. . . .

PENELOPE. And yet you might have told. . . .

ODYSSEUS. Would that have comforted you?

PENELOPE. You could have given me the feeling that the two of us were thrusting away together the woman you took so completely into your arms.

ODYSSEUS. Why torment you with what was no longer a pleasure to me?

PENELOPE. And to think that during your long absence I wove and unwove the cloth upon my loom, loosening at night what during the day I'd spun, as if bringing my life back again to the point where you departed from it; and all to the end of keeping the suitors from my bed, that I might pass the night's best hours—unfondled, undelighted, and betrayed! That you did not spend your nights alone, during your absence, that I understood. But I did not think a rival would bear you a son, and that by his hand I should be deprived of you forever. . . .

ODYSSEUS. You forget that you, too, bore a son to Odysseus. His name, Telemachus. He shall fight in my place.

PENELOPE. Is the issue certain?

ODYSSEUS. Yes, that is, no. . . . In battle, nothing is certain. But Telemachus has fire—and youth. As for Telegonus, it is true that he is a great warrior.

PENELOPE. Greater than Telemachus, you mean.

ODYSSEUS. I did not say that.

PENELOPE. Odysseus. . . .

ODYSSEUS, *uneasily*. Yes?

PENELOPE. The Oracle has said that you are to die, and at the hands of your son.

14

ODYSSEUS. Yes, but I shall not meet him on the field. Telemachus will fight for me.

PENELOPE. But if Telemachus is not the victor, is not your life forfeit?

ODYSSEUS. To that I have agreed.

PENELOPE. Then . . . if the gods desire that you should fall, have you not drawn Telemachus into the pit prepared for you? If he fights and dies, you too die. And if the gods want you to die, what to them is the life of my son?

ODYSSEUS. I do not want to even consider that Telemachus may not be the victor.

PENELOPE. Shall I be deprived at one stroke of both Telemachus—and of you?

ODYSSEUS, *reassuringly*. I pledged my word to yield up my person if Telemachus falls but . . . I am not so ready to comply. . . . I shall not readily leave you alone. . . . If the moment for surrender comes, who knows, I may yet find some other course of action.

PENELOPE. Then your life is not really staked on your word, for which Telemachus shall risk his?

ODYSSEUS. I tell you I cannot even imagine Telemachus defeated. But if that be his fate, be sure that I shall have something to say about my own. Remember, I always had some trick that saved me at the last. Besides, I tell you, I have every confidence in Telemachus.

Re-enter TELEMACHUS, *armed*.

And here is our son. Is he not a brave sight arrayed for battle, Penelope?

ODYSSEUS *takes down his bow and hands it to* TELEMACHUS.

Here, carry my bow; you know the merit of it. But do not ask me for instructions. We have different qualities. My virtue lies in a certain craftiness. Rashness is just as much your virtue as it is your defect. So I am not the one to advise you. Fight your own fight.

PENELOPE. Must you fight, Telemachus?

TELEMACHUS. Yes, Odysseus has placed his whole trust in me.

PENELOPE. Odysseus never placed his whole trust in one other person; just as he never placed all of his love in one woman or his hope of continuance in one son. . . .

ODYSSEUS, *warningly*. Penelope!

PENELOPE. Very resourceful is Odysseus! At the moment he counts on you, Telemachus, but do not imagine that you are the only resource he has. If you live, he lives. But if you die, he does not intend to die. He will not keep his pledge to surrender his person. He will dishonor his word. He admitted as much to me. . . .

TELEMACHUS. I don't believe you.

PENELOPE. Telemachus!

TELEMACHUS. It is just that you do not want me to fight.

PENELOPE. Then ask Odysseus if he will keep his pledge if you should be the loser.

TELEMACHUS, *nobly*. If I asked him that I would show mistrust of him, and I want him to trust in me.

But it is evident that he has been shaken.

PENELOPE. How can you deceive him, Odysseus?

ODYSSEUS. I see that you will need my help if you are to betray me with success, Penelope. Do you want me to repeat to Telemachus what I said for you alone?

PENELOPE. Yes, tell him the truth. Do not deceive him. As you deceived me!

ODYSSEUS. Very well, then. For your better education, Telemachus, it is not absolutely certain that I shall surrender my person if you are defeated—though I count on you to win. Does this disturb you? Your mother evidently hopes it will keep you from fighting. But reflect: only a fool goes to certain death. When you risk your life, you possess it all the more powerfully; but when you surrender it without a struggle, you are more dead than are the dead.

TELEMACHUS. But you pledged your word!

16

ODYSSEUS. This would not be the first time I broke my word and lived to forgive myself for so doing.

TELEMACHUS, *bitterly*. I had faith in your honor and felt honored by your faith . . . but you do not trust me. . . .

ODYSSEUS. One can only trust a man who has decided to be reasonable. After all, when you meet Telegonus on the field it will be your life or his. I count on you to like yours best.

Trumpets sound. Enter CAPTAIN.

CAPTAIN. The enemy has accepted and is waiting on the field, Telemachus.

TELEMACHUS, *unsteadily*. Plan well and astutely, Odysseus. Plan now what you can do next. I fear for your life. . . .

Exit TELEMACHUS, *very unsteady*.

ODYSSEUS. I don't like that.

PENELOPE. His last word to you was a threat.

ODYSSEUS. Why, the boy counts on being beaten!

PENELOPE. You think that, too?

ODYSSEUS. This was your doing, Penelope.

PENELOPE. It was not I who sent him to fight, it is not my life he is to shield with his!

ODYSSEUS. It was send him or fight myself.

PENELOPE. Who but you should meet an enemy who is your enemy alone, of whose life you are the cause?

ODYSSEUS. That was the very reason—anyway, one of the reasons—I gave myself for not meeting him. It would have been father against son. What is he to Telemachus?

PENELOPE. But Telemachus is not a stranger to you. You can't let him fight now, Odysseus.

ODYSSEUS. No, I can't let him fight. There is no sense in letting him throw away his life, and with no gain to me.

PENELOPE. Then call him back now. At once! Odysseus! I am asking you for his life!

17

ODYSSEUS, *who is facing her from one end of the stage, does not move toward her.*

ODYSSEUS. I have no reason to let him lose it. I have every intention of saving him, even against his will. But it is not easy to thrust my breast before that of the one I hoped would defend me. I've never done that before, Penelope. It is something new and painful. It is like learning to walk.

PENELOPE. Odysseus! You will have to run now, if you are going to save him!

ODYSSEUS. I'll save him, never fear.

He slowly crosses the stage, reaches and embraces her, and then, turning swiftly.

Captain!

Enter CAPTAIN.

Stop Telemachus. He is not to fight. Bring him back here. Use force if necessary. Use force preferably!

Exploding.

The imbecile!

Exit CAPTAIN, ODYSSEUS *following him to the stairway and shouting after him.*

And announce to the enemy at once that Odysseus himself will meet the challenger in the field. That was what he wanted originally.

Looking at PENELOPE.

He will welcome the substitution. Quickly!

After a brief pause TELEMACHUS *is brought in held by two* SOLDIERS.

Ah, Telemachus, what a sight you make now, you who were so superb in arms before! Two strong men have to hold you back to keep you from rushing out to be soundly thrashed. So great is your desire to cast away your life and mine with it. And why? I never considered but that you would win. Your mother stirred up your suspicions, I know. Never mind about that. As if your death would make no difference to me!

Enter CAPTAIN.

CAPTAIN. The enemy awaits you on the field, Sire.

ODYSSEUS. Well, let him wait a bit. I shall meet him in good time.

CAPTAIN. I will see that he is so informed.

The CAPTAIN *exits.*

TELEMACHUS, *still held by the two* SOLDIERS. You are going to fight?

ODYSSEUS. Yes, Telemachus, despite my years, despite the Oracle.

Loudly.

Bring me my arms!

Softly.

Make me look fit for battle.

A SOLDIER *enters bearing a breastplate which he helps* ODYSSEUS *buckle on;* ODYSSEUS, *so fitted, notes that* TELE- MACHUS *has not relinquished his bow, and snatches it from his grasp; but* ODYSSEUS *is unable to string it.*

I should have liked to carry this bow. But no matter. Another may serve as well. Yes, I shall fight, Telemachus. And do you know why? Because I am a better risk, I think, than you would be. Besides, if you had flung your life away, and just to spite me, I might have given way to some slight inclination to die, too. That is a feeling I do not wish to have, one I abhor as much as I do death itself. . . . Always I sacrificed to life. . . . Today my sacrifice to it may be my life. . . .

TELEMACHUS. Father, forgive me for doubting you, accusing you. The truth is that I doubted my own courage. You do not inspire courage, though I see you have it. I thought you feared only for yourself. Let me fight. Even now.

ODYSSEUS. Too late, Telemachus. The enemy would not accept. Why should he? I can't make myself ridiculous at this point, changing my mind each moment like a woman, revealing to my opponent my fear. Since I am unlikely to win, I must at least think of the impression I make. There's a good reason for losing sometimes. Would anyone care about the impression he left who always came off victor?

TELEMACHUS. Your luck was always good; now I, too, depend on it. If you win, I'll forget my failure.

Exit TELEMACHUS.

PENELOPE. Forgive me, Telemachus!

ODYSSEUS. The next king of Ithaca!

PENELOPE. Then it wasn't true.

ODYSSEUS. No, it was not.

PENELOPE. You had no trick this time other than to fight yourself.

ODYSSEUS. You must have known that . . . for a while I thought your fear was for me.

PENELOPE. It was for you; you weren't wrong about that. But tell me, Odysseus, why did you grant the charge I made against you to Telemachus if you could have denied it fairly?

ODYSSEUS. I care nothing about fairness. But I had to know, when I saw Telemachus shaken by what you told him, whether my defender was a boy or a man. A boy could never beat Telegonus.

PENELOPE. Can anyone beat this son of Circe?

ODYSSEUS. Penelope, he is my son also.

PENELOPE, *bitterly.* You show your admiration whenever you speak of him.

ODYSSEUS. He has my craft, my skill in arms; my very recollections of Ajax are in his shoulders.

PENELOPE. What shall you feel when at last you stand before him? When the moment comes to strike—or yourself be hit—shall you wish him length of days?

ODYSSEUS. I don't know.

PENELOPE. Poor Odysseus. It is from the years of your life spent away from me that this threat of ruin has come to us both. This son of yours came here as your enemy.

ODYSSEUS. But what does he know of me? Only what Circe told him. And didn't I see you today turn Telemachus against me with only a few words? Think of what Circe must have told her son of me during all these years.

PENELOPE. This is the moment for frankness, Odysseus. Is not your life with me the truth of your life? Didn't you prove that by returning to me?

ODYSSEUS. Part of my life was in my wandering. It is as true—and as false—as the part I share with you. Can you forgive me?

PENELOPE. What is there to forgive?

ODYSSEUS. Forgive me my son by Circe.

PENELOPE. I could forgive you that.

They embrace.

ODYSSEUS. Then what else is there to forgive?

PENELOPE. There is the fact that he is going to kill you.

Exit PENELOPE.

ODYSSEUS, *alone, seated on his throne.* Is he going to kill me? I am filled with wonderment. Telemachus might have killed him and I would have approved. I would have pushed off the responsibility if Telemachus had laid claim to the deed. Once dead, this son so splendid would not trouble my night's sleep. He lives, and I shall never sleep to wake, or wake to sleep again.

He drowses. Enter CAPTAIN *bearing a sword, which he presents to* ODYSSEUS.

ODYSSEUS, *waking.* I am still king, am I not?

CAPTAIN. Yes, Sire.

ODYSSEUS. Surely, there are some affairs to set in order before I leave for combat.

CAPTAIN. Everything is in order.

ODYSSEUS. No one to be pardoned?

CAPTAIN. No, Sire.

ODYSSEUS. Then there must be someone to be punished.

CAPTAIN. There is just the deserter you questioned earlier, who is momently to be executed.

ODYSSEUS. That man is pardoned. Moreover, I must see him at once. Bring him to me.

CAPTAIN. Yes, Sire.

ODYSSEUS. *That man must live.*

He crosses over to the front of the stage and addresses the audience.

You see, it is always well to leave a task or two unfinished, a question not quite settled, a disorder in the making, so that there will remain something or someone still left for you to tamper with, when the unmending moment comes in view.

Enter CAPTAIN *with* DESERTER, *whose head has been shaved.*

ODYSSEUS, *to* CAPTAIN. Untie this man, Captain.

CAPTAIN. Yes, Sire.

Exit CAPTAIN.

ODYSSEUS, *to* DESERTER. You are well shorn.

DESERTER. That is how they prepare us for execution.

ODYSSEUS. The gods are stricter barbers to those they are set on destroying. They cut us from our very selves.

DESERTER. You are melancholy, Sire.

ODYSSEUS. In a few moments I am to face the enemy leader.

DESERTER. The whole army knows this and hopes for your success.

ODYSSEUS. What success can Odysseus hope for? The enemy chieftain is my son.

DESERTER. Is it possible?

ODYSSEUS. You recall your dream, I suppose. In my opinion, being a loyal subject, you dreamed for me. And now tell me this. Would it matter much whether I win or lose?

22

DESERTER. No, Sire.

ODYSSEUS. Suppose I kill my son, which I am not likely to succeed in doing?

DESERTER. Sire, that would be a great misfortune.

ODYSSEUS. And if I myself am slain?

DESERTER. I should have an impulse to take my own life.

ODYSSEUS. But . . . you would resist that impulse?

DESERTER, *ashamed.* Yes.

ODYSSEUS. Good. You are a good fellow, in fact a man after my own heart. You may go. You are free.

Exit DESERTER. ODYSSEUS *regards his throne, and addresses it.*

A judgment on your life, on your whole life, Odysseus, whose insufficiency is now laid bare. You are not serious enough, not simple enough, not severe enough, and not spiritual enough—no not to kill your son. For that, you haven't the gravity. Each peril you passed through successfully left you something less grave, though a little less lighthearted. Odysseus, I like you better than anyone, you see, I know just how much I like you. But I do not stand in awe of you. No, you may not kill your son. . . . So now I shall have to separate from you, Odysseus. I do not need your qualities. Cleverness will not help me, nor even the kind of courage I know you to have, the courage to find a way out, when there is a way out. In your own words, O wise Odysseus, only a fool goes to certain death. When I march from these halls, I must be more dead than are the dead.

He goes to the stairway, and turns to face the throne once more.

How could you go with me?

Halfway up the stairway.

Alas! At the end of its Odyssey the soul may not take counsel of Odysseus. . . .

Trumpet.

23

THE TICKLISH ACROBAT

Robert Hivnor

CHARACTERS

ELLIE SPROCKET, *American, plus or minus thirty.*

UNCLE HENRY, *fifty, firm holder of an unimportant post in the U.S. State Department.*

GORJO, *a very old native waiter.*

BABA MARCO, *thirty-five, wife of a local artist.*

JOE ZANELLI, *American, suitor of Anna.*

BASSETT PRATT, *an American archeologist.*

BOMOGRICA, *Mayor of all of Pomo.*

SUFI, *a doctor.*

ANNA
PAPA } ZUGO, *an ancient family of acrobats, now*
MAMA   *self-employed.*
UNCLE

LADY, *a native.*

Entire play takes place in a square of Pomo, a town in Dalmatia.

Act I.

Scene 1. *The square before the excavation.*
Scene 2. *First stage of excavation, Bohemia.*

Act II.

Scene 1. *Second stage of excavation, The Fort.*
Scene 2. *Third stage, The Temple.*

Act III.

Scene 1. *Temple restored.*
Scene 2. *The same.*

ACT ONE

Scene One

*The place is the square of a tiny hill town in Dalmatia.
Three stone houses compose the sides of the square.
Between the houses are two entrances to the square.
The center house is a café and wineshop.*

*It is early morning and the café is shuttered when the
curtain goes up but it is now opened by* GORJO. *He is
half-blind from sleep and a quarter-blind from old age
but he unstacks and places three of four tiny tables,
hangs up napkins and so on, with the grace of long-
established habit. Now through the east entrance comes—
slowly, feeling his way and with the serenity and caution
of a man who is used to hangovers—*MR. ZUGO. *He pauses
for support by a stone pole in the middle of the entrance.*
GORJO *sees or rather senses this and gracefully gets
brandy from the shop and puts a glass of this on the
table for the man at the post. The window of the house
on our right is now opened from within and we perhaps
get a glimpse of the woman's arm that does it and perhaps of a bluish tattoo upon that arm.* GORJO *puts another
glass of brandy on another table. Now a small, wizened,
ageless man comes out of the door of the house at right
and comes to the brandy.*

*The house on our left is more West European in style,
with French windows opening out onto a balcony over-
looking the square. Now these are thrown open and an
American lady, tallish, wide-ish, good-looking,* MISS ELLIE
SPROCKET, *comes out on the balcony. She is at the time of
her life when people are intrigued to guess her age.
26? 29? She is thirty, and good bones and good health
will enable her to remain so for years. She is in a robe*

27

and slippers and her hair is in some night style. She smiles with pleasure and breathes deeply.

ELLIE.

I must insist you come out now,
Otherwise you'll miss it all.
Come out, *please,* Uncle Henry!
(*With ponderous civility*) God bless you, Gorjo.

GORJO.

God bless you, Madame.

Her UNCLE HENRY, *a distinguished—but not offensively so—looking man of fifty-plus, comes out as if fearing the light. He speaks with filial grumpiness.*

UNCLE HENRY.

Miss what, the dawn?

ELLIE.

No, no.
The sun is the same everywhere.
I mean the *people* getting up.

UNCLE HENRY, *down his nose.*

These people?

ELLIE.

Look.
Like sailors coming out on deck
And hoisting up the Past
So it can be used once more.
Yes, Old Europe is good for yet another day.

UNCLE HENRY.

You call this Europe?

ELLIE.

Paris and Florence aren't Europe.
They're market places. Here, in old Dalmatia,
Here is the true Europe.

UNCLE HENRY.

Sailors?

ELLIE.

Not really.

28

I meant everyone in Pomo seems to have his little task
Like on a boat.

UNCLE HENRY.

What's-his-name there would be Albanian,
But the other one—

*Although Uncle Henry has been looking down his nose
at the two native men, his attitude is not that of snob.
He is saddened and made uneasy rather than confident
and superior.*

ELLIE.

Listen!

We hear a cry of a muezzin in the distance.

UNCLE HENRY.

What's that?

ELLIE.

The muezzin. He's calling the faithful to prayer.
Isn't it lovely!

The cry.

UNCLE HENRY, *nodding toward* BROTHER ZUGO.

But that one isn't a Moslem, I see.
Anyway he's not facing toward Mecca.
He doesn't seem to be facing in any particular direction.

ELLIE.

Oh, no, not Brother Zugo.

UNCLE HENRY.

What is Pomo, I mean as far as religion goes?

ELLIE.

A beautiful combination, I'd say. Moslem.
Orthodox. Roman Catholic. Yes, here
A call to the faithful wakes us up.
Not a rooster, not an alarm clock,
But a celibate on a tower! He calls,
The town stirs, and then the mores start.

UNCLE HENRY.

The what?

Two ladies, introduced to us later as MOTHER ZUGO *and*

*her daughter, come on bearing vases. They are partially
veiled.*

ELLIE.

                The mores.
The prehistoric habits of Pomo.
Look. It never fails. Those two
Each morning come up to the square
Then down again.

UNCLE HENRY.

    Up and then down?

ELLIE.

                I don't know why.
You would say they were emptying the slops,
But I say they are performing
A ballet of bodies and souls.

UNCLE HENRY.

    Ellie!

ELLIE, *a trifle loud for this time of day.*

    God bless you, Brother Zugo.

BROTHER ZUGO, *startled.*

    What? What?

ELLIE.

    God bless you.

BROTHER ZUGO.

    God bless you, Madame.

ELLIE.

Now look at the mountain. Why does one always develop
a kind of veneration toward mountains?

When he looks in the wrong direction.

That way! That way!

UNCLE HENRY.

    Not much snow up there. Too bad.
Ellie, I know you have to watch your pennies,
Or your drachmas or dinars or whatever they are,
And you have to have a house and a little help,

An expensive proposition in Paris,
Or Indianapolis, for that matter, but—
But *Pomo!*

ELLIE.

I love this town.

UNCLE HENRY.

Couldn't you love it from a distance?

ELLIE.

One of the reasons I love it is
That I'm part of the life. I don't sojourn:
I reside, I live, I help.
You know about the local wine. . . .

UNCLE HENRY, *a shudder.*

Ugh.

ELLIE.

And of course there is no local water.
The cheese is bad. The goats are wormy
And the wheat has the smut. But what's that?—
Economics. The faces of the people are right as rain.
My dear, troubles make them more human, not less.

UNCLE HENRY.

Oh, yes?

ELLIE.

And that is civilization, isn't it?
That woman there.

BABA MARCO *has come out of her house, despising the light, pains in every joint, and aims herself toward a table.*

Her husband left her.
Then one at a time her four children left her, yet
  she lives,
She lives. . . .

BABA *takes a nip of brandy.*

UNCLE HENRY.

She lives very well.

31

ELLIE.

> I remember the government man, Bomogrica,
> Who came here to try to get them to leave.
> He failed. Then he asked me—
> "What have they to live for here?"
> I said I didn't know. Then he asked me,
> "What have you to live for here?"
> And I replied, "For *them!* For *them!*"

UNCLE HENRY, *after shaking his head at this illusion.*

> What can you do "for them," Ellie.

ELLIE, *never sad, but sometimes reflective.*

> Well. Not much. Very little.
> I have my medicine cabinet, my advice.
> I write letters to interested parties.
> I bring persons like yourself to Pomo.
> And then, I share their grief. That's something.

UNCLE HENRY, *who has ceased to listen.*

> What is that grand odor I'm smelling?

ELLIE, *pleased.*

> Oh, the last of my Paris waters. *Eau de* something
> or other.

She gives him a filmy sleeve.

> Sniff?

UNCLE HENRY.

> No, I meant something cooking.

ELLIE, *disappointed but serene.*

> Shall we have breakfast?

They go off the porch.

At the table BABA *finishes her brandy with a cough.*

GORJO. God bless you, Baba.

BABA. God bless you, Gorjo.

BROTHER ZUGO. God bless you, Baba.

BABA. God bless you, Brother Zugo.

These are grumbles and greetings at the same time, expressing a kind of low-keyed fellow-feeling.

BABA. Did you see him?

She has referred to UNCLE HENRY. *They first nod, then shake their heads.*

I found a gray hair in my bedroom last night. It must have blown in from the street.

BROTHER ZUGO. What a joke on you!

BABA, *glancing at Ellie's house.* Politicians are vultures.

BROTHER ZUGO. Well.

He drinks.

BABA. They live on the dead. When they show up it's the beginning of the end.

BROTHER ZUGO, *the thoughtful drinker.* Well, a year off this life is a year on the next.

GORJO. Every morning she says it's the beginning of the end.

BABA. Should I say it's the end of the end?

A clenched fist.

Growing old in this town! Think of it. *Me.* I don't ask much. A laugh a week. How do I sound when I laugh, huh? Do you remember? I don't.

GORJO. I remember you laughing during the festival.

BROTHER ZUGO. I remember. Marie was living then.

BABA. A festival? What was it for?

BROTHER ZUGO. A harvest.

BABA. A harvest. Some towns have them every year.

JOE ZANELLI *has entered. He shakes hands all around in a way that indicates that he, although a foreigner, an American, is accepted as a friend. He is handsome, manly, athletic, and his swagger and somewhat overly violent movements contrast with the tighter, economical movements of the natives.*

33

ZANELLI. Are you sure it's a laugh you're talking about, Baba?

BABA. Are you sure you want to get up today, Joe? Have you thought it over?

To GORJO.

Tell him the bad news.

ZANELLI, *sitting down at a table.* GORJO *serves him.* Later—later—

BABA. Why do I stay in this hole, eh? Is it because I think my husband will come back?

She laughs bitterly.

ZANELLI. Let's all pretend we're happy. You first, Baba.

BABA. Happy!

She snorts.

You know who came last night . . . ?

ZANELLI. Yeh.

BABA. You know who he's going to see?

GORJO, *when* ZANELLI *doesn't answer.* He knows.

BABA. And you know at what time of day?

GORJO. If it had been good news he would have seen him last night.

All nod but ZANELLI, *who sighs.*

GORJO. That's right, Victor.

BABA. Gorjo, what are you chewing on?

GORJO, *with genuine perplexity.* I don't know.

BROTHER ZUGO, *gently.* Something he ate yesterday and forgot to swallow.

BABA, *fiercely, while* ZANELLI *laughs.* Oh this town! Ah!

This last refers to ELLIE SPROCKET *and her* UNCLE HENRY, *who move somewhat, or relatively, pompously down to a table apart from the natives and* ZANELLI. *As they do this the jug-bearing ladies cross the square.*

34

ELLIE, *her hand on his arm.* Oh, look. Now they're carrying empties.

A sigh.

That's how they walk in Heaven.

UNCLE HENRY *sits down. Nods to* GORJO.

UNCLE HENRY. Coffee?

ELLIE. You don't want to meet them?

UNCLE HENRY. You said they had to honor the stranger. Let them do that for a while.

GORJO *serves him with a flourish.*

Now ELLIE *shakes hands with* GORJO *and* BABA, *trying after the simple one-shake-per-person method of the country, but she is at once too feeling and too physical.* BABA *makes a face behind* ELLIE'S *back when the latter shakes hands with* GORJO, *who, in his position as waiter, would just as leave not just then.* ZANELLI *and* ELLIE *nod.* ELLIE *returns to her* UNCLE HENRY.

ELLIE.
Touch. How much better than words.
Every morning each of us wakes up into his separate
    mysteries.
Then we come down into the square and touch.

UNCLE HENRY. You missed the young man over there.

ELLIE. He's an American, actually.

UNCLE HENRY, *a quick look.* No! Well, thanks for warning me.

ELLIE.
                I'll tell you about him,
    If he doesn't tell you himself. Besides,
    I nodded.

UNCLE HENRY, *to* GORJO. Could you tell me, did a Mr. Pratt arrive this morning?

GORJO. Nobody came but Bomogrica.

35

BABA, *to* ZANELLI. That's a sad statement.

UNCLE HENRY. Then he'll be here this morning.

BABA. You see. Something is dying. The politicians are gathering.

UNCLE HENRY. What's this?

ELLIE. Unleavened bread. Yes, the kind Christ broke with his disciples.

Breaks it.

Perhaps St. Stephen in his wanderings ate such in this very square.

UNCLE HENRY. I know, but I *like* bread.

UNCLE HENRY *motions for* GORJO.

BABA. Jump, Gorjo, the foreigner.

GORJO *comes over.*

UNCLE HENRY. Brandy.

ELLIE, *disappointed.* Uncle Henry! In public.

Now BOMOGRICA *comes in the east entrance of the square. He is an official-looking person of (a guess) Turkish origin, but what kind of official, prefect, commissioner, it is impossible to say. But he seems to be a man of importance, even of power. His stomach and head are large. When he is speaking he is pompous—not so much so when listening. He would like to be cautious, but is unable to be so.*

UNCLE HENRY. Ah, Bomogrica.

ELLIE. Well, hello.

BOMOGRICA *smiles, bows to them, then shakes hands with the natives, bowing to* ZANELLI. UNCLE HENRY *drinks his brandy. Then* BOMOGRICA *comes over and shakes the hands of the two Americans.*

ELLIE, *of* BOMOGRICA. Did you see that bow?

BOMOGRICA. Madame. Sir.

UNCLE HENRY. Sir.

ELLIE, *to* UNCLE HENRY. Oh dear, I'm always confused

about how to address this gentleman. Is it Mayor, Prefect, Commissioner?

BOMOGRICA. Madame, my worries have no name. Just call me 'friend.'

To UNCLE HENRY.

At last we meet, so to speak, in the midst of our problem, in poor old Pomo.

UNCLE HENRY. Won't you sit down.

BOMOGRICA. The last report I made to the people here was from the wine-tasters. I hope I don't come to mean bad news to my friends here.

ELLIE, *to* UNCLE HENRY. They wouldn't even taste the wine; they just smelled it and passed on.

UNCLE HENRY. Speaking of bad news, your petitions have been rejected.

ELLIE. No!

BOMOGRICA. All those papers!

ELLIE. We'll fill out more.

UNCLE HENRY. I must discourage you both from re-applying.

BOMOGRICA. Was it—that American word—a technicality?

UNCLE HENRY.
No, no. I have all the stuff in my room.
We can go over it if you like.
But briefly the situation is, a dam
Is not practical because there's no snow on the
 mountain.
But I wish to compliment you on the fact
That the site you chose was a splendid one—
Had there been water.

BOMOGRICA.
Thank you. What about the—

ELLIE.
The minerals! Minerals!

37

UNCLE HENRY.

No deposits of any kind.
The geologists were amazed, I'm told.
To find soil so devoid, so pure, rather, of—

BOMOGRICA.

The Germans said that years ago.

ELLIE.

The bridge.

BOMOGRICA.

Yes.

UNCLE HENRY.

The point they made about the bridge is
You have to have something to cross a bridge *for*.
A bridge in itself is nothing. Your bridge
Led nowhere.

BOMOGRICA.

It led to here.

UNCLE HENRY.

Oh.

They look glum.

BABA. Ha, ha, ha, you see?

BROTHER ZUGO. What?

BABA. Bad news, ha, ha, ha.

UNCLE HENRY. However, there is one more thing.

BOMOGRICA. No more. Consider this local problem: How to keep my heart from breaking.

UNCLE HENRY. Let me say this first. One project has been accepted. Not by the government, but by a foundation.

ELLIE. But how interesting!

BOMOGRICA. A foundation . . . project . . . yes! But what are they going to do for Pomo?

UNCLE HENRY. Dig it up.

BOMOGRICA. What?

BROTHER ZUGO, BABA, GORJO. What? What? What?

38

UNCLE HENRY. I mean, of course, that this fund is willing to support an archeological investigation of the town.

BOMOGRICA. Is this a good thing?

ELLIE. A wonderful thing!

UNCLE HENRY. Won't you come in and have a look at the details?

They rise. BOMOGRICA *is pleased but mystified.*

BOMOGRICA. When do they start?

UNCLE HENRY. Right away.

ELLIE. I'm so glad. You know about Diocletian.

BOMOGRICA. Who?

They go off to ELLIE'S *house.*

BABA, *furious.* Gorjo!

GORJO, *contritely.* I know.

BABA. Why is it when he listens he breathes like this. *She wheezes.*

GORJO. I know.

BABA. No one can hear anything.

BROTHER ZUGO. I heard. No dam.

BABA, *to* ZANELLI. Did you hear anything?

ZANELLI. I was eating.

BABA. No dam. No electricity for another hundred years.

ZANELLI. Baba, people like you and me don't need bright lights at night.

BABA, *clutching her side.* That pain again. Right here. *Another place.*

Right here.

As ZANELLI *pats her arm.*

Well, I'm leaving. Going. If Marco—

Shakes head in anguish.

—if Zoë—if Paul—

GORJO, *severely. Speech broken up by his chores.* This

39

beautiful woman in her prime thinks she's unhappy. If I were to count her blessings I would need twenty or thirty fingers. Wife of a gifted artist. I look forward to the day when I can welcome him back to Pomo. Four children. If they could write, how many letters they would write home to their mama.

BABA's *attention is seen to be on something she hears.*

BABA. What's that?

She holds her finger up and beats regularly, her face showing a certain amount of dread. What she has heard is a man counting paces and approaching the square.

That awful noise! Oh!

Then BASSETT PRATT *enters and they all stare at this man of thirty-five dressed in loose khaki clothing. He seems to be combining walking with pacing out some measurement and what partly amazes them is that he enters the plaza not in one of the usual four ways but comes on a straight line and undeflected by any obstacle.*

PRATT *is a thin man of generally intellectual appearance. His face is handsome enough but what mars it, setting aside the essential glasses and curiously youthful haircut, is a certain overfocused look, an almost birdlike concentration, when he is at work. On the other hand, when not at work he relaxes very far from this into a listless, spasmodic, disarmed, boyish pleasantness.*

PRATT. Fifty-six, fifty-seven, fifty-eight. . . .

Now PRATT *sees them all, nods, smiles.*

Fifty-nine, Sixty. . . .

Stopping without losing step, to them all.

Good morning.

ALL. Good morning.

PRATT. Sixty-one, sixty-two, God bless you.

ALL. God bless you.

PRATT. Sixty-three, sixty-four.

Makes mark.

Any chance of getting some coffee?

All glance at GORJO, *who goes through the series of movements which have to do with a tiny cup and saucer and filling it with the "coffee" of the region.* PRATT *now stops, perched awkwardly on the ruin of the fountain in the center. He takes out a notebook, an eversharp pencil, and holding the notebook close to his eyes (he either writes small or is near-sighted), puts down his figures. After this he picks up the coffee, downs it with a gulp, suffers the dregs, then catches with his eye the sizable shoes of* ZANELLI. *He looks* ZANELLI *over.* ZANELLI *looks him over.*

PRATT, *finally, with mild cheerfulness.* North American?

ZANELLI. Yeh . . . North American.

PRATT. Say, ah—

A beginning of something, then he breaks off.

My name's Pratt.

ZANELLI *nods.*

I'm from Indiana.

ZANELLI, *finally.* Where at in Indiana?

He finishes his breakfast, pushes it from him.

PRATT. Bridgewater.

ZANELLI. Never heard of it.

PRATT. It's near Indianapolis.

ZANELLI, *extending his hand with sudden hospitality.* Man, I see you're the kind of Yank that speaks to other Yanks. I'm Joe Zanelli. Cleveland.

PRATT. Fine place.

ZANELLI *nods.*

What would you say about the people here?—Friendly?

ZANELLI. At first you're sorry they're unfriendly and then you're sorry they're friendly. Say, Jack, what's all this?

PRATT. What?

ZANELLI. Countin' things.

PRATT. I'm a—well, I'm with an archeological party.

ZANELLI. What's that?

Mainly suspicion.

PRATT. I'm going to have a look into little Pomo's past. I'm an archeologist.

ZANELLI, *after an instant of brooding.* I had a cousin who went to college.

Explaining.

Something wrong with one hand.

PRATT. What do you do?

ZANELLI. Before the war I played a couple of years of semi-pro ball.

PRATT. That explains the—

He points to the shoes.

ZANELLI. Yeh, before the war I was optioned by the Cards.

PRATT, *with true respect.* You were?

ZANELLI. Yeh.

PRATT. What position?

ZANELLI. Short. Second. Infielder. Then came the war.

PRATT. Then came the war.

ZANELLI. I got outa condition and I'm still outa condition. I'll die outa condition.

PRATT. How long have you been in Pomo?

ZANELLI. If this is July, about a year and a half.

PRATT. You must have a good reason to stay here that long.

ZANELLI, *after nodding in solemn agreement.* A woman.

PRATT, *a respectful pause, then.* The women are beautiful in this part of the world.

ZANELLI. Damn right.

42

PRATT. Everything else gone to pot. It's as if all the energies of the community were bent on producing one thing—beautiful women.

ZANELLI. Yeh.

He frowns at the other's eloquence.

PRATT. The men, on the other hand—

ZANELLI. A bunch of characters!

A moment of silence while they share their contempt for the local male population.

PRATT. You met this girl during the war?

ZANELLI. Yeh. Then I went back to Cleveland. Then I came back. I guess I'm stupid. Let me tell you how it happened. Fantastic.

PRATT. Well.

He glances at his watch.

ZANELLI. I'm a tail gunner. The *Mama Mia*, B-17. August, 1944. The big deal is almost over. We were coming back from Austria to Italy and got hit by some Messerschmidts which had made a mistake 'cause they wasn't supposed to be where they were. They shot us down just the same. I jumped.

PRATT. What happened to the others?

ZANELLI. I don't know. They jumped down the line somewhere. Anyway. Here I was floating down here and there was this carnival going on in this square. Up there hell busting out all over, down here—bagpipe music, yeh, that's what I heard first of all. Then there was these acrobats. I'm just coming to, still in the air, blood all over my face and I hear this music and then I see coming up toward me through the air this babe—her hands were together like she was praying—praying in tights—yellow hair—little tiny feet—beautiful eyes—and she smiled. Then she fell and her old man or somebody caught her. And guess where I came down! In the net! It was like I was part of the act.

GORJO. More coffee?

PRATT, *hurriedly.* No, no.

GORJO. Fizzy water?

PRATT. What?

ZANELLI. That keeps the coffee down.

PRATT. That's what I call a romantic meeting. And since then you've been looking for her.

ZANELLI. I *found* her.

Abrupt change of subject and expression.

Say, Jack—this job you're doing. Need any help?

PRATT. Hadn't thought much about it.

ZANELLI. I'm gettin' a little low.

PRATT. I think we can get together, Joe. Take this—

He thrusts the end of tape unwinding from a large spring drum type tape into his hands, rises and starts measuring again.

ZANELLI. Hey, just a—

But PRATT is walking to the west side of the plaza with the tape.

BABA. What are you doing, Joe?

ZANELLI. I don't know, Baba.

BROTHER ZUGO. What is the man going to build, Joe?

ZANELLI. I don't know, Victor.

BABA. He's an engineer. Isn't he, Joe? An American engineer.

GORJO. Someday there'll be shiny motor cars lined up right along here.

ZANELLI. How would they get here, Gorjo? By mail? You have to have roads.

BABA. Maybe that's what the man is making.

GORJO. Yes!

BROTHER ZUGO. I've always been a man who likes to watch things going up.

PRATT, *with his end of the tape, is standing under, or*

beside, ELLIE's *porch. She appears at the window, laughing politely from some social situation inside. But when she sees* PRATT *below her she stops and regards him with intense interest*

ELLIE. Uncle Henry, I believe our man has come.

UNCLE HENRY *comes to the balcony. He is joined by* BOMOGRICA. BABA *refers a contemptuous laugh to them.*

BABA. Look. Hah. Here's a man who gets things done.

BROTHER ZUGO. Bomogrica is drinking English whiskey.

GORJO. He shouldn't do that. Where? Where?

GORJO *looks the wrong direction, and this wrings a sigh of impatience from* BABA.

UNCLE HENRY. Yes, that's Pratt.

ELLIE. I had expected an older man.

BOMOGRICA. Shall we welcome him?

ELLIE. Yes, shall we?

UNCLE HENRY. I thought you avoided other Americans.

ELLIE. I meet them first. The poor boy will have his problems.

UNCLE HENRY. All right. Let's go down.

BOMOGRICA. When I was a boy there were German archeologists in Spurros and before the last war I met some English ones. But this will be my first American. . . .

They go in from the window and reappear soon at the west entrance of the plaza. In the meantime PRATT *has been putting chalk marks at various points.*

UNCLE HENRY. Doctor Pratt. Good to see you again.

PRATT. Mr. Sprague.

UNCLE HENRY. I see you found Pomo, at least. This is my niece, Ellie Sprocket. This is Director Bomogrica, who, I warn you, is a power in these parts.

ELLIE. Welcome to Pomo, Doctor Pratt.

PRATT. How do you do.

45

BOMOGRICA. I see you are losing no time. Good.

PRATT. How do you do.

ELLIE. Tell me, sir. What mysterious quest brings you to our little city? The lost arms of Venus or something like that?

PRATT, *smiles; he knows its a joke.* Well.

ELLIE. What satisfaction it must be—disrobing a town and seeing what it's really like.

PRATT. Well, uh.

ELLIE, *to* UNCLE HENRY *and* BOMOGRICA. What intellectual satisfaction!

PRATT. To tell the truth, I've never had that satisfaction. I've been digging, off and on, for ten years and I've never found anything.

BOMOGRICA. Nothing at all?

PRATT. I've dug in Idaho, Columbia, Iran, Egypt, and in every case we failed to find what we thought we might find. But of course scientifically that was very valuable: we proved what we were looking for *wasn't there.*

He laughs. They do not.

BOMOGRICA *reaches and grasps* PRATT *by the arm.*

BOMOGRICA. You'll find something here.

PRATT. I might come up with something spectacular, but that's not our main interest.

BOMOGRICA, *to* SPRAGUE. He has to.

To PRATT.

I have the honor of speaking for the citizens here, and I insist—

UNCLE HENRY, *smiling to* PRATT. Our friend thinks only of Pomo.

BOMOGRICA. Or rather I have the honor of whispering for Pomo. Speeches are for the common people but to you, I whisper.

Whispers.

Robert Hivnor

You *must* find something. We have no oil. No water. No sheep. No wine. Our only produce is—men. Our only export —human souls. Our only resource—our past.

BOMOGRICA *has gone into a florid speech-making manner.*

PRATT. Anything the matter with him?

UNCLE HENRY. He's not used to our gothic drinks.

BROTHER ZUGO, *to* BOMOGRICA. Well, what is it? What's the plan?

BOMOGRICA, *back to* PRATT. You'll find it. It's there!

BROTHER ZUGO *and* GORJO. What? What?

BOMOGRICA *now confronts the group of natives and we see him explain in native pantomime the "project."*

ELLIE. Is your wife joining you later, Doctor Pratt?

PRATT. I'm not married.

ELLIE. Oh. She would have enjoyed it, I was going to say.

Now we overhear what BOMOGRICA *is saying to* BABA, BROTHER ZUGO, *and* GORJO, *with the politician's jollity, which causes no one to be jolly.*

BOMOGRICA. Houses falling down—fountains broken— so you want me to fix them? Are you crazy? They're ruins! *Smiles.*

Pomo is the oldest city in the world.

All watch PRATT, *who is busy with an operation which concerns the door of* GORJO's *café.*

ELLIE, *to* UNCLE HENRY *and for* PRATT. The word "archeology" sounds so romantic to me.

BOMOGRICA, *to* BROTHER ZUGO. Ask him. He knows. In the race to be oldest, Pomo will be first.

ELLIE, *to* PRATT. One remembers scientists returning to dead cities and making them live again.

PRATT. Well. Oh. The trouble with this one is that it was never sacked or buried under an avalanche. It's been lived in continuously. That confuses the picture.

47

BOMOGRICA, *sincerely, almost bowing.* We beg your pardon.

PRATT *is becoming more and more engrossed with the problem of the door. He directs* ZANELLI *applying the ropes.*

UNCLE HENRY. I was thinking, Pratt. . . .

PRATT, *to* ZANELLI. Over. Over. Ah. Yes.

UNCLE HENRY. A thought occurred to me. . . .

PRATT, *to* UNCLE HENRY. Yes, sir.

UNCLE HENRY. Maybe a small museum would be possible here.

ELLIE. Yes!

PRATT, *busy again.* I—don't—know.

BOMOGRICA, *to* GORJO *and* BROTHER ZUGO. Did you hear that?

GORJO, BROTHER ZUGO, BABA. What? What? What?

BOMOGRICA, *to them.* Museums! Revolving doors. . . . Respectable people in Pomo again. Men with their wives. Museums!

We see him continue to explain.

ELLIE. That door. The warm complexity of it!

PRATT. Um.

ELLIE. Is it Roman?

PRATT. Oh, no, Miss Sprocket.

BOMOGRICA. Not Roman.

BROTHER ZUGO.
I've never been in a museum.

BOMOGRICA, *to* PRATT.
Understand you're looking for a museum.
Well, it's all down there.

Stamps foot.
You'll find it.

UNCLE HENRY.
Not *looking* for one.

48

BOMOGRICA.

> Egyptians used to come here
> To see how a really ancient people lived.
> Centaurs lined the entrance hall. . . .

PRATT. Are there any records of this museum?

BOMOGRICA. Crumbled to dust. That's the trouble with being the oldest country in the world. The museum fell down among the ruins—and ruined the ruins!

UNCLE HENRY, *to* PRATT. May I ask what that rigging is for?

PRATT, *almost happily.* You'll see. It's a good system. Used it before. Over the corbel, Joe!

ELLIE, *to* BOMOGRICA. Corbels! How renaissancy! The— the almost Shakespearean daring of it.

BOMOGRICA.

> Our Shakespeares lived before your Christ. We had
> a French Revolution before Charlemagne.

ELLIE, *to* PRATT. It *is* Renaissance, isn't it?

PRATT. No, no.

BOMOGRICA. No?

PRATT. It's nineteenth century.

ELLIE, *let down.* Here?

PRATT, *to* UNCLE HENRY. Simple block and tackle.

ELLIE, *to* BOMOGRICA. A scientist. . . .

BOMOGRICA.

> *Our* miracles of science came before the wheel.
> Hence civilized love was first made in Pomo.

ELLIE. I beg your pardon.

UNCLE HENRY. *Civilized* love?

BOMOGRICA.

> That's right. Ask Baba. Ask anyone.

UNCLE HENRY. Before then it was uncivilized?

BOMOGRICA.

> I won't describe it. Yes,
> The first lovers came from Pomo.

49

Over there there used to be shade
—Medieval trees—and out of there
Came our great surprise.

BOMOGRICA *totters near* ELLIE.

ELLIE, *to* UNCLE HENRY.

Hold up this amusing man.
                            The nineteenth century!
So that is history too! Already?
And all I can think of is men with beards,
And Queen Victoria sitting down.

This has been said watching the increasingly eager motions of PRATT, *as he prepares to pull down part of the door.*

PRATT. O.K.?

ZANELLI. O.K.

PRATT. All right, folks, watch and watch out.

BABA. Look!

GORJO. Which way?

Pratt laughs for the first time. He pulls at his rope, ZANELLI *pries, and rotten jambs, corbels, lintel give way and fall—or, in some productions—are flown.* BABA *and* ELLIE *scream and all shout.*

PRATT, *to* ELLIE. You don't believe there was a nineteenth century? Well, now, if you'll go over and pick some of those pieces up, I believe I can prove to you there was such a thing.

ELLIE. Oh, I believe, sir, I believe!

ACT ONE
Scene Two

Same place but not the same scene, for PRATT'S *willful little pick and knife have transformed—or de-transformed —the styles, if not the structure, of the houses from provincial Mediterranean simplicity into a more ornate, colorful folk architecture.* PRATT *has not peeled off all the walls, of course, but where he has we see bright pinks and blues and around windows and doors and along cornices somewhat schmaltzy peasant painting of, on the one hand, out-of-scale classical ornament and, on the other, those strange designs of circus wagons.*

The actions begin very much as the first scene: the light of dawn on the houses. The cry of the muezzin. ELLIE *comes to her balcony as before and again her gown tells us what a handsome figure she has.*

The muezzin calls.

ELLIE. Listen! I wish I could do that! . . . Wake up, Pomo. Wake up, Gorjo, it's time.

GORJO, *as if summoned, half-blind eyes half opened, opens shop and employs his habits to set the tables right.*

Ah, old faithful!

A horrible, viscous yawn from GORJO.

That face!—one of God's larger flowers opening to the sun. Good morning, Gorjo.

GORJO *is startled but doesn't respond.* BROTHER ZUGO *comes tentatively on.* BABA *kicks open her door. The muezzin again.*

How happy he calls this morning, as if he expected some mail from home.

She sees BABA.

Oh, that robe! I wonder—is ugliness just comic relief? I didn't mean that. Wise, worldly Baba. You have sinned and you will sin again. But you get up early in the morning.

51

In her own agonies of awakening BABA *has started for the wine shop, but half-way there she stumbles and falls.*

ELLIE. Oh, dear.

BABA *sits, dismayed.*

BABA. Gorjo, didn't you hear anything?

GORJO. Good morning, Baba. How are you feeling?

BABA. I fell down!

GORJO. Poor Baba!

BABA. I'm not drunk, you fool. I don't know what's the matter. My feet just went this way and that.

She gets up.

ELLIE. Unhurt, thank goodness.

BABA. Think of it. Me—mountain-bred, falling down!

ELLIE. Why don't these natives use their native intelligence? Can't she see our Mr. Pratt has changed her little pathway to the bar?

BABA *finds her morning table.* GORJO *places a brandy before her.*

BABA. Now kiss my hand

He does. She stares at the place where she fell.

GORJO. Baba. Baba.

Now the vase-bearing lady appears at the entrance to the square and UNCLE HENRY *joins* ELLIE.

ELLIE, *whispering.* Look.

To MRS. HURABI.

Well come, Mrs. Hurabi. Well come.

But as the lady passes through the square she loses her customary stateliness, her feet puzzle over the pavement, and her calm smile becomes more intense. Finally in a quiet panic she falls. The vase is protected, much as a baby is, but it is otherwise a catastrophe of bracelets, veils, shirtwaists, and three or four petticoats.

ELLIE. Oh, dear, Mrs. Hurabi.

BABA *offers to help but is waved aside by* MRS. HURABI, *who however does not rise but sits and thinks.*

UNCLE HENRY. Is she all right?

ELLIE. They would come to me if she weren't.

BROTHER ZUGO *has come in and has complained that his table is not set squarely on the ground.*

GORJO, *to* BROTHER ZUGO. No, no. My father taught me where to put these tables.

BROTHER ZUGO *jiggles a table.* BABA *jiggles hers.* ZANELLI *now enters, shakes hands with* BABA, GORJO, BROTHER ZUGO.

ZANELLI. What's the matter with her?

BABA. She fell down, poor old lady. Let her alone.

ZANELLI. Gorjo, my table—

GORJO *hops about, putting little wedges of wood under the legs. Now* PRATT, *in khaki working clothes, joins* ELLIE *on her balcony.*

UNCLE HENRY. Good morning, Pratt.

ELLIE. Doctor Pratt. Did you sleep well?

PRATT. Very well, thank you.

ELLIE. You didn't find the bed too soft? Too big? Isn't it enormous!

PRATT. It's very comfortable.

ELLIE. Austrian, I think. It's really *my* bed.

PRATT. Oh, then—I—

ELLIE. I've always found it comfortable.

PRATT. I don't want to put you out.

ELLIE. But I use the cot in here.

PRATT. I had planned to stay at the Buenavista, and—

UNCLE HENRY. You wouldn't like it there.

PRATT. Then let's make this a business proposition.

ELLIE. I'm a friend of Pomo, of science, of you, sir. Let it go at that.

UNCLE HENRY. Every morning Ellie comes out here and watches Pomo wake up. But has it ever occurred to you, Ellie, that just coming out here in that robe may wake the town up?

ELLIE *laughs and pulls her wrapper about her.*

ELLIE. One feels—in Pomo—one wakes up—further.

PRATT. Well, they all seem very awake this morning.

The fallen-down lady is whimpering. BROTHER ZUGO *and* GORJO *are trying and failing to stop a table from jiggling. Now the other three* ZUGOS *enter, in colored tights and cloaks, very tense for acrobats, looking for someone.* FATHER ZUGO *is, as usual, scowling. Their movements and stances will be parodies of the usual family group.*

UNCLE HENRY. Yes, what has happened to the "ballet of bodies and souls"?

ELLIE, *to* PRATT. Look, Doctor Pratt.

Quickly.

Must I call you that?

PRATT. Not "Doctor."

ELLIE. I mean—

PRATT. Bassett is my name.

UNCLE HENRY. Bad luck.

ELLIE. I *like* it. Those three, Bassett, with Brother Zugo there, the only one who drinks and smokes, are the famous acrobats.

PRATT. I've heard of them.

ELLIE. This is their first appearance in months here in the square. And do you know why they're here? I think it's the changes you've made, Bassett. So colorful. It's like—like they must remember it.

UNCLE HENRY. A little schmaltzy, isn't it?

ELLIE, *to* PRATT. You see the four I mean.

PRATT. I see the one on the end.

He has referred to the beautiful ANNA.

UNCLE HENRY. Beautiful girl.

54

ELLIE. In that cute Balkan way.

FATHER ZUGO *suddenly sees* ZANELLI *and reacts with controlled fury.* MOTHER ZUGO *at the same time puts her arm around* ANNA, *who smiles calmly at him.*

PRATT. That's Zanelli's girl.

Suddenly BABA *gasps and points at the pavement by the wineshop door and pulls over* GORJO.

BABA. Your wine's leaking.

GORJO. What!

BROTHER ZUGO. Oh, oh. Wine leaking!

GORJO *leans over, samples it with a finger, tastes, smiles.*

GORJO. It's all right, Baba. It's blood.

BABA. "It's all right, it's blood."

She hits her forehead. The table jiggles. The fallen lady moans. The ACROBATS *argue.* BROTHER ZUGO *joins them. Now* ELLIE *adds to this confusion by leaning over the balcony and shouting.*

ELLIE. Good morning!—May I explain?—May I explain?

At the top of the noise, enter DOCTOR SUFI *through the west entrance. Silence. Behind, making himself secondary to* DOCTOR SUFI, *is* BOMOGRICA. DOCTOR SUFI *is dark, slow, impressive. He is dressed in a long white coat and white hat (sikke). A stone amulet hangs from a long chain about his neck. He has rag leggings, and what is most remarkable about his costume are his shoes, on the tips of which are little bells.*

UNCLE HENRY. Well, look who's showed up.

DOCTOR SUFI, *quieting them.* Children—children—children of children.

He comes down. His walk is stately, not quite pompous, his dignity of the religious rather than the military order. SUFI *bows but does not shake hands. Sometimes as he walks—he is doing so now—he straightens his legs slightly so that the bells on his shoes jangle.*

SUFI, *when they have grown silent—except the occasional sufferings of* MRS. HURABI.

55

So much noise I didn't hear a little song of love. Do you hear it now?

He leans over and picks up a bug and holds it before his smiling face.

ELLIE. Isn't he priceless! His name is Doctor Sufi.

PRATT. I've seen sandals like that in India.

ELLIE. They're to warn insects to get out of the way.

UNCLE HENRY. I wish all the frauds of this world had bells on.

SUFI, *of the insect.* Wearing your jewels today, little one? You are not the only creature whose house has been disturbed. But what is home? A stop on the holy way.

PRATT, *to* UNCLE HENRY. Fraud?

UNCLE HENRY. With bells on.

ELLIE. He's very good for a back rub, actually.

SUFI. Goodbye, fellow traveler. Buzz buzz!

He gently launches the insect, which, judging from the recoils of BABA, MADAME ZUGO, *and* ELLIE *from its path, circles the plaza and then flies up and away. Now the moans of* MADAME HURABI *attract* SUFI'S *attention; he frowns and approaches her, examines her without touching her, while she jabbers beneath the veil and curtain of an unknown tongue.*

PRATT. It comes back to me now. He may be a member of the Moslem order of *Bektashi*—yes. They were chaplains to the . . . what were they?—Janissaries. They were celibates.

ELLIE, *a sigh of approbation.* Ah, yes.

PRATT. And mystics. I thought they were defeated by Mahmud a hundred or so years ago.

ELLIE. Oh, Europe. Dalmatia. Mystics! Celibates!

She has gone back to her usual mood of exultation when DOCTOR SUFI *suddenly kicks* MADAME HURABI *in the backside. She springs up, grabs her vase and disappears up*

56

the east entrance to the square. SUFI *smiles impassively and clasps his hands together while the bells jingle.*

UNCLE HENRY. The blow that cured.

ELLIE, *to herself.* How lucky to have that jar empty.

SUFI *moves up to* GORJO, *who is still kneeling over the rivulet of "blood."* SUFI *goes in the wineshop.*

PRATT. I see Bomogrica staring up here. Perhaps I should go down and face the music.

ELLIE. Leave it to me, Doctor Pratt!

They go in off the balcony. SUFI *comes to* GORJO.

SUFI. Gorjo, you must lower the price.

GORJO. What!

SUFI. Listen.

Drip, drip, drip.

Your cask is sprung. Drip, drip, drip. Sell it as it drips out.

GORJO. I can put it in skins.

SUFI. Are we shepherds? Peasants?

UNCLE HENRY, *remote and bored,* ELLIE, *wide-eyed and in front, and* PRATT *come down the west entrance.* BOMO-GRICA *greets them. There is much shaking of hands. Then—*

BOMOGRICA, *to* PRATT. May I present Doctor Ali Sufi.

SUFI BOWS.

PRATT. How do you do.

SUFI. Bless you.

ELLIE. You will be most interested in my friend and countryman, Doctor Bassett Pratt, Doctor Sufi. He is an archeologist and is responsible for the digging here.

SUFI. Yes! But I knew an archeologist had come last Tuesday when my men, I mean to say, my patients, told me of a stranger walking not along paths but over the hills, not over bridges but through the brooks. I knew then someone was following the old Roman road.

PRATT. That's right. I was.

SUFI. I welcome you not only to Pomo but to cities Pomo was built on. The mayors of those cities are all dead. I welcome you in their place.

PRATT. Thank you.

ELLIE, *to* SUFI. So very well said.

SUFI. After 1878 a German of your profession came here.

ELLIE. How interesting.

SUFI. He's buried in Spurros. Then after World War I some English came. And now an American. Well, I'm glad to meet you before you go.

ELLIE. Doctor Pratt will be with us a month.

SUFI. A month!

A step backward.

I thought you were finished.

PRATT. Oh, no. Coming up the valley I heard of your reputation as a healer.

SUFI. Bless you, *I* don't *heal,* I merely tailor the costume of death so it fits a little better under the arms.

PRATT. But you *are* a medical doctor.

SUFI. Yes. I was trained for better things, but my Order (*Sighs.*) was disestablished. Our monasteries are now hotels. Now you have to be married before you can get in. (*Laughs.*) However, I *am* a doctor, I am of this world, I heal, I serve bodies. And I come to Pomo to cure.

MRS. ZUGO *puts her arm around* ANNA *in the background.*
But what brings you here?

PRATT. Work.

SUFI. So I see. But what in *particular?*

ELLIE. He won't tell us, Doctor Sufi.

PRATT. I don't know.

ELLIE, *archly.* You must be looking for something.

BOMOGRICA, *to* DOCTOR SUFI. He has official permission.

Robert Hivnor

SUFI. But he says. . . .

PRATT. I'm not on a quest. I'm a scientist. We take one step at a time.

SUFI. Why didn't I know about this before?

BOMOGRICA. We only knew last week. I was going to send a boy. Was I wrong not to?

SUFI. No, I mean why didn't I foresee—

UNCLE HENRY. Of course, this might bring some money in.

BOMOGRICA. That's right.

PRATT, TO SUFI. Surely a lover of truth like yourself could have no objection to the digging.

SUFI. That depends on what you find.

UNCLE HENRY *laughs.*

PRATT. Well. Uh. I wouldn't be surprised if I found something of a religious nature.

SUFI. Everything is of a religious nature.

PRATT. Well. I mean—

SUFI. Not a Greek temple.

PRATT. Possibly.

SUFI, *to* BOMOGRICA. Another Greek temple.

SUFI, *to* PRATT. Some of us here are Greek, but many, like our friend here—

BOMOGRICA *bows.*

—are Turks.

SUFI. Why not a Turkish temple?

BOMOGRICA. It would be certainly better than this Serbo-Croatian gimcrackery.

UNCLE HENRY. Gentlemen. I appeal to your common sense. Doctor Pratt has no control over what he finds. He isn't looking for anything Greek—he's just looking. And I'd like to point out that as an American he can afford to be fair. He's not looking for American ruins, is he?

PRATT. That's right.

SUFI, *with hands clasped, head to one side in resignation.*
So be it. What a bright day! But to work! And what
deformities must Doctor Sufi gaze on now?

BOMOGRICA *whispers in* SUFI's *ear. He turns and regards
the acrobats.* PRATT *picks up his tools.*

PRATT, *to* ZANELLI. Well, Joe, on your feet.

UNCLE HENRY, *to* PRATT. If I were you, I'd cease and
desist for a while.

PRATT. Why?

UNCLE HENRY. You'll see.

BOMOGRICA *and* SUFI *have gone upstage, and after a quick
confabulation with the four* ACROBATS, *there are shouts
of joy from* BABA *and* GORJO. *The word passes around.
The* ACROBATS *go off.*

ELLIE, BABA, UNCLE HENRY, BOMOGRICA. A performance.
They're going up. Today? Right now! *etc.*

All take seats at the tables. GORJO *skips gracefully about
doling out coffee.* ELLIE *and her* UNCLE HENRY *sit at one
table, but* ZANELLI *and* PRATT *sit nearby.* BOMOGRICA *and*
SUFI *are apart.*

ELLIE, *calling to* BOMOGRICA. The new festive look has
inspired our little acrobats.

BOMOGRICA. Perhaps, Madame.

ELLIE, *to* UNCLE HENRY, *but for* PRATT's *benefit.* "Madame"
again. Dear me, will they never accept me.

SUFI, *to* ELLIE. You are right, my child. This new bright
bohemia the American has brought us has, as you say,
infused these artists with new confidence.

BOMOGRICA. Just artists. That's right, but an economic
asset to Pomo at one time. I think of the old days, when
the foreigners used to go to Venice and Paris and Rome,
and the Venetians and the Parisians and the Romans came
here.

BABA. I remember!

BABA *stands up, eyes sparkling.*

BOMOGRICA. Yes, you have the right to remember, Baba Marco.

BABA *goes to* BOMOGRICA *and they talk quietly together.*

PRATT. Who's she?

He has addressed the question to ZANELLI, *but* ELLIE *answers.*

ELLIE. Old Pomo was probably the last place in Europe where the old tumblers and acrobats and tattooed ladies and sword-swallowers and that sort of thing could be seen. This lady is such a relic, poor thing, of those days.

BABA *suddenly takes off her cloak, revealing a large shapely figure covered with bright tattoos.*

PRATT. I see what you mean.

ELLIE. The tattooed lady.

ZANELLI. But she's no freak. She's *somebody!* She's the town whore.

PRATT. Well—during my travels I've got to be very understanding of prostitution.

ELLIE. Oh?

BABA *is displaying her charms. The natives laugh good-humoredly. She performs for* PRATT *and* UNCLE HENRY.

BABA.

> As you can see, I'm the wife of an artist,
> The great Alexander Marco, son of Alexander Marco,
> Official tattooer to the Maltese Navy.
> He tattooed "Hold fast" on the hands of sailors
> To keep them on the yards, when the windjammers
>   sailed the sea.
> He tattooed smiles on the faces of the kings of Middle
>   Europe.
> But his son, my husband, was not interested in politics.
> God knows he believed in only two things,
> And one of them was Art.

ELLIE, *exulting again.* Oh, Art!

BABA *shoves a picture under Pratt's interested eyes.*

BABA, *pointing.*

> A popular group. Opus 8 to 12.
> When young, the son, my husband,
> Came under foreign influences—impressionism—
> Chartres cathedral. Note the diffuseness
> Of outlines lost in an atmosphere of color.

PRATT. Very good.

BABA. Circa 1910.

Turning to another area.

Now the reaction to all that. He returned to the Renaissance one February. Came home shouting, "I want to do a Rubens on a Rubens."

PRATT.

> His pictures were better than his jokes.

BABA.

> During that time I had five children.
> Me, blue all over with Agonies in the Garden,
> Annunciations, and St. Francis feeding the pigeons,
> Giving birth to pure white things!
> See the herds grazing here, and see the wise men
>   coming.
> They got real milk from this Madonna,
> School of Parma, and with their little fingers
> Pinched pilgrims going to Jerusalem.

PRATT.

> Very pretty.

BABA.

> Then came World War I.

She turns.

> Postimpressionism. Cubism. Vorticism.
> My god, I've been through them all.

PRATT, *laughing and pointing.*

> Surrealism.

BABA.

> Silly period.

PRATT.

A scar
With imitation stitches over it.

BABA.

That's not a tattoo, son.

PRATT, *peering close*.

This looks familiar. Eighteenth century. Something
ordo seclorum.

BABA.

It's the design on your dollar bills. Would you like to
kiss me there? Do you love money?

All the natives laugh.

BABA, *walking away and more to them all.*

Alexander Marco's
Mind was sharp and his needle was sharp,
And when St. Paul was crucified, see, in Rome,

Pointing out details.

He's upsidedown, all except the eyes,
I felt the pain in those little hands
And screamed, I can tell you. I screamed,
But it is a masterpiece.

ELLIE.

Poor woman. How it must have hurt!

BABA.

There is no art without suffering.

PRATT.

I thought it was the artist who did the suffering.

BABA.

Great art makes everybody suffer.

An appeal to PRATT *and* UNCLE HENRY.

Let's drink a toast for Art,
And to all those who gives themselves to Art,
As I have, God knows. I mean in wine.

ZANELLI, *setting* GORJO *in motion.*

Wine!

PRATT.

Wine.

ELLIE.

So early in the day . . . !

PRATT, ZANELLI, BABA *drink.*

BABA.

A toast to my husband-artist, Alexander Marco.
He believed in two things, Art
And the resurrection of the body.
Doomsday!

The natives gasp.

The fire which is prophesied.
Is it good that *all* will burn, I mean *Art* too?
But wait, Baba is in Paradise.
The blessed hosts are smiling on me there,
Remembering in Heaven the Louvre,
In Felicity remembering *The Rape of Europa.*
What? Who! How? Which? And
The believers (who believed so much) will doubt
Ulysses Setting Forth,
And *Hannibal Crossing the Alps.*

ZANELLI.

What Alps!

ELLIE.

As a child, I haunted museums.

The barks and yippees of the tumblers, and suddenly the
ZUGO *family run in. They, mother, father, brother, and
daughter* ANNA, *are all beautiful people dressed in tights
of contrasting and somewhat faded colors, but yet we
see that with all this beauty and the grace of their professional stances, uncle is limping, the father bandaged,
the mother humming nervously. Only* ANNA *seems whole.
She smiles at* ZANELLI.

BABA, *calling.* How do you feel now, Brother Zugo?

He shrugs. The ACROBATS *go through their preliminary*

64

movements. *They are at one moment rather melancholy semi-cripples searching out their pains with their hands in a more or less realistic way and at another moment smiling and graceful with professional and formal lightness.*

ELLIE, *to* PRATT. And *now* is Pomo softening your cold, scientific heart?

PRATT. Very entertaining.

ELLIE. And notice how clean their tights are. Dear Mrs. Zugo washes them out for every performance.

PRATT. They don't seem in very good shape.

ZANELLI. They used to work out on the high wires. Have you ever seen high wires? Man, eighty feet in the air!

During the period of entrance of the ACROBATS, BOMO-GRICA, *ever whispering, has led* UNCLE HENRY SPRAGUE *to* DOCTOR SUFI. *They observe but do not watch the acrobatics, instead seem interested more in* ZANELLI *and throw him several intense glances while they talk. The* ACROBATS *in the meantime are standing together with arms behind each other's back. Now* FATHER ZUGO *joins the three men and they all come over to* ZANELLI.

UNCLE HENRY. May I see your passport?

ZANELLI. Sure.

ZANELLI *gives it to him from his leg pocket.* UNCLE HENRY *has to straighten it out.*

UNCLE HENRY. This is in order. (*Returning it.*) Don't lose this.

To FATHER.

Now, Mr. Zanelli here wants to marry your daughter. But is she of age? She *looks* of age,

UNCLE HENRY *has looked.*

but what do the records say?

FATHER *and* MOTHER ZUGO *don't know what he means.* Or, if you and Madame Zugo were to tell me that she isn't—

65

ANNA. I'm sixteen.

UNCLE HENRY. Yes, yes, now
To the parents.
how old do *you* say she is? Fifteen?

ZANELLI. The age of consent here is fourteen.

BOMOGRICA. First thing those Americans learn.
To FATHER.
But you see how he works. Technicalities. This one failed, the next one won't.

UNCLE HENRY, *to* ZANELLI. Your passport tells me that you have to leave the country in three months.

ZANELLI. Yeh.

UNCLE HENRY. And unless you're married you can't take her with you.

FATHER ZUGO.
Sir, you see before you the Zugo family.
We are, with the principal royal houses,
The purest blood in Europe.
We never ruled kingdoms, but we ruled ourselves,
And kept before the walking masses
The somersault.

BROTHER ZUGO.
The handstand.

MOTHER ZUGO.
The cartwheel.

FATHER ZUGO.
Our performances please you, I hope,
But they save us. Remarkable—
To lead a disciplined and virtuous life,
Like great men, and cause no harm to anyone!

BROTHER ZUGO.
Except ourselves.

FATHER ZUGO.
Remarkable to have stood on our heads

66

Each day while the crusaders passed.
Remarkable to have practiced our art
Six hours before noon and ten hours after
And still find time to reproduce ourselves.

MOTHER ZUGO.
Remarkable.

ANNA ZUGO.
Remarkable.

FATHER ZUGO.
Love sanctifies us all.

Murmured agreement.

But we Zugos have not passions but ways:
All husbands have their duties.
But imagine, if you can, your wife falling through
the air.
Imagine catching her by the fingers.

BROTHER ZUGO.
Imagine not catching her.

FATHER ZUGO.
Each day we grow a little larger.
I must take this into account.
She must take this into account.
We play with a growing ball.

MOTHER ZUGO.
When you look up, think how carefully we must argue
To catch each other right. It's not only
Our gymnastics the Kings and Ministers of Europe
applaud.
Some of them are married too.
These days it is hard to maintain families
Even on the ground.

Murmurs of agreement.

UNCLE HENRY. I'm a bachelor but I think I can appreciate
your achievement.

ZANELLI. I'd like to say something.

FATHER ZUGO, *appealing to* UNCLE HENRY. He's not going to—

BROTHER ZUGO, *sternly, to* ZANELLI. Watch your language.

MOTHER ZUGO. Come here, Anna.

ANNA. Don't say you love me, Joe. It embarrasses father.

FATHER ZUGO. Embarrasses us all!

ZANELLI, *to* ANNA, *quietly*. I'm not going to *say* I love you, Anna.

The ACROBATS *cringe with embarrassment, especially* ANNA.

What I'm going to say is, they think I'm a peasant or something. Imagine a peasant at second-base for the Cardinals! But that's not the big thing. The big thing is she doesn't want to be an acrobat or an acrobatess or whatever you call them. She can't be. She's ticklish.

UNCLE HENRY. What's that? I don't have an ear for language.

ZANELLI. Look at 'em. They look like they been in a wreck. Of course everyone looks a little shook up in this town, but let me tell you what used to happen every Thursday. They used to climb eighty feet in the air, Papa, Mama, Victor here, and Anna. They would toss each other around until someone put his hands on her and she'd giggle and down they'd come. Mama. Boom. Brother. Boom. Papa. Boom. Then my Anna.

Doubling fist.

It made me feel like lamming somebody.

ELLIE. Could this happen anywhere else?

SUFI. This ticklishness keeps her from performing. It also keeps her from being a wife.

ZANELLI. Agh!

ANNA. I don't feel ticklish tonight.

UNCLE HENRY. Are you saying that to your father or Mr. Zanelli.

DOCTOR SUFI. To me, perhaps.

To ANNA.

You think you're cured?

ANNA. Yes, I have that feeling.

FATHER ZUGO. But we asked the Doctor over especially to see you.

BROTHER ZUGO, *with hand on his bandage.* And me.

DOCTOR SUFI. Well, let's see. On with the show.

Applause and a scattering to give the ACROBATS, *or rather, tumblers, room. As they take their stance all signs of disability vanish; they become smiling, agile, professional. Now follows a tumbling act at the climax of which* ANNA *is carried and during which, at the crucial moment, she giggles. They all fall down, and while they quickly recover, and bow and smile,* ANNA *cries and all their hurts and pains come back.*

ZANELLI. See what I mean.

ELLIE, *applauding.* I thought you were so good.

To those around her.

Gifted artists, all of them.

ANNA *sobs.*

SUFI, *to* FATHER ZUGO.

Now Hugo, I'll confess to you,
I'm no demigod, no saint, no virgin
Casting out the devil. I'm just
The greatest psychotherapeutic human being in the
      world.

FATHER ZUGO. Ah.

SUFI. If man can cure her, I can.

FATHER ZUGO. Just cure her of the ticklishness, nothing else.

SUFI. That's a great deal. Confess, Papa, none of us can stand being laughed at by a woman. And one's daughter too.

FATHER ZUGO. Cure her!

DOCTOR SUFI *takes* ANNA *over to the other side of the stage.*

ZANELLI. You know, back in the States we know a little bit about curing hiccups and ticklishness and things like that. Right, Jack?

BABA. They've tried everything.

ZANELLI. I mean it's *deep*. It has something to do with the sex set-up.

BABA. Is that your idea of something deep?

ZANELLI. This doesn't worry me a bit. They got the cart before the horse. I'd marry her first—that'd cure the ticklishness.

BABA, *nodding.* She'd never smile again.

PRATT. There's something in what you say.

Watching ANNA *and* DOCTOR SUFI *in consultation.*

Surely they're not going to let that quack fiddle with her.

ZANELLI, *rising.* Hey! Take it easy. You're not going to let that quack fiddle with her!

SUFI. Quack?

ZANELLI. I don't mean anything personal, Doc, but man alive, let's be civilized about this. I'm getting tired of people putting spoons down her back and making her sit in a tub of cold water. Anna, I think I can cure you. Will you give me a chance?

ANNA *turns to her mother, who embraces her.*

PRATT. What are you going to do, Joe, seduce her?

UNCLE HENRY. He'd never live to tell about it.

ZANELLI. Hypnosis.

SUFI, *interested.* What's that?

ZANELLI. Back in the States I was quite a hypnotist.

SUFI. How do you spell it?

70

ZANELLI. Some of us guys in the gang used to hypnotize girls at parties. You know, get them to wash the dishes and that sort of thing.

PRATT. It might work.

SUFI. Would this be an experiment?

ZANELLI. Yeh!

SUFI, *pleased.* Ah. If you want to *experiment*, Yank, well, go ahead.

FATHER ZUGO. What?!

BROTHER ZUGO, *to* FATHER ZUGO. Don't you believe in science?

FATHER ZUGO. Is *this* science?

ZANELLI *approaches* ANNA, *bows, takes her hand and leads her to steps of wineshop center.*

MAMA ZUGO. Tell the man the troublesome area, Anna.

ZANELLI. I'll find it, Mama.

They sit down.

Anna, honey, first I'm going to put you to sleep. Sleep is a very natural thing. So don't be afraid. Don't be afraid to feel your eyelids getting heavy . . . eyelids getting heavy. Relax.

ZANELLI *lifts up one arm and lets it fall; it is dead weight.*

UNCLE HENRY. A very willing subject.

SUFI. A beautiful trance.

ZANELLI, *back to business.* Now, Anna, you are in America. It is night in America, practically morning, as a matter of fact. You are sitting in the front seat of a Buick.

ANNA. A what?

ZANELLI. A car. O.K., a big front seat. We're parked. The radio is playin'. It's a little bit chilly.

ANNA *shudders.*

You move over to me in the driver's seat. Your leg touches the sharp crease in my pants.

71

ZANELLI *is seated beside her and acting out his part.*

ZANELLI. It's Saturday night. We've been out dancin' or somethin'. We always go out dancin' or somethin' on Saturday night. You're a little tired. Just a little. But your back is way back in the seat. That's the way the girls sit in the States.

ANNA *lolls in an ungainly fashion.*

Yeh, that's right, one leg out. You're lickin' the corner of your mouth where you got a tooth filled or something. You don't care how you look 'cause we're goin' steady. Everybody expects us to get married.

ANNA *sucks her tooth, lolls, yawns.*

You've been around. Tried the pack. I've been around. Played the field. We like one another. That old radio playin' soft. The lights whizz along the superhighway. Then I say something. "Anna! Anna!" My voice sounds queer. You know something's up. You stop chewing your gum. You know this is it. I move over. "Anna," I say, "I—I love you." Then—then—

He fits action to the word and touches her. She bursts out laughing, snaps out of the trance, jumps up and runs away from him.

DOCTOR SUFI. Results negative, wouldn't you say? Negative or positive, I forget which it is.

ZANELLI, *with disappointment and disgust.* Ah.

PRATT. Do you consider that a fair experiment?

SUFI, *shrugging.* In human life. . . .

FATHER ZUGO. Well, now let a *doctor* try.

PRATT. Doctor!

ZANELLI, *turning on* SUFI. Are you registered with the Medical Association?

DOCTOR SUFI *comes to* ZANELLI *and takes his arm and side by side they walk in a circle around the plaza.*

SUFI, *turning away wrath.* Your question is germane.

ZANELLI. This ain't no side show. . . .

SUFI. You have a point.

ZANELLI. Beautiful women. Everyone thinks they're public property. But they're human beings.

His speeches have lost some speed and edge.

SUFI. I wish I'd said that.

PRATT. Joe! Joe! He's giving you the old eye.

ZANELLI. . . . human beings. . . .

SUFI *stops but* ZANELLI *continues to walk around in a circle.*

SUFI. Now you are in my power.

Laughter, especially from ELLIE *and* FATHER ZUGO.

ELLIE. Serves him right.

SUFI. I want you to leave us for a while. No. Not that way. Backwards, on your hands and knees,

Before ZANELLI *can comply.*

but first a spray—I mean a shower bath. In America they wash standing up.

He simulates the sound of water.

Shshshshsh.

ZANELLI *recoils slightly from the water, then smiles blissfully.*

ZANELLI. This is what I been needin'.

ELLIE. I hope he isn't going to take off his clothes.

SUFI. Soap. Catch.

Tosses him a cake.

ZANELLI *soaps himself.*

GORJO. First time I ever seen a shower bath.

SUFI. Water suddenly too cold.

ZANELLI *frantically struggles with imaginary faucets.*

That's better. Towel? No towel.

ZANELLI, *groping.* Towel . . . towel. . . .

PRATT, *throwing one.* Here, bud.

73

ZANELLI. Ah.

SUFI. Now you are a little child, obsessed with your national game of baseball. You are "batter up." The bases are what is known as "full." You are nervous. You face a master bowler.

PRATT. Pitcher.

ZANELLI. Why did I take a shower *before* the game?

SUFI. Strike one!

ZANELLI *heads, turns quickly as if watching a fast one go by.*

CORJO. So this is baseball.

To BABA.

What do you think?

She shrugs.

SUFI. The winding-up. The pitch. Strike two.

ZANELLI *swings and misses.*

ZANELLI. What the—

Shakes head. He now grips bat tensely.

SUFI. The pitcher gets some tobacco from the umpire and puts it in his mouth.

BROTHER ZUGO. In his mouth?

SUFI. Strike three!

ZANELLI, *heartbroken.* I can't understand it. Fanned by a—a—

SUFI, *gaily.* Strike four!

ZANELLI. What!

PRATT, *to* SUFI. He's already out.

ZANELLI. Strike *four*. What a country!

ZANELLI *has snapped out of it apparently and is smiling at* SUFI.

Say, Doc, you're pretty good. You must be a yogi or something. But I'll tell you something. I wasn't really under.

PRATT. Be a sport, Joe.

SUFI. No?

74

ZANELLI. I was just playin' along. Another thing, I was hypnotizin' you all the time.

Advances on the DOCTOR.

Yeh, and now you're standing an eighth of an inch off the ground. You ain't touchin'.

SUFI. What's that in millimeters?

ZANELLI. You're floatin', man. Now I understand. You're in an airplane. One thousand feet up.

SUFI. Flying?

BABA. He looks a little worried.

GORJO. He's never been up before. Have you?

BABA. Of course I haven't.

ZANELLI. There's the coast of Albania. Greece. There's Pomo. There's the square. What's that?

SUFI. What's what?

ZANELLI. The engine coughed. Good God, the wing's red hot. Fire! You'll have to jump.

SUFI. I'm glad I have a parachute.

ZANELLI. How quiet when the engines shut off!

SUFI. Engines shut off . . . we must be losing altitude.

ZANELLI. Jump, man, jump!

DOCTOR SUFI *swallows, bends knees, jumps.*

SUFI. Why can't I remember that prayer forwards as well as backwards.

ZANELLI. You're falling through space. Will your chute open?

SUFI. What a silly question. Where's the ring?

He makes as if to find the ring.

ZANELLI. That's right, where's the ring?

SUFI. —ring. . . .

ZANELLI. There is no ring.

The DOCTOR's *form and face express, in a certain dignified way, anguish.*

The earth comes up. Well, it's a dramatic way to end.

ACROBATS. That's right.

But the DOCTOR *suddenly seems to regain control of himself.*

SUFI.

> Rather than be crushed on the earth,
> I bow to a power greater than I am.
> To the young American who has many courses
> In high school. He is the greatest
> Unmarried psychotherapeutic second baseman in the
>   world.

ZANELLI *smiles with triumph and relaxes.*

ZANELLI. Yah, well, no hard feelings. It was those four strikes that brought me to.

SUFI. How lucky for us who are from small countries that these gentlemen from large countries have a sense of humor.

ZANELLI. Yah, well. . . .

PRATT. Hey, Joe!

SUFI. And now will you bid us all one of those gracious, formless, American farewells.

ZANELLI, *beginning to back out.* Say, it's been nice gettin' to know all you folks. If you're ever in Cleveland . . .

He is now down on all fours going out the East entrance backwards.

give me a ring. I'm not in the phonebook but my brother is and he'll always know where I am. . . . Just tell him. . . .

SUFI. I hope no one else demands my credentials.

Silence.

> Now where is the ticklish acrobat? Now child,
> Come to me. Sit on this bench. Now will you others
> Please leave. Such a delicate treatment,
> Such a delicate constitution requires it.

FATHER ZUGO. I'm staying.

SUFI. I don't insist, but by staying you endanger the consummation of the test.

Robert Hivnor

FATHER ZUGO, *to* MOTHER ZUGO. I don't like that word consummation.

SUFI. Well, well, *giggling.* Let's see.

To himself.

Young girl thinking about the ends of things instead of the ends of life.

ANNA. I think you're wrong there, Doctor Sufi.

SUFI. Who is ticklish, you or me? In church, in school, and in the lover's bed, you giggle.

ANNA. I've never been in that bed.

She giggles.

SUFI.
    You see.

He becomes the hypnotist again.

    Now child, I'm getting out of patience.
    As for you, your eyelids are getting heavier.
    Your eyelids are getting heavier.

They do.

                You are no longer young.
    The world has gone round the sun fifty times.
    Your bosom, once the wonder
    Of the trapeze, is shriveled to nothing.

ANNA.
    Oh!

SUFI.
    Your dreams are entirely of food.
    Gone the young men, the babies, the romance
    Of distant lands. You think only of
    Luke-warm consommé, tea, milk toast
    And the ground-up kidneys of the lamb.

A sigh from ANNA.

    Old. Sick. The trapeze hangs motionless
    In the heights. Your father and mother
    Have long since gone into the grave and now **you**
        welcome

77

Death. Your heart, weak and leaking in three places,
Feels about it the hand
Which everybody recognizes,
Although no one has seen it.

A moan.

Yes, Death has come into your room, Old Lady.
Dignified: see with what astounding politeness
He stretches out his secretarial hand.

DOCTOR SUFI *enacts the part.*

And touches you.

On your side.
Once
You giggled when they touched you there
But now—

He touches her, but she begins to giggle.

Anna! I am Death! Death!

She springs to her feet giggling and laughing.

To hell with it. What a silly girl!

MADAME ZUGO *comes and embraces* ANNA.

FATHER ZUGO, *to* SUFI. Well?

SUFI. My first failure. Why did I have that heavy lunch?

FATHER ZUGO, *to* ANNA. Are you all right?

She laughs.

SUFI. A hopeless case. She's good for nothing. She can't love without laughing, therefore, and this is the first time this week I've said therefore, she can love nobody.

FATHER ZUGO. She loves her father.

MOTHER ZUGO. She loves me.

ANNA. I love Joe Zanelli.

But ANNA *giggles as the curtain comes down.*

ACT TWO

Scene One

Pomo weeks later. BASSETT PRATT's *creative excavation has again changed the spirit of the place. Remnants of the previous two scenes remain—to remind us of them— while we see mainly that the plaza was once (and is again) the court of a fort, or strong point. Some walls seem to be crenelated. Surfaces are composed of huge stones and we see some of that forbidding hardware we associate with medieval castles. The effect is grim but still in the spirit of the comedy.*

We occasionally see and sometimes hear PRATT *and his helper,* ZANELLI, *working behind the wineshop-fortress wall. At certain moments without seeing them we see their chisels and picks coming through the spaces in the stones.* SUFI *is eating.* ANNA *and* BABA *watch him.*

ANNA. Yes, I would. I think I would.

BABA. But you're happy here. How could you be happy there? They're different. You'd hate America.

SUFI, *after wiping his mouth with an enormous napkin.*

No, you wouldn't like America.
The rich foods there! The puddings!
The milkshakes! All that unfermented sugar!
When I was there a bubble this big
Went up and down my esophagus.
At night it quivered
Like in a carpenter's level
When those big trucks went by
Taking cow's milk to the city of New York.

ANNA. I wouldn't mind going over for a visit. Did you get around much in the States?

SUFI.

Yes, yes, Pittsburgh, Baltimore, Minneapolis,

79

All those not-yet-sacred places. But
Travel is a waste of time.
Animals vary from place to place,
But people are the same the world over.

ANNA. What did you do in America, Doctor Sufi?

SUFI. Gorjo, I've finished this course.

GORJO *is not his old self. He slouches out of his waiter's
stance and does not now respond with his usual natural
willingness.*

BABA. Gorjo!

*He blinks and picks up a plate. Now through the follow-
ing action runs the familiar—familiar and unfunny to
hungry men the world over—of the incompetent waiter.
In the second scene of the play he had his problems and
was unsuccessful in his thinking about them. Now he has
given up and seems to be in a state of alternate shock
and overeagerness. But his old grace and balance keep
his disasters minor.*

SUFI.

It's a strange place. No culture
Yet everybody reads and writes.
That put me at a disadvantage:
I had culture, but I couldn't read or write.

ANNA. Can't read!

SUFI, *to* ANNA.

I was brilliant from birth,
Took only scientific subjects,
Went directly to medical school.

GORJO, *having expertly taken the plate away, polishes
the table, disturbing the* DOCTOR, *who endures it with
dignity, but now he starts to take the table away. The*
DOCTOR *holds onto the table.*

BABA. Gorjo, what are you doing now!

SUFI, *as he holds onto the table.* This is in a sense *my*

table too. Think back, I had my salad. Now comes some-thing else.

GORJO *lets go of the table.*

GORJO. You were hungry today, Doctor.

SUFI. I'm still hungry.

GORJO. Beautiful day. Sharpens the appetite.

BABA. He said that twice before.

SUFI. Now for the *pièce de résistance,* as they say in America.

GORJO. Today *is* Monday. Yesterday was Sunday.

He goes nodding and blinking.

SUFI. Learn to read! I saw if I was to stay in America I'd have to become a child again.

BABA. Is that bad?

SUFI. I, who have known Platonism, or whatever it is, should learn to read? I came home.

BABA. Home! He never had a home.

ANNA. Bachelor.

BABA. Celibate.

SUFI. I belong to an order which is celibate. As an old Mohican sage told me: Let us harvest all the distinctions we can; we may have to eat some in the winter.

BABA. He joined that order when he was fifty. When he was a young man he fell in love with an American woman.

ANNA. Oh, yes?

They see GORJO *putting on his coat and hat.*

SUFI. Gorjo!

ANNA, *to* BABA. The only American lady I've ever known is Ellie Sprocket.

SUFI, *to* GORJO. Where are you going?

GORJO. It's nice here. But I must go back to Pomo.

SUFI. This *is* your shop, Gorjo.

81

BABA. Smell, Gorjo. It looks different but it smells the same.

GORJO *takes off his coat, puts on his apron, goes into the shop.*

ANNA. Poor Gorjo.

To SUFI.

What was she like?

BABA. The American woman.

SUFI. Lucy? Beautiful.

BABA. And they weren't introduced. They just met.

SUFI. Our eyes introduced us. They have a strange phrase over there: They were meant for one another. That's what they said about us.

ANNA. Mama says we were meant to do good and think about God.

SUFI. Lucy was meant for *me.* But there was a certain firmness about the mouth, a straightforwardness about her eyes, that indicated character. What a blow!

SUFI *sighs.*

ANNA. What did you do?

SUFI. I taught her to smoke tobacco, drink wine, dance two-by-two. No use. She had character. She lost her virtue between yawns, so to speak, but she still had character. It was at that moment that I realized I was in the grip of an historical situation.

ANNA. But what did she look like?

SUFI. As a mystic I don't like historical situations.

A wave of his hand.

For instance I don't like this.

ANNA. I don't either.

SUFI. Well, I was sitting on what they call a sofa with this Lucy and I realized—

ANNA. Is it true American women have longer legs than other women?

82

SUFI. —and I realized that in America love-making is the pleasure of the male and the politics of the female.

BABA. Pooh.

SUFI. In a democracy nakedness is a crown! Every woman can be a Queen!

They laugh.

I am not a Marxist. I've never had the experience. But I believe those who control the means of production run the country. In the States the men are the means of production and the women control them.

BABA. Shush.

She has seen ELLIE *enter the square. She looks at the three, sits down at a table, is served the inevitable coffee by* GORJO, *who then comes over to* SUFI. *With a plate* ELLIE *tries to attract the attention of* PRATT *and fails.*

SUFI, *to* GORJO. I was hoping for a slice of lamb.

GORJO. Don't you know this is cheese Monday?

SUFI. Cheese Monday!

GORJO. Mr. Pratt reminded me. It's the first Monday in September.

BABA. Already!

SUFI. But you haven't honored that old-fashioned holiday since—

GORJO. He gave me a little speech, put his hand on my shoulder—anyway I couldn't serve any meat today.

SUFI. So I'm eating cheese today.

GORJO. He said we could have a bloodless mollusk, if we wanted.

SUFI. Give me that cheese. Since when have you been going to that foreigner for advice about food?

GORJO. Since—

He spills the cheese.

—excuse me.

SUFI, *catching it.* All right, I got it.

83

Indignation.

Goat cheese!

GORJO. He said—

SUFI, *taking a bite of the cheese and wincing.* All right.
A bitter glance at the chisel coming through the wall.
I know what he told you.

GORJO *isn't listening.*

Pious observance of old customs is good for you. Yes,
but *he* isn't eating any goat cheese.

To BABA.

You don't think *I* worry about such things. *I* don't work
hard? Your doctor? Your friend? Today I looked down
twenty throats, down past the tonsils, past the stomach,
through the small intestines, right out onto the ground, for
I know that sickness can lie in the land.

PRATT *and* ZANELLI *now come on carrying between them
a tray of stone objects.* ZANELLI, *tired, lets his end down
first.*

BABA, *disdainfully.* Work, work, work.

ANNA. After lunch, too.

BABA. Like a couple of convicts.

SUFI *has finished his lunch at last and blinks with
drowsiness.*

SUFI. People say, "What's wrong with me, Doc?" With
them! Such egotism. Maybe the canals of the moon are
overflowing.

PRATT, *to* ZANELLI. What's the matter, Joe?

BABA, *to* ANNA. Don't you look, dear.

SUFI. That's right.

BABA. And don't be nervous.

SUFI. You know the proverb?

ANNA. Look? I close my eyes and see Joe.

*She imitates him without looking, by some prescience,
as he wipes his brow, etc.*

84

SUFI. "Out of sight, out of mind," was the proverb I was thinking of.

He rises.

BABA. Anna, it's time.

ANNA. I don't care.

They prepare to go off to their siesta. GORJO *yawns.*

SUFI. One no longer sleeps well in the square.

BABA, *in confidence.* They say the plans came from New York.

SUFI. No, no. This is a Venetian Fortress, Baba. Yes, once we were under the thumb of those damned gondoliers. Pleasant dreams, Baba.

BABA, *to* ANNA. I feel a little sick again.

ANNA. Poor Baba.

They leave the stage to PRATT *and* ZANELLI.

PRATT. You've lost your old pep, Joe.

ZANELLI. Yeh. Look at that poor bastard Gorjo. He didn't know he was practically blind until you started movin' things around. Now he knows.

PRATT. Ellie is going to fix him up a place over there.

ZANELLI. Jack, don't you think things are approaching a crisis? You ever been to one of those Yurpeen movies? Everyone dresses different. They're nobody but they dress different—the baker has a skirt, the shoemaker has an apron, and the farmer wears skirts. But listen, along comes a crisis and they all dress up like Americans. Street suits! Yeh. Well. Old man Zugo—today he's dressed up.

PRATT. I hope it doesn't mean more trouble.

ZANELLI. It always did in these movies.

PRATT. Sleep it off, Joe. I'll see you later.

ZANELLI. Today, I will.

He goes off. PRATT *resumes work.* ELLIE *comes down.*

ELLIE. Working through siesta again!

PRATT. Hello, Ellie.

ELLIE. They say of the siesta, it enables one to see the two best parts of the day, dawn and midnight, but as for myself—

PRATT. I need all the daylight I can get.

ELLIE. Off schedule?

PRATT. I don't know! My watch stopped two days ago and no one in Pomo has the time.

Picks up axe.

I'm living by the muezzin.

ELLIE, *laughing.* Does it matter?

PRATT. Of course it matters.

He swings the axe and startles ELLIE.

ELLIE. Oh.

PRATT. Sorry.

ELLIE. My poor Pomo. I'm not objecting, Bassett, but sometimes you seem to be taking those bricks right out of my mind.

PRATT. You and Baba.

Ellie notices an object among the stones PRATT *and* ZANELLI *had been carrying.*

ELLIE. That little stone man. It used to be in Gorjo's shop—above the wine cask. So thirsty looking.

PRATT. It's a devil. Used to be part of the plumbing of the fortress. The face sinks in, see there, and a stone pipe came out of that.

ELLIE. Oh.

PRATT. Came from one of the larger underground rooms, a sort of guardroom. Also a torture chamber. Those chains came from there. What this little man was thirsty after was blood.

ELLIE, *wistfully.* Don't you ever find any prayer wheels?

PRATT *picks up a fragment.*

PRATT. Well, Joe broke through to Greco-Roman times about ten this morning. I think it was ten. . . .

ELLIE. Lovely pink.

PRATT. Not native stone at all. Must be a part of some votive object. Look at that curve. That's a 200 B.C. curve, if I ever saw one. Pure. . . .

ELLIE. I see that.

PRATT. —there was a place there all the natives avoided. All the paths went near but not too near. This must have come from there.

ELLIE. But what was it?

PRATT. Something holy—

ELLIE. Something to be avoided?

PRATT. Something we can put under a glass case where it won't do any harm.

ELLIE. How different we are, you and I! Both Americans. The same generation—I wouldn't say you were really older than me. Yet when you see these beautiful cultural things you think of them as—evil. All I can think of is how much love went into their making.

PRATT. Love! Baba Marco represents what that culture means to me. There's St. Francis feeding the pigeons on one shoulder, and an ikon in every niche, and what is she? —a whore.

ELLIE. Bassett!

PRATT. A nice one. Still—

ELLIE. You're so wrong!

PRATT. And tattooed as she is on the outside, it's nothing to what must be on the inside. There are the real masterpieces!

ELLIE. You'd like to climb into our minds, wouldn't you, and go smash—just like this.

PRATT, *muttering.* I don't need to.

ELLIE. Although, of course, I don't particularly like Baba as a person, I rejoice that she exists, both inside and out.

PRATT. You're corrupted, too.

ELLIE. But I went to school in America. . . . No, I didn't reach old Europe until I was twenty-two—twenty-two . . . then. . . .

She tries to remember, then abruptly.

Do you know dogs?

PRATT. What!

ELLIE. I suppose I mean American dogs. I buried one here. Well, when you bring a dog home after a long trip and let him loose in his own back yard, how he leaps, how he goes round and round! Bow wow! Sniff, sniff! That's how I felt when I came to Europe.

PRATT. That's how I felt when I came over as a boy. Then I came as a man—with a gun. I don't mean I was carrying a gun. It was a big gun. Took forty men to operate it.

ELLIE, *real interest*. Oh?

PRATT. Culture! Art! Their art is the engraving on sword handles.

He kicks one of the fragments.

ELLIE. Oh.

PRATT. Yes, I grew up. You never did, Ellie. Going oo and ah about things you don't understand. At your age. A Greek orthodox mass one day. Clipping a Protestant cemetery the next. Treating the natives like children. If you want to be mother hen, why don't you have some children of your own?

ELLIE. Bassett!

PRATT. It's all right. Everyone's asleep.

ELLIE. *I'm* not.

He directs his attention back to his work.

ELLIE.

"Oo and ah." I suppose I do. Yes,
That's my way. I did in America too:
I oohed and ahed about muddy rivers
And Pennsylvania Dutchmen.

88

But isn't that all right to do? To be amazed?
I am amazed. The chances! The possibilities!
And Sir, I'll have you know, it's not only cathedrals,
And fountains, and officials, that touch me.
                                        Yesterday I
Saw something on a shepherd's face in Pozlitz,
Oohed, aahed, brushed penicillin in it,
And sent his specimen to the Clinica Medica.
You search the world over for something,
But in Europe, in America, I find.
Morning, noon, and some afternoons, like this one,
I find.

PRATT.

What do you mean by that?

ELLIE.

Oh, Bassett, you dig, dig, dig, night and day,
Finding nothing, ever, but worst of all,
Destroying yourself, it seems to me. . . .
You're unhappy—didn't you know?—unhappy,
And as you get deeper you get unhappier,
And more hopeless. Why?

PRATT *shows an interest.*

PRATT.

Others have wondered about that.
Two years ago I had a nervous breakdown.

ELLIE.

Poor thing.

PRATT.

My mind went blank in Persia.
                                        Overwork.
A doctor there, Swiss or Austrian, I forget,
He had the opinion that I was looking
For something not in the world's past
But in my own past.

ELLIE, *illuminated.*

I see.

89

PRATT.

What was his name? Well, he lived long enough
To have every idea in his head discredited.

ELLIE.

He meant you were looking for your lost home.

PRATT.

No, for my lost childhood faith. For God.

ELLIE.

Not under rocks, I don't think.

PRATT.

He couldn't accept the idea that
It is enough for me to destroy false gods,
To tame—to purify—history.

ELLIE.

He was right—you're searching for home—*your* home.

PRATT.

No, no.

ELLIE.

So search we all in our way. You seek—

PRATT.

No, no—

ELLIE.

—a house of love.

PRATT.

Quite the opposite. He said—

ELLIE.

I'm glad you told me this. May your search
Be over soon!

PRATT, *pointing, pick upward.*

But Ellie, it's the divine . . . !

ELLIE.

My heart goes out to you, and to the little doctor,
Who knew, wise man that he was—

PRATT.

But—

ELLIE.

> Who saw in your peevishness, your swearing,
> Your perpetual scratching, your untidy bathroom,
> Your eyes on the dump heap, your violence toward
>   beauty,
> Your way of saying, "I love you."

PRATT, *a moan.*

> Oh.

ELLIE.

> When I was a little girl I lived in a big happy house.
> All eight of us were very happy, yet in all those years,
> Not one of us said, "I love you." But there was a
>   little toy.
> A bunny, I think. When you squeezed it it said: "I
>   love you."
> Bless things that say, "I love you."

PRATT, *fleeing upstage to his digging.* Good Lord!

ELLIE.

> That's right. Go seek your house of love.

ELLIE *sways from side to side. Were the atmosphere of this Earth not so thin she would be dancing, for she is very happy. Now* UNCLE HENRY *appears at the east entrance, dressed as a traveler and carrying two large knapsacks. He is surprised both at the new version of Pomo and at* ELLIE.

UNCLE HENRY. Ellie, is that you?

ELLIE. Uncle Henry.

UNCLE HENRY. For a second I thought I was in the wrong place.

ELLIE. Then you saw my familiar face.

They kiss.

UNCLE HENRY. It looks a little different, too.

ELLIE. Much mail for me?

UNCLE HENRY. You have a separate sack at the consulate.

They seat themselves and ELLIE, *with remarkable efficiency, sorts her letters. Her* UNCLE HENRY *surveys the new Pomo.*

UNCLE HENRY. Y' know, I like this!

ELLIE, *reading.* Um.

UNCLE HENRY. Has real character.

ELLIE, *enraged.* I'm off the board of the Sidesaddle Club.

UNCLE HENRY. Oh?

ELLIE. Blast Mrs. Hofstetter!

UNCLE HENRY. Ellie.

ELLIE. All right, don't blast her. But what does she know about delinquent girls?

Sound of demolition and of PRATT *swearing.*

ELLIE. Will he never stop?

UNCLE HENRY. Just doing a job of work. By the way, I made some telephone calls. Nice trans-Atlantic ones. I have news about our scavenger.

ELLIE. I'd love to get my hands on a telephone for just one morning.

UNCLE HENRY. Got Charlie Goodhue at the bank. You know his cough. Well, with that and transmission noises I didn't get the full picture, but he was glad that you and Pratt were over here together.

ELLIE. What about him?

UNCLE HENRY. He has money.

ELLIE. Much money?

UNCLE HENRY. Hard to say. More than I have. You're right about one thing, his mother was a Gillis. The story I got from Charlie was that he has the money in a kind of fund—anyway, it's his own money he's using for all this. He's the foundation.

ELLIE *rises.*

ELLIE. I'll get you some tea. I'm glad for his sake he has money, but of course no man, however rich, can afford to be unhappy.

92

She goes off and UNCLE HENRY *approaches* PRATT.

UNCLE HENRY. Hello, there.

PRATT. Oh—back—hello.

They shake hands.

UNCLE HENRY. Well, my boy, now you're getting some-where. A fort. Now this town makes a little sense. Why live in a place like this? It's clear now—to control that valley.

PRATT. That's one reason.

UNCLE HENRY. Look at those walls. You need a three-inch gun to blast through those and you don't drag them up donkey roads. Who built it?

PRATT. This bit is Roman. The walls—Venetian.

UNCLE HENRY. Tactics change. Strategy remains the same. Now I admit I had the guidebook approach to poor old Pomo. Flora and Fauna. Saints. Artists. Festivals.

Dismisses them with a laugh.

Now I see. I think there should be plaques on hills like this, saying something like this: It is important that this beautiful hill, where poets walk *et cetera*, should not fall into the hands of the enemy.

SUFI *and* BOMOGRICA *come on. The latter is dressed in an over-elaborated uniform of some romantic general staff.*

ELLIE *also comes on, carrying a cup of tea.*

SUFI. Welcome back, Sir.

BOMOGRICA. Mr. Sprague.

UNCLE HENRY. Well, well, look at this.

ELLIE. How very becoming. And impressive, too.

UNCLE HENRY *and* ELLIE *shake hands with* BOMOGRICA. PRATT *observes the uniform sardonically.*

UNCLE HENRY. I see you're in the Bicycle Corps.

BOMOGRICA. Oh, yes. I understand it's still dry down there.

UNCLE HENRY, *shaking head.* Yes—

Cheerful again.

But what do you think of all this?

SUFI. Very disturbing to the poor in spirit.

UNCLE HENRY, *to* BOMOGRICA. I mean you, sir.

BOMOGRICA. Very, very pretty, and perhaps our salvation.

PRATT. Beautiful Europe. Every hill has a castle on top of it. And beautiful dungeons underneath the castles. Forts. Walled cities. You can have 'em!

UNCLE HENRY. I admire it and I admire the sons of Pomo who built it.

BOMOGRICA. We're all walking a little straighter these days.

UNCLE HENRY. The blood of good men has been shed inside there. You're going to quarter a battalion here, are you, with a local command?

BOMOGRICA. Yes, the sound of the bugle will once more ring through Pomo.

BABA *comes on sleepily.* ZANELLI *comes on.*

UNCLE HENRY. There'll be reveille and not that damned Mohammedan. Congratulations.

BABA. A battalion?

BOMOGRICA. We're a proud and hardy people. Soldiering comes naturally to us. Uniforms, guns, pensions.

UNCLE HENRY. Well, I think the problems of Pomo are solved.

PRATT. Wait a minute.

To BOMOGRICA.

In the first place I don't see why this Fort appeals to you. It has never been *your* fort. *Your* proud and hardy people have never manned it. They died in heaps outside it. That's the way it was when the Romans were here. They gobbled up what soldiers were left into their own army. What about the Turks? What about the Serbs?

BOMOGRICA. But now we'll use it ourselves.

PRATT. I don't think so.

UNCLE HENRY. Why not?

PRATT. I'm going to tear it down.

BOMOGRICA. What!

ELLIE. Already?

PRATT. The underpinning is out now. It's just a question of which way it will fall.

BOMOGRICA. It held off the Visigoths for forty days.

SUFI. But not this goth.

BOMOGRICA. I feel defeated—outmaneuvered.

UNCLE HENRY. Really, Pratt, sometimes—

SUFI, *to* ELLIE. What a hero! What a general! He sacks more cities than Hannibal and all his elephants.

PRATT. You're lucky to see this at all. I remember some Indian sites out in Colorado. They were going to flood the area. Use it for a dam. Well, to save time we took a bulldozer and just cleared off the overburden.

ELLIE. "Overburden!" What a word.

UNCLE HENRY, *to* PRATT. You'd never get a bulldozer up here in peace time.

To BOMOGRICA.

I'm sorry about this.

PRATT, *to* BOMOGRICA. You'd save *this?*

BOMOGRICA (*he would*). Well.

PRATT. Ugly!

UNCLE HENRY. A monument to the reality of power, my boy.

PRATT *kicks aside a large chain.*

PRATT. Look at that. For animals? No. For men—Europeans.

BOMOGRICA, *unshocked.* Well.

UNCLE HENRY, *to* BOMOGRICA. Power is the dirty work. Someone has to do the dirty work.

BOMOGRICA *considers this, blinks.* PRATT *kicks a stone.*

PRATT. Civilization . . . !

95

The ZUGO *family enters in a sad, (early) Picassoesque formation, with the* FATHER *dressed, as* ZANELLI *has warned, in a shiny suit.* BROTHER ZUGO *carries a large impractical sword in his arms.*

ZANELLI, *to* PRATT. Here comes the crisis.

FATHER ZUGO. Put the sword on the table.

Gasps from the natives.

BOMOGRICA, *to* FATHER ZUGO. Are you sure?

UNCLE HENRY, *to* SUFI. What now?

SUFI. He wants to talk of matters of blood, tribe and that sort of thing. The sword is the sword of justice.

PRATT. Rusty, isn't it?

BOMOGRICA, *to* FATHER ZUGO. All right, on with the preliminary talks.

FATHER ZUGO. No. Final talks.

Pointing.

The sword—wrong direction.

BROTHER ZUGO *turns it around.*

UNCLE HENRY, *to* BOMOGRICA, *preparing his excuses.* I've come a long way today. If you don't mind—

FATHER ZUGO. No! It is an important public complaint I am making. A foreigner—we don't speak his name—

THE ZUGOS. No, no.

FATHER ZUGO. He is making advances to the daughter of this house without first approaching father.

ZANELLI. I ain't touched her since that day in the square.

UNCLE HENRY. Sure?

ANNA. I'm sure, Sir.

BOMOGRICA.
    Zanelli has obeyed the law. Hasn't called
    On her, met her in private places, nor even spoken,
    Except to say good morning, God bless you.
    He's been watched.

96

FATHER ZUGO.
  The *law!* Who says he breaks the law?
  Armies, they don't break the law,
  Yet we build forts.

He indicates Fort Pomo.

BOMOGRICA.
  Once we did.

FATHER ZUGO.
  We have laws against robbers, but against lovers—
  None. Against enemy force there is force.
  Against enemy love?

Spreads hands helplessly.

  Even if—

Glares at ZANELLI.

ELLIE.
  Dear me. Is it the same? I don't think so.
  War hurts people.

FATHER ZUGO.
  What!

PRATT.
  I don't see the comparison. War
  Takes what is not offered. Love—

FATHER ZUGO.
  You!

To them.

  They work together.
  He—

Points to PRATT.

  —rapes Pomo a little at a time.

Now at ZANELLI.

  He does the same to Anna.

BROTHER ZUGO.
  The trouble is, we worry and he doesn't.

MOTHER ZUGO.

> The trouble is, the weather has been so good.
> They say good morning all the time.

ELLIE.

> Yes, it has been lovely.

ZANELLI.

> Yeh. Nice.

ANNA.

> Yes, lovely.

FATHER ZUGO.

> You see!

MOTHER ZUGO.

> It upsets the house. The house was
> Not made for love, I mean this kind.
> The cups get broken. Beans spill
> Out on the floor and go down little holes.

ZANELLI *wants to say something*.

ZANELLI.

> Say—

BROTHER ZUGO.

> No.

MOTHER ZUGO.

> Stop him.

FATHER ZUGO, *to* BOMOGRICA *and* SUFI.

> Stop him loving! Stop him loving!

UNCLE HENRY.

> I thought all the world loved a lover.

ELLIE.

> Love. Can it be stopped? Just like that?
> No more than it can be started just like that.

FATHER ZUGO, *to* BOMOGRICA.

> You and I have served. The great retreats.

BROTHER ZUGO, *reminding* BOMOGRICA.

> Paragezzo. Solipoli.

98

FATHER ZUGO.

    That uniform. That bicycle pump in gold
    Upon your shoulder. It means nothing?

BOMOGRICA, *to* SUFI.

    To stop loving. It shouldn't be hard.
    So many have done it.

SUFI, *with sadness.*

    Ah.

MOTHER ZUGO.

    If on Monday he did it a little less, on Tuesday
    A little less—

SUFI, *appalled.*

    Oh!

ZANELLI.

    I'll never stop loving her until we're married.

ELLIE.

    Dear me.

ZANELLI.

    You know what I mean. Never!

FATHER ZUGO, *who for the past few moments has had his quivering head in his hands, now with a sudden commanding assurance begins to chant in definite units of short lines in an unknown tongue.*

ELLIE. What's that?

PRATT. Sounds serious.

ZANELLI. Yeh.

PRATT. What language is that?

SUFI. Old Pomonian. He says he is rejoicing as only a native of Pomo can rejoice.

PRATT. Oh?

FATHER ZUGO *chants more lines.*

SUFI. He is up to his neck in joy because the fort exists again. Now it is like it was a thousand years ago. Except then there were no Americans present.

More Old Pomonian.

SUFI, *translating*. America does not exist. It's not mentioned in the Bible.

FATHER ZUGO *chants*.

SUFI. No really great writer ever mentions America. For example, Aristotle. And where were the Americans at the Battle of Sevastopol?

FATHER ZUGO *chants with growing aggressiveness*.

ELLIE. Oh, dear.

SUFI. I can't translate that.

BOMOGRICA, *now translating*. Pomo not afraid of American soldiers. We have two billion population.

UNCLE HENRY. Two *what?*

PRATT. They count the dead in their census.

FATHER ZUGO *shouts two words*.

BOMOGRICA, *to* SUFI. To arms?

FATHER ZUGO *repeats*.

SUFI, *translating and agreeing*.
Yes.
Let England control the narrow passages
Of the physical world.
What is Gibraltar or Singapore
To the straits in the sea of blood?
Let America have the city, so necessary to victory.
Let us control the house:
Control the mouth, not of the Ganges
But of our daughter. And hold the female delta,
Outflank the husband,
Post the dog in the vestibule—
It hates the new.

ELLIE.
The dog?

SUFI.
Let America rule the Pacific,
Ireland the North Sea, and Russia the rivers.

What's in them? Fish. Let Pomo
Control the past. What's in it?
Minds, souls, survivors of love,
And the Pomonian Constitution.

PRATT, *to* UNCLE HENRY.

He couldn't control his stomach muscles.

UNCLE HENRY.

Upon his dominion the moon never sets.

FATHER ZUGO *shouts*.

BOMOGRICA.

The battle cry.

SUFI.

It means: Put out the light!

FATHER ZUGO *now whips out a large eighteenth-century pistol and aims, with his brother's help, in the general direction of* ZANELLI. *He, warned by screams, differently pitched by* ELLIE, BABA, *and* ANNA, *darts toward the fortress.* UNCLE HENRY *and* BOMOGRICA *grapple with the* ZUGOS *while* PRATT *maintains a stunned calm. Now the gun goes off and hits a rope, which lowers a boom, which knocks down an important underpinning. Fort Pomo, or some prominent parts of it, now begins to fall, a piece at a time. And all, including* SUFI, *jump downstage and to the sides to get out of the way.*

PRATT. It's all right.

A piece falls.

VOICE. All right?

PRATT. It was supposed to do that.

ELLIE. Anybody hurt?

PRATT. Nobody's hurt.

FATHER ZUGO, *to* BOMOGRICA. I did not mean to shoot the rope.

BOMOGRICA. I believe you.

FATHER ZUGO. Besides, it was bird shot.

ELLIE. First aid, anyone?

As the confusion clears and they adjust to the new lighting, they see that the wall of the fort was supported by a colonnade of the pillars of a Greek temple. They see through them to the mountains.

BABA. Brandy . . . brandy. . .

MRS. ZUGO, *to* ANNA. You can see the mountains from the square.

BOMOGRICA, *to* PRATT. Isn't that a Greek temple?

PRATT. Yes, there it is, your old Greek temple.

ELLIE, *to* BOMOGRICA. How lovely. At least it's not Serbian.

SUFI *takes on the manner of the sacred teacher.*

SUFI. Dear Doctor, we thank you.

PRATT. That's all right.

SUFI. We were living inside a temple all the while.

This is true, for we see that the walls of ELLIE'S *and* BABA'S *houses were also sustained by pillars and that they respectively compose the ends of the temple.*

UNCLE HENRY, *to* BOMOGRICA. He's going to make a lot out of that.

SUFI. Praise God, now all is clear to me.

UNCLE HENRY. What's all clear?

To BOMOGRICA.

He's happy about something.

SUFI. Shall we sing? I'm faint with happiness. Hold my arm.

BOMOGRICA. Why? Tell me why?

SUFI. I know the reasons!

BOMOGRICA. For what?

SUFI. The reason the grapes shriveled on the vine. The springs. The infirmities of our children. The poverty. The fleas. The family quarrels.

Robert Hivnor

Cheerily.

Pomo all this while a sacred city. These streets lead nowhere—of course not—they are holy.

ELLIE. Yes, I see that.

SUFI. We thought we were starving. Not so—we were fasting.

MOTHER ZUGO, *understanding.* Oh.

SUFI. We thought we were sick—no, no, we were learning how to die. We thought we were lazy. Children, we were not meant for work but to celebrate eternal things. I declare therefore a festival to celebrate this divine revelation.

ELLIE, *to* PRATT. Wonderful. The famous festival.

PRATT. A festival! How long will it last?

SUFI. Three days.

They cheer and FATHER ZUGO *leads them in a rhythmic song. This has to us a weird oriental sound. Monotonous and yet with feeling. As the curtain comes down we see* UNCLE HENRY *in a posture of gloom and* BOMOGRICA *is having a drink.* SUFI *is wide-eyed in an attitude of piety with hands together gazing upon his temple.* ZANELLI *and* ANNA *look at each other fondly.* PRATT *is contemptuous.*

ACT TWO

Scene Two

Scene: the temple is revealed to us. BABA'S *and* ELLIE'S *houses still stand, but along their sides we see in bas-relief the same type of column which composes the rest of the temple. We see through the back columns into the foothills and this gives a new rustic feeling to the set. It is deep twilight. Most of the tables are gone but now* UNCLE HENRY *and* PRATT *sit at one of those remaining.*

UNCLE HENRY *is somewhat drunk,* PRATT *very sober.*

UNCLE HENRY. My boy, this is the third day of the festival and tell me—sincerely—not that you're not always sincere—nothing if not sincere—tell me—I want the truth—never once did you let yourself go?

PRATT. I did not.

UNCLE HENRY. For a certain type impossible. As a four-year-old boy I couldn't cry. Now I can.

PRATT *grimaces contemptuously.*

My boy, you ought to let yourself go. Do you good. You're gettin' tenser and tenser. Co on. Have fun.

PRATT. I intend to have some fun.

UNCLE HENRY. Real fun?

PRATT, *smiles, nods.* Without letting myself go.

UNCLE HENRY. No . . . he's a paleface . . . a paleface. . . .

PRATT. You remember driving on a parkway in the States. There you are in three or four lanes of traffic. Each car going at a carefully regulated speed. Keeping in line. Figuring the margin of safety. Then one car comes weaving in and out. It can do this because the others keep their position. Tonight I'm doing a little weaving.

UNCLE HENRY. How's that?

Music. Sound of monotonous singing.

PRATT. Listen to them. You say they're letting themselves go. But it's not really abandon. No. They do things they wouldn't ordinarily do. Drink. Dance. But the dance—have you seen it?—is so complicated and rigorous that they all seem on the point of exhaustion. They hold hands but it isn't each other they feel, but something larger. . . .

UNCLE HENRY. They've lost themselves in the group. Wish I could. Never found a group I liked.

PRATT. Let them. But one man isn't drinking. One man isn't singing.

UNCLE HENRY. He's sitting down thinking how different he is.

PRATT. Just thinking. Anticipating an hour of hanky-panky with one of the beautiful women of Pomo.

UNCLE HENRY. What! You—you wouldn't.

PRATT. I will.

UNCLE HENRY. But *they* don't do that.

PRATT. For them it would be sacrilege. Not for me.

UNCLE HENRY. May I ask a question? Does it matter whom with?

PRATT. No.

UNCLE HENRY. It has to be *somebody*.

PRATT. At the terrible moment, yes. Before and after, no.

UNCLE HENRY. I didn't know you were that kind of fellow. A gentleman wouldn't do a thing like that.

PRATT. Listen to the music.

UNCLE HENRY. You weren't thinking of Ellie?

PRATT. An American girl? No, not Ellie. Why, we couldn't even *tell* Ellie. Listen to that music.

UNCLE HENRY. Ah, you're just talking—

PRATT. You know me better than that. Tonight—a lady from Byzantium. Why not? I've worked hard. Don't I deserve it?

105

As an afterthought.

Besides—I want to. Some good ought to come from this primitive blow-out.

Enter ZANELLI *dressed in a baseball uniform.*

UNCLE HENRY, *bowing elaborately.* The King of the Feast.

PRATT. Hello, Joe.

ZANELLI. I'm disgusted.

He goes through the wind-up of a baseball pitcher.

UNCLE HENRY. Aren't you havn' fun? Can't you lesh yourself go?

ZANELLI. I'm just disappointed. I expected something different.

UNCLE HENRY, *laughing.* And we know what.

ZANELLI. I wouldn't ha' agreed to be King of the Feast if I'd known it was just goin' to be a lot a—geez . . . give me another drink outa that basketball bladder.

Takes swallow from the wine-skin.

PRATT. Joe, did old Sufi approve your costume?

ZANELLI. He likes it. He wants me to give it to him when I go. Y'know, I never thought I'd ever wear it here. Kept it in the box. Looked at it when I got a gloom on. Hey, here they come around the track again.

The DANCERS *come on. They are serious of face and so closely interlocked that any freedom of movement is impossible.* ELLIE *is there with the rest of the natives we have seen. A few moments on the stage and off they go.*

UNCLE HENRY. Good ole Ellie, she's letting herself go.

ZANELLI. It's so gloomy. I feel like bawlin'.

PRATT. An outdoor wake.

ZANELLI *winds up again.*

ZANELLI. I'm sick at my stomach.

UNCLE HENRY. Ellie writes letters all morning and lets herself go at night. She's alive.

ZANELLI. If it hadn't been for that damn war I'd been in the minors.

Takes another pitch.

This uniform makes me feel kinda—I don't know—clean. I don't like to get mixed up in this sort o' thing.

UNCLE HENRY. I played baseball as a youngster.

Sweet melancholy.

I never made the school varsity, nor even the class team, but I played right field for the dorm.

ZANELLI *pitches*.

PRATT. I don't suppose you'd believe this, but when I was fourteen or fifteen I was the best hitter in my neighborhood.

ZANELLI. I didn't know I was talkin' to a couple of athletes.

PRATT. In the town where I lived. . . .

UNCLE HENRY. Bridgewater.

PRATT. Yes. There was a high hill where most of the so-called middle classes lived. Lawns, trees, ivy-covered churches. Our social life—if boys can be said to have such a thing—are you interested?

UNCLE HENRY. *I* am, m'boy.

PRATT. We hung around the church and Peterson's Drugstore and Ice Cream Parlor. It was a very pleasant place—old-fashioned. Big fans going around on the ceiling. The smell of candy. First-rate ice-cream sodas. Well, we had a team and it was in a league—and we had a chance for the championship that year. But I remember our chief competitor was a team from another part of town, the slums.

ZANELLI. Now you're makin' *me* homesick.

PRATT. Their home base was the Bagdad Athletic Club. It was really a poolroom.

ZANELLI. Good ole Bagdad A.C.

PRATT. So at the end of the season you had two teams fighting it out, the Bagdad Boys, and ourselves, the Green Park Presbyterian Church. Well, they had a boy named Louis, that was his last name, who was a *good* pitcher.

ZANELLI. He had a fast ball.

PRATT. Right. He terrified us with it. I was the only one who could hit him. Well, came the time for the big play-off. Our coach was the Preacher, Reverend Campbell, and before the game he gave us a long talk, about what advantages we had over the poolroom boys. But this is the point— on the day of the big game I didn't show up.

UNCLE HENRY. What?

ZANELLI. Yeh?

UNCLE HENRY. You didn't play the game?

PRATT. No, but I couldn't stay away from the ball field. It was a scoreless tie. Then Reverend Campbell sent one of the boys after me. I went back with him and then Reverend Campbell put his arm around me and asked me why I wasn't playing. Then I told him. I couldn't play first base for the Green Park Presbyterians because I no longer believed in God.

ZANELLI, *in the middle of a wind-up, stops and sits down.*

ZANELLI. Have you ever read a book called "Great Moments in Baseball"? Boy, there's a book.

The DANCERS *in their tight pulsating formation come in again. But this time they bow before* ZANELLI. ELLIE, BABA, ANNA *carry flails.* SUFI *watches from behind a column.*

DANCERS. The King!

They bow.

BOMOGRICA. The King of the Feast must be cured. Cure the King.

ZANELLI. Cure? What's wrong with him?

BOMOGRICA.

The King must be cured of his anger.

108

The bean must be cured of its pod.
The King must be cured of his soul.

DANCERS. Cure the King.

ELLIE, *stepping out.* With this holy flail I part the chaff from the corn.

MAMA ZUGO. With this holy flail I part the good from the evil.

ANNA. With this holy flail I part the life from death.

All cheer.

Sudden skirl of music and the dancers envelop ZANELLI. BOMOGRICA *and* PAPA ZUGO *pick him up and the rest start beating him with their flails, so that he doesn't join in the laughter of the* DANCERS *as they carry him out.*

PRATT. Good old Joe.

UNCLE HENRY, *to* PRATT. But what happened? He reconverted you, prayed, and you went in the last half of the ninth and hit a home run.

PRATT. No. It wasn't like that. I forget who won. I only remember I felt I didn't want to play the game.

UNCLE HENRY. Boy, you're peculiar.

A man's cry is heard in the distance, overtopping the music.

UNCLE HENRY. What was that?

The celebrants come in singly. ANNA, *heartbroken, comes in on the arm of her mother; the others file back guiltily.* FATHER ZUGO, *an exception, appears happy.* ELLIE *runs to her* UNCLE HENRY.

ELLIE. Uncle Henry!

UNCLE HENRY. Whatsa matter, lil' girl?

ELLIE. We just threw Mr. Zanelli over a cliff.

UNCLE HENRY *and* PRATT, *rising.* What!

UNCLE HENRY *and* PRATT *run off. Music bridge. Dimming of lights to indicate passage of time.*

Enter UNCLE HENRY *and* PRATT.

PRATT. What's a sprained ankle and a few bruises.

UNCLE HENRY. It's not that. It's doing that to an American citizen.

PRATT. It was a compliment.

UNCLE HENRY. Suppose he had been killed. How would I have written that one up?

PRATT. It's all nonsense. . . .

Suddenly.

Ah.

They focus on a point off stage.

Look at that tired little bacchante limping home. What a pity I got myself dirty pulling up Zanelli.

He starts to go off.

UNCLE HENRY. You're coming back?

PRATT. What! I'm just going to wash.

UNCLE HENRY. I thought perhaps . . . you still have plans . . . ?

PRATT. Certainly.

UNCLE HENRY. But the fun's over.

BABA *comes on wearily, making a long cross in front of them to her house.*

PRATT. God bless you, Baba.

BABA, *startled.* What? Oh.

UNCLE HENRY. Pleasant dreams, Baba.

BABA. Yes, Sir.

PRATT. See?

UNCLE HENRY. See what?

PRATT. The answer to my prayer, I mean, my problem.

UNCLE HENRY. You wouldn't. You—you debase yourself.

PRATT.

What? You flatter me and confuse, Old Boy,
The kingdom of heaven with the whoredom of art.
She is a temple of night, and Europe, and now let
The last Goth put a penny in the box.

UNCLE HENRY, *as* PRATT *leaves.* Right now?

PRATT. First I must wash.

UNCLE HENRY. Yes, I see that.

He catches BABA *just as she is about to enter her door.*
Baba, my dear. Our friend, the sacker of cities—
He whispers.

BABA.
I wouldn't let that man come near me.

More whispers.

All right. I'll accept your money.
When he comes I'll be silent as the grave.
But suppose it's my husband Marco come back again
And I don't answer the door?

UNCLE HENRY. He's been away for twenty years.

BABA. That means he's due back any time.

UNCLE HENRY, *giving more money.* Here.

BABA. Thanks and good night.

UNCLE HENRY. Good night.

He goes off, avoiding PRATT, *who comes on eagerly.*
BABA *goes in hurriedly.* PRATT *knocks on her door.*

PRATT. Baba. Baba. Baba!

*He clenches his fist in frustration but retires from the
door when he sees* ANNA *and* ZANELLI *come on. For the
first time we see them with their arms about one another,
in the attitude of lovers. They are oblivious to* PRATT *and
to much else as they cross the square.*

ANNA. What was it called?

ZANELLI. Basketball! Basketball!

ANNA. But you said you played it in church.

ZANELLI.
Not *in* church. Downstairs.
You see, Anna, over here you bury people
Underneath your churches.
In America we have gymnasiums.

I don't know why I talk about America—
You'll never understand.

She begins to cry.

Anna!

ANNA.

Joe.

They embrace.

ZANELLI.

Anna, what we did tonight was wrong.

She cries again.

But we had to do it. Look, Anna, if we
Were in an earthquake together
Or lost at sea on a raft for months without water,
That would be bad, sure, awful, but
It would bring us together, wouldn't it?
We'd sort of be proud of it later.
That's the way sex is—horrible, but
There you are, together, and never giving up!

They kiss and leave.

PRATT *with even more eagerness now tries* BABA's *door again.*

PRATT. Baba! Baba!

He seems about ready to break down the door when he sees ELLIE *come on. She is in the remains of the weird pastoral costume of the festival and seems tipsy.*

PRATT. Good heavens.

ELLIE. Oh. Did I scare you, Bassett?

PRATT. No, no.

ELLIE. Didn't you recognize me in this?

Holds up a remnant.

Somebody pulled this off. Didn't you recognize me?

PRATT. I did and didn't, Ellie.

ELLIE. Oh, I'm a living paradox tonight. Feel good—

look like hades. Bound for beddy-bye but wide awake. Perfectly exhausted yet thrumming with second wind.

PRATT. You had a good time at the festival.

ELLIE. Think so? Are you sure? Not my usual good time, so it's a question whether it was a good time or not. But then it was a holiday. Nobody works but everybody took the holiday, but I had more fun since I work. Oh, that dance! I think I came in first. Oh, dear, two hours ago I felt so young. You know, the more people the younger. Where's that thing?

PRATT. Is the holiday over, Ellie?

ELLIE. What? More games? Where?

PRATT *takes her arm.*

PRATT. This way.

ELLIE. And then will you take me home?

PRATT. I'll take you home, Ellie.

ACT THREE

Scene One

The scene is the same but everything is cleaned up and the temple is very bright and cheerful in the midafternoon sun. A few more stones have been restored to their ancient places. GORJO's *wineshop is not visible but his tables are inside the columns and seem to have spread there from its new location, out of sight but nearby.*

ELLIE *and her* UNCLE HENRY *are sitting at a tiny table on her balcony. He is reading the paper; she is writing letters.* BABA *comes through the plaza.*

ELLIE. Isn't it a beautiful day, Baba.

BABA. Yes, God bless you, madame.

ELLIE. Do you think you will like your new house?

BABA. Yes, but the cat might be worried.

ELLIE, *to* UNCLE HENRY. I would like to leave that lady something when we go. A hand mirror or something. I suppose money wouldn't be the thing.

UNCLE HENRY, *firmly*. You don't have it to give, Ellie. Not yet.

He reads.

ELLIE, *sighs, smiles*. To think I once disliked her.

UNCLE HENRY. Now you've more in common with her.

ELLIE, *hurt*. Uncle Henry.

UNCLE HENRY. You amaze me, Ellie. That morning after the carnival or whatever it was. You get up at the usual hour, prepare the usual breakfast, write letters. Did you sleep in the big bed with all the curlicues on it?

ELLIE. It's just an ordinary, eighteenth-century, baroque Austrian bed.

UNCLE HENRY. I'll bet *he* didn't think it was just another morning. I'd like to have been there when *he* woke up!

114

ELLIE. He sprang out of bed rather earlier than usual and took a long walk.

UNCLE HENRY. You amaze me.

ELLIE. I am calm in the security of my love for him. You're a cold man. You don't understand that one sometimes has to sacrifice that thing which is dearest to one.

UNCLE HENRY. You sound so old-fashioned.

ELLIE, *laughing.* I didn't mean what you mean. I meant— well, I had to sacrifice something to the gods that night— my conscience. Love is greater than morals, as the builder of this temple knew.

UNCLE HENRY. I hope the gods appreciated what they got, and that you're not confusing a sacrifice with an investment.

ELLIE. It *was* a good conscience, as I remember. . . .

BOMOGRICA *comes on. He is being talked to by* SUFI.

SUFI. Good morning.

ELLIE *and* UNCLE HENRY. Good morning.

ELLIE. We were saying how much we enjoyed the festival.

UNCLE HENRY. Yes, yes.

SUFI, *after bowing.* I'm not superstitious but as I told Bomogrica, it is snowing in the mountains. In my opinion the festival was a success.

ELLIE. I did all *I* could.

SUFI *joins* BOMOGRICA *at the table.*

UNCLE HENRY. Yes.

SUFI. Another example of its mystic power is that Anna Zugo is no longer ticklish.

UNCLE HENRY. Who isn't what?

ELLIE. The cute little acrobat—no longer—

Enter PRATT, *brisk, pretty much the same, carrying rope and tackle.*

UNCLE HENRY. Ah, the sacker of cities.

115

PRATT, *with a look of worried concentration on his face,
crosses toward his digging.* UNCLE HENRY *calls.*

Could I see you a moment, Pratt?

PRATT. Certainly.

He joins them and ELLIE *smiles casually.*

ELLIE. How's the headache, Bassett?

PRATT. Not so bad today.

UNCLE HENRY. Bassett, first of all, I want to tell you how
much I admire the work you've done here. You know your
job—you, ah, are industrious, ah—but the main thing is—
I like you.

PRATT. Are you going away?

UNCLE HENRY. No-o.

Smiles.

—What I am getting at is that I feel that what happened
between you and Ellie is perhaps all for the best—well,
there's no question about it, is there?

Jovially.

Perhaps old Sufi is right after all, these festivals have a
kind of mystical power of some kind.

PRATT *is stunned.*

PRATT. I had hoped that a man of your tact would not
learn about that.

UNCLE HENRY. You made no attempt to conceal it.

PRATT. Of course, I mean that you would not notice it.
But since you have, let me tell you what, in substance, I've
told Ellie. First of all, I more than apologize. I think that—
although no real harm has been done—that the weeks and
months will reveal to us both that it was perhaps a mistake.
As for me, I'd rather not talk about it. To me it's just another
one of those incidents which show how weak and irresponsible we all are these days.

UNCLE HENRY. I don't feel irresponsible, do you, Ellie?

ELLIE. Well.

116

Robert Hivnor

PRATT. You see the situation: we two alone, living in the same house, me—overworked, with the digging—and both of us grown-up, sophisticated . . . getting nowhere. Everybody behaves with more freedom abroad. Some people get away with murder!

UNCLE HENRY. I don't know what you're talking about.

PRATT. Surely you're not going to hold me accountable for—

UNCLE HENRY. The point is, a lady of good family has been seduced.

PRATT. What!

UNCLE HENRY. She has been publically embarrassed.

PRATT. What public? Here? In this end-of-the-road rural bohemia?

UNCLE HENRY. Pomo is a healthy mountain town of much military and religious significance.

PRATT. My god!

UNCLE HENRY. But the public I was thinking of is in the States.

PRATT, *to* ELLIE. You've—those damn letters—don't you realize that you could damage my whole financial position by letting this thing get out?

ELLIE. Oh?

UNCLE HENRY. How so?

PRATT. It's a sad fact that my money is administered by two small-town puritan lawyers of great age by the name of Postlethwaite and Bliss. Those two religious bluenoses have no idea what I'm doing or how I live, yet—

UNCLE HENRY, *breaking in firmly.* I'm familiar with the duties of Harvey Bliss and his partner.

PRATT. How?

UNCLE HENRY. I believe it came out in the course of Ellie's correspondence with her club.

PRATT, *regarding* ELLIE. Seduced!

117

UNCLE HENRY. As a matter of fact, Harvey is fond of you. Thinks you're brilliant but unstable.

PRATT, *muttering*. Seduced her like a river seduces the ocean—

UNCLE HENRY *is looking through his wallet for a paper*.

UNCLE HENRY. Rivers, oceans—talk about anything but yourself.

ELLIE. Has the word *love* disappeared from the councils of men?

UNCLE HENRY. Ah. For two weeks I looked into my troubled conscience, then to protect the good names of all of us, I acted. A clipping from the Bridgewater *Signal*.

He gives it to PRATT, *who takes it, reads and droops*.

It announces your engagement to Ellie. There's a note of congratulation with it. I don't recognize the signature.

To ELLIE.

Your Uncle Harvey thinks marriage will be the making of both of you.

PRATT, *to* ELLIE. Mr. Bliss is a relative?

ELLIE. My mother's uncle. What a coincidence!

PRATT, *to* UNCLE HENRY. May I say to all the uncles that this engagement will not last long.

He gets up.

UNCLE HENRY. Breaking the engagement is one way to handle it.

PRATT, *to himself*. Must do something. . . .

ELLIE. Bassett—apply to your friends. Get their advice. What's good for you is good for me.

UNCLE HENRY. He has no friends.

ELLIE *goes in and* PRATT *walks away. As he does so he meets* DOCTOR SUFI *and* BOMOGRICA *coming on*.

BOMOGRICA. Hello, my friend.

SUFI *bows to* PRATT.

PRATT. Have you seen Joe? I need Joe.

BOMOGRICA. Mr. Zanelli sleeps late these days.

PRATT *drags out his demolition equipment.*

Why should he want Zanelli? Surely he isn't going to begin again.

SUFI. I don't think so.

UNCLE HENRY *joins* SUFI *and* BOMOGRICA, *shakes hands with the latter.*

BOMOGRICA. What's he doing now? Isn't he finished?

SUFI. Ah, Doctor Pratt!

He is ignored.

UNCLE HENRY. Well, Bassett boy, what are you up to now?

PRATT. Well, on the one hand I'm continuing my research. On the other hand I'm tearing down a heathen temple.

SUFI. I pray that isn't so.

BOMOGRICA. What would be left?

PRATT. A flat place. Air. Sunlight. Freedom.

SUFI. A flat place. Indiana. . . .

BOMOGRICA. The sun has come up. I don't think he ought to work in the sun.

SUFI. He's not looking well.

PRATT *laughs and attaches rope.*

PRATT. When I say boo you jump.

BOMOGRICA. I thought he found what he was looking for.

PRATT. I'm not even warm.

A discussion between the three older men.

BOMOGRICA. I must ask, Sir, I must ask—are you listening?

PRATT. So far.

He goes on digging.

BOMOGRICA. Sir, I must insist that this excavation be—

PRATT *pulls down a fragment.* SUFI *approaches.*

SUFI. My boy.

PRATT. Out of the way, medicine man.

Waves hammer at him.

UNCLE HENRY. Take it easy, boy.

SUFI. Threatening Sufi with death is like threatening to take milk from a cow.

UNCLE HENRY *and* BOMOGRICA *now come up behind* PRATT, *grasp him, wind some rope around him and sit on him.*

BOMOGRICA. A double knot.

UNCLE HENRY. I think this is the best thing.

SUFI. No violence.

PRATT. What is this, a lynching party?

UNCLE HENRY. Will you stop the work for a while, Pratt?

PRATT. Do you think I could leave it at this? A temple! Don't you see we have to purge these things from history?

BOMOGRICA. He doesn't like this? I thought everybody liked things like this.

SUFI. Isn't this the source? Isn't this Journey's End?

PRATT. We must have earlier beginnings!

BOMOGRICA, *to* UNCLE HENRY. The dust when he took down Fort Pomo! Got me right in here.

Coughs.

SUFI. And the profanity!

To PRATT.

Mr. Pratt, we have been very tolerant of the disorder caused by your work because we thought you were getting somewhere. Don't you believe that this is the somewhere?

PRATT. No.

SUFI. I think it is. Look at the sun shining on it. God is running his finger along the edges. Sir, I think it is possible that God caused you not to believe in Him so you might get better grades in school. So you might better dig us up our temple. Do you believe that is possible?

PRATT, *with scorn.* Hah.

SUFI. Don't you believe in anything?

PRATT. I believe in what is left.

BOMOGRICA. Maybe he doesn't believe he's tied up. Let's get this rigging out of here.

ELLIE *comes out.*

ELLIE. What are you doing to Bassett?

UNCLE HENRY. It's all right, Ellie.

ELLIE *gives a sympathetic sob and comes down.*

ELLIE. Untie him. Untie him this instant.

PRATT. No . . . no. . . .

GORJO, *pointing.* He's. . . .

He has seen that a change has come over PRATT.

SUFI. Is that a smile?

PRATT *has ceased struggling.*

BOMOGRICA. The sun has got him at last.

SUFI. No, this is what they call in the States a nervous breakdown.

GORJO. First time I ever saw a nervous breakdown.

UNCLE HENRY, *to* PRATT. Easy boy. Can you hear me?

ELLIE *unties* PRATT. *Sits beside him.*

PRATT. That's mine. That rope is mine and that pick is mine.

ELLIE. All right.

BOMOGRICA *drops the equipment he was about to take away.*

PRATT. Do you like sand boxes?

ELLIE. Yes, I do.

He seems to be making something in the sand.

PRATT. So do I! Would you rather play Panama Canal or house?

ELLIE. I think I'd rather play house.

He smiles.

ACT THREE

Scene Two

The last scene opens as the first one did, but the idea is that many of the same actions (avoiding the center of the square, and so on) make sense in the religious context of the temple.

ELLIE. Good morning, Gorjo.

GORJO. Good morning, Madame.

ELLIE, *to herself.* In two hours I will be madame, blast you.

BABA *comes out of her house.* ELLIE *begins to do squats and bends.*

ELLIE. Good morning, Baba.

BABA. Good morning, Madame Sprocket. That's the right name. You're not married already?

ELLIE, *with a laugh.* Of course not!

BABA. You have a beautiful clear day for it.

ELLIE. You can see every mountain in the world.

Her UNCLE HENRY *comes out on the balcony. He is carefully dressed in a dark suit with flower.*

UNCLE HENRY, *kissing her on cheek.* Brides don't see, Ellie. They don't do anything. They just wait.

ELLIE. How true, in a poetic sense.

Three lady vase-bearers come on, push through the square.

Look, now we know why they always went out of the way to visit the temple. And why Baba and the others always avoided the center of the square. Some goddess was stationed there. It all fits in, doesn't it, Uncle Henry?

UNCLE HENRY. Brides think so.

BASSETT PRATT *comes quietly and slowly on from stage east. He is not exactly somnambulistic for sleepwalkers*

122

seem to know where they are going. He wanders over to the tables but examines the columns at odd moments with professional interest.

Lo, the bridegroom cometh.

ELLIE, *a whisper.* Yes.

UNCLE HENRY. I consider it tasteful to have had him sleep elsewhere for a few weeks. And I consider this a good omen for the success of your marriage.

ELLIE. What is a good omen?

UNCLE HENRY. The fact that he showed up at the wedding.

ELLIE. Go to him, Uncle Henry. Comfort him. I mean, calm him down.

They go in. UNCLE HENRY, *coming out of* ELLIE'S *house, meets* SUFI *coming into the plaza.*

SUFI. Good morning.

UNCLE HENRY. Good morning.

SUFI. Do you think he's well enough to be married?

UNCLE HENRY. You mean sick enough, don't you?

SUFI. Why are bachelors so witty at weddings? But seriously—his state of mind—I wonder—

UNCLE HENRY. I wanted him to wait until we got back to the States, but he was determined to do it here.

SUFI. Well, it is a good day for it. Surfaces very active today—jackasses rubbing their sides against the buildings. By the way, I have a friend in Indiana. Would you like his name?

UNCLE HENRY. No, thank you. There are two weddings today, I believe.

SUFI. Here comes the other party now.

Enter BOMOGRICA, FATHER ZUGO, BROTHER ZUGO, ZANELLI, ANNA, MOTHER ZUGO. *The women are in peasant costume, the men in suits.*

ZANELLI. Jack!

PRATT *comes down smiling.*

PRATT. Congratulations, Joe.

ZANELLI. Thanks, pal.

They shake hands.

Look at that.

He pushes ANNA *forward.*

All mine. Even if I never make a million, man, I'm a success. A success.

BOMOGRICA, *to* SUFI. Oscar here now believes America exists.

FATHER ZUGO. Yes, Joe convinced me. He cured my daughter of her tickles. However, after that she began to get sick in the mornings. It was like a mist lifting—I began to see America.

The ZUGOS *laugh.* FATHER ZUGO *slaps* ZANELLI *on the back.*

ZANELLI, *mainly to* PRATT. Yeh, a month ago they tossed me over a cliff. I was a scapegoat! Now, I'm a *husband!*

He smiles, but a certain consciousness clouds his face.

FATHER ZUGO *laughs and slaps him on the back.*

FATHER ZUGO. Yes, Joe is all right. Last night we teach him acrobatics.

BROTHER ZUGO. Very good. Watch.

FATHER ZUGO *claps his hand. The family takes its stance.* ZANELLI, *a little tardily but smiling, jumps apart and to the center of the plaza. Another yipee and clap and* FATHER ZUGO *is on* ZANELLI's *shoulders. Another one and the other three* ZUGOS *perch on his arms so that he is supporting all of them.*

ZANELLI. You don't think there's anything symbolic about this, do you?

The ACROBATS *shout and amid applause descend, and the whole party forms a festive group and goes off.* BABA *follows them.*

SUFI. You can say what you want about that fellow Zanelli, but he has a fine set of teeth.

124

Robert Hivnor

UNCLE HENRY. The old man shows commendable flexibility—admitting that America exists.

He smiles and shakes his head.

BOMOGRICA. Yes, but—

SUFI. Of course I know America exists. But think—if it didn't! If it never had! Columbus would have discovered Hawaii. The Irish would have immigrated to China, the Shakers settled among the Hindus. The English would have been orientalized by a culture instead of brutalized by a frontier.

Rises.

The Atlantic and the Pacific oceans would be the same. You must admit it is a conception. Almost a vision!

PRATT. Goodbye, Ali Sufi. You have won. I have lost.

SUFI. God be with you. Won? Lost? No, no, there has been a solution—of sorts.

PRATT. But you got your way. The temple stands.

SUFI. Part of it does. My child, it stands because you are powerless. You destroy _all_ the past and naturally find yourself alone. It takes much power to rule, much more to purify. In this connection, I am reminded that I have a lecture. Untranslated into English but printed up. Shall I send it to you? It is called—

PRATT _turns from him sadly._

At this moment ELLIE SPROCKET _runs on. For the first time in the play she has on that most formidable costume —make-up, hat, stockings, bag, everything—the female street dress. She trips on, carrying a shallow basket of fresh fruit and small squashes and gourds, and shouts hellos. She runs to_ PRATT _and kisses him on the cheek._

UNCLE HENRY, SUFI, BOMOGRICA. Bless you. Lovely dress. You look so. _Etc._

ELLIE. There were no flowers to speak of, so I decided to carry this basket of fruit.

SUFI. You were right, my child, for marriage is a harvest as well as a planting.

ELLIE. And these grapes are so good in midmorning.

SUFI. Would *I* think so?

He picks off one, is pleasantly surprised, nods.

Yes, indeed.

BOMOGRICA. And now comes a moment I've looked forward to so long.

He looks at ELLIE.

ELLIE, *smiling*. Oh?

BOMOGRICA. In the name of the citizens of Pomo and of the government, such as it is, I present to you this letter, as a token of recognition for your services.

ELLIE. Oh, thank you. I thought you were going to kiss me.

SUFI, *to* UNCLE HENRY. It was written for Mr. Pratt, but at the last moment we decided to give it to Mrs. Pratt.

UNCLE HENRY. It was a nice thought, Doctor.

ELLIE. Thank you so much.

BOMOGRICA. And now I shall kiss you.

Does so.

UNCLE HENRY, *looking at his watch*. It's time.

A powerful formal smile to SUFI *and* BOMOGRICA.

Gentlemen, I may not see you again for some years. I want to say now that there are three great pleasures in coming to Pomo. One is the experience of arriving, the unforgettable visual experiences; and second, getting to really know Pomo and its people; and third, leaving Pomo.

ELLIE *and* PRATT *and* UNCLE HENRY *shake hands with* BOMOGRICA. SUFI *stands apart smiling, palms together. The three Americans start off up through the colonnade. As they approach the colonnade* PRATT *stops long enough to turn and wonder. They go off.*

BOMOGRICA, *to* SUFI. I meant to say something about them having a lot of little Pratts but it stuck in my throat. Tell me, Doctor, are good people always ridiculous?

126

sufi. Yes, it's a law. Let us hope the converse is also true.

Suddenly to him.

Watch out!

He kneels and picks up an insect.

Amid all this married joy, this autumnal fruition,
This being fruit in the garden of Allah,
This being fruit on a tree that is being shaken,
And this falling to the ground at the feet of the beloved,
Amid all this, I regret to say,
Someone has stepped on a beetle.

He holds it up.

One leg out of six gone. A small thing

With sternness.

Compared to the thoughts
That have today been bent, crushed, squashed
In this plaza. Come, more than brother,

They walk slowly upstage, ali sufi *being careful to jangle out his warnings to creeping kind.*

Let's take no more steps today, for steps
Even on the holy way can hurt,
As we have seen. Genuflections can kill bees.
Careful!

Points to ground.

Any violence today,
Any gross movements of any kind,
Let them be done by others.
Watch out!
We will sit down and be harmless.

They sit down at a table with tranquil smiles and bomogrica *pours wine as the curtain comes down.*

TWILIGHT CRANE

Junji Kinoshita

translated by A. C. Scott

INTRODUCTION

To the outer world the drama of Japan has for long been represented by the Noh and Kabuki theaters which have made such a great contribution to Oriental drama as a whole; the birth of a contemporary theater is an event which has remained unnoticed by a majority.

This is accounted for by a number of factors. The history of modern Japanese drama is a very brief one covering a period of little more than fifty years, a period, too, which was sadly disrupted by war and all its attendant evils. Much of the achievement of the new theater in its early years lay in the interpretation and imitation of Western drama, and the troubled years of the last two decades effectively blocked any real development of a movement, which at best was only in an experimental stage. So far Japan has not succeeded in creating a significant modern drama movement of her own, a theater which is as much an expression of her inner being as were the Kabuki and Noh in their time.

The postwar years have brought many problems to the younger artists of Japan, not the least of which in the field of drama has been the problem of building on the great traditions of the past and yet creating a living art out of the present. Mr. Junji Kinoshita is one of the younger playwrights who is making a significant attempt to solve this problem.

Japan is rich in its wealth of folklore, which, more than anything else, epitomizes in simple fashion the spirit and nostalgia of its people and the poetry of its countryside, and it is to folklore that Kinoshita has gone, as others have done in the West before him, in an attempt to preserve tradition and yet create from it. The play, *Yuzuru, Twilight Crane*, is a measure of the success obtained by Mr. Kinoshita in his work for a new theater. Based on an old folk tale, the play uses colloquial speech to express a theme which is universal, the contest between materialism and spiritual values; it is a fantasy which draws a conclusion applicable to human nature the world over and perhaps never more obvious than today.

The important thing about this play is that it dispenses with the spurious sophistication which occasionally tends to encumber contemporary artistic development in Japan. The theme is developed against a background of folklore which appeals to something fundamental within us all, the child listening to a fairy tale. A crane, in gratitude for the kindness rendered to her by a simple-hearted peasant, Yohyo, when she was wounded by an arrow, turns mortal and becomes his faithful wife. She possesses the power of weaving beautiful cloth from her feathers, which eventually proves her husband's undoing. Overcome by greed and urged on by two mercenary villagers, he demands more and more cloth from her until in the end she can no longer continue, and resuming her form as a crane, she flies away at sundown leaving the materialistic human world for ever. In its simple dignity the play contains a great depth of poetic feeling. It has caught something of the very spirit of the Japanese people in that it gives us that intangible reflection of the inner self of a country any true work of art must possess. Mr. Kinoshita's play bridges a gap which has long been open in the dramatic art of his country.

Twilight Crane was first performed in Osaka in 1949 with the actress Yasue Yamamoto in the leading role. The play received public and official acclaim, and Kinoshita was awarded the Mainichi Press Drama Prize for his work, whilst in 1950 Miss Yamamoto received the Ministry of Education prize for her acting as Tsu. A major performance was staged at one of the leading Tokyo theaters in 1952, where it was received with even greater enthusiasm than before. The partnership of Mr. Kinoshita and Miss Yamamoto and her company, the Budo no Kai, has been a happy omen for the Japanese theater and much may be expected from **their** continued collaboration.

It was while I was making a special study of the Kabuki

theater in Tokyo that I first saw *Twilight Crane* staged.
My work in the classical theater had not prevented me from
seeing a certain amount of contemporary drama being
played in Tokyo, but I had remained unimpressed and
sometimes bored by such modern developments as came
my way. Then one evening a Japanese friend took me to
see *Twilight Crane*. It was an unforgettable experience that
fired my imagination immediately. Here was a play which
preserved the poetry and feeling of the ancient theater in
the best possible way; tradition was not cast overboard and
yet it was not allowed to dominate simply because it was
tradition. The production owed much to Western stage
technique, but used in a creative not an imitative sense—
in short it was excellent modern Japanese theater.

Shortly after this I commenced my association with Mr.
Kinoshita, which has resulted in the production of this
English version of his play. In considering a translation like
this, several points must be borne in mind. *Twilight Crane*
is written in colloquial Japanese speech which might almost
be termed dialect, not the dialect of any one district but
those familiar speech forms common to the nation at large.
In this way the author makes his play appeal to the widest
possible audience. It follows that in many cases it is impossible to give literal renderings in English. The natural
rhythm and euphony of the Japanese language are also
qualities impossible to reproduce in another tongue, but
they have been used with great delicacy of effect by the
playwright in the original. Perhaps one of the simplest
examples is the use of the beautiful Japanese word of
farewell, *sayonara*. Tsu's final words in the play, when
taking leave of her husband, are, "*Sayonara, honto ni,
sayonara. . . .*" They contain a quality of wistfulness which
the more prosaic English "goodbye" cannot possibly reproduce.

The aim of this English version has been to preserve as
far as possible the simplicity of the Japanese without becoming slangy in the process, whilst at the same time retaining

the quality of drama spoken on the stage. It is hoped that it may serve to introduce to a wider public a play which is an important addition to the postwar drama of all nations and a milestone on the way to a vital modern theater in Japan.

A.C.S. *Tokyo.*

PUBLISHERS' NOTE: Mr. Kinoshita writes the following about the game played by the children in *Twilight Crane*: "The game, Nengara, is played by several children at once. A long nail or pointed piece of wood (the nengara) is held by each child. The first one hurls his down to stick upright in the ground. The next child throws his nengara and tries to strike down the first one, if he succeeds, he is the victor. If not, the third child tries to strike down the two stakes and so on. The one who succeeds in knocking a nengara or several out of the ground is the victor."

134

CHARACTERS

CHILDREN

YOHYO

TSU

SODO

UNZU

A solitary peasant's hut stands in the middle of the wide snow-covered countryside. CHILDREN *can be heard singing in the distance.*

Let's cover Grandpa with the eiderdown we sew,
Let's cover Grandma with the eiderdown we sew,
Chin kara kan kara,
Ton, ton ton. . . .

Inside the hut YOHYO *is stretched out asleep before the hearth. The singing stops and the* CHILDREN *appear running before the hut.*

CHILDREN, *chanting in chorus.*

Tsu! Tsu! sing us a song,
Tsu! Tsu! come and play with us,
Tsu! Tsu! sing us a song.

YOHYO, *opening his eyes.* What's the matter, what's the matter?

CHILDREN.

Tsu! come and play with us,
Tsu! sing us a song, Tsu! Tsu!

YOHYO. Oh, you're looking for Tsu are you? Well she has gone out.

CHILDREN. She's gone out? Truly? Where has she gone?

YOHYO. I don't know where she's gone.

CHILDREN. Where has she gone, when is she coming back? Tell us, tell us, Yohyo!

YOHYO, *standing up.* Hey, you noisy children, be quiet!

CHILDREN, *scattering.* Yah, yah, Yohyo's getting cross, Yohyo, Yohyo, silly old Yohyo!

YOHYO. He! he! he! all right, all right, don't run away, stay and I'll play with you.

137

CHILDREN. What shall we play?

YOHYO. What *shall* we play?

CHILDREN. *Nengara?*

YOHYO. All right, nengara.

CHILDREN. Let's sing!

YOHYO. All right, let's sing.

CHILDREN. Snowball fights?

YOHYO. All right, snowball fights.

He joins the children.

CHILDREN. Bird in a cage, bird in a cage?

YOHYO. All right, bird in a cage.

CHILDREN. Stag, stag, how many horns?

YOHYO. All right; stag, stag, how many horns. Now let's go, let's go!

CHILDREN. Stag, stag, how many horns!

They run off repeating the words.

YOHYO, *about to follow.* Oh, I forgot! It will be too bad if Tsu comes back to find the soup cold. She is so dear, so dear.

He puts the pan on the fire. TSU *comes out from a back room.*

TSU. Yohyo!

YOHYO. Oh Tsu! where have you been?

TSU. Oh nowhere particular . . . you shouldn't. . . .

YOHYO. He! he! he!—I was putting the soup on. It would be no good if you came back to find it cold, he! he! he!

TSU. Oh thank you, and now I must get supper ready for you.

YOHYO. Um . . . then I will go and play nengara.

TSU. Nengara eh?

YOHYO. And after that snowball fights and then singing.

TSU. And after that bird in a cage, and then stag, stag, how many horns. Am I right?

138

YOHYO. Yes! Stag, stag, how many horns. Tsu, won't you come too?

TSU. I would love to, but I must get the meal ready.

YOHYO. Oh come on!

He starts to drag her off.

TSU. No, you mustn't, you mustn't!

YOHYO. Oh come on, come on, let's go and play together!

TSU. No, stop it, stop it!

She is dragged away laughing. The children's singing is heard in the distance. SODO *and* UNZU, *two villagers appear.*

SODO. What! That woman over there? She's Yohyo's wife, you say?

UNZU. That's right, Yohyo is a lucky fellow to get such a nice wife; he has done nothing but sleep by the fireside since she came.

SODO. Stupid though he was before, he was a hard worker, but how does a foolish fellow like that come to have such a pretty wife?

UNZU. It's a mystery. Where she appeared from and when nobody knows, but Yohyo has never had an empty purse since.

SODO. I say, Unzu, is that story about the cloth true?

UNZU. It's true all right, if we take that stuff to the city we can sell it for ten *ryo* the piece every time.

SODO. Did you say that his wife weaves it herself?

UNZU. That's right, but she won't let anyone see her at work in the weaving room. Simple Yohyo never tries to peep, and next morning when he gets up the cloth is woven, and what beautiful cloth it is, too!

SODO. *Semba ori,* that's what you called it, isn't it?

UNZU. That's what the townspeople call it, they say you can only find such stuff in heaven.

SODO. Unzu, you must have acted as agent between her and the townsfolk and made plenty of money out of it

139

UNZU, *laughing meaningly.* A small commission, that's all!

SODO. You're a wily one, but if it's really semba ori it should fetch between fifty and a hundred ryo at least.

UNZU. What! Do you think so? But what on earth is semba ori?

SODO. Well, it's rare stuff made from a thousand feathers plucked from a live crane.

UNZU. Where the devil does that woman gather such feathers, I wonder?

SODO. Um . . . is this the weaving room?

Forgetting where he is, he looks into the weaving room. There's a loom all right. Oh. . . .

Enters the room.

UNZU. What's the matter?

SODO, *picking up a feather.* —we thought. . . !

There is a pause and TSU, *who has returned unnoticed, slips out of the inner room.* UNZU *gives an exclamation of startled surprise.*

SODO. Er . . . I'm sorry to have entered your house while you were out.

TSU *says nothing, but stands looking at him with her head on one side like a bird.*

UNZU. Yes, I'm Unzu from the village over there and I'm much obliged to Yohyo about the cloth.

TSU *remains silent in the same position.*

SODO. Oh—er—madame, I should like to talk to you—er—about your cloth, which I heard about from this fellow here. . . . I'm Sodo from the village yonder, I came over for a little chat. . . . Is it true that it's absolutely genuine semba ori?—though it's rude of me to talk about it.

TSU *only looks at them suspiciously and then goes back into the inner room with a fluttering movement as though she had heard a sudden sound.* SODO *and* UNZU *look at each other.*

SODO. Well?

UNZU. What do we say to that. . . ?

SODO. She didn't seem to understand a word . . . she looked just like a bird.

UNZU. That's a fact, just like a bird.

Twilight gradually falls, and inside the house the fire in the hearth flickers red.

SODO, *looking at the crane's feather.* You know there's a certain story about a crane who took a liking to a man and became his wife.

UNZU. What! What are you talking about?

SODO. Um . . . I see now . . . yesterday a villager told me that one evening four or five days ago, he saw a woman standing by the edge of a pool on the mountain over yonder, and thinking there was something mysterious about her, he watched her secretly and she, not knowing she was being observed, glided into the water and turned into a crane.

UNZU. What!

SODO. And after wading about in the water for some time she changed from a crane into a woman again and slid away.

UNZU *gives a loud cry and rushes from the hut.*

SODO. Hey, stop making such a noise!

He rushes out of the hut in spite of himself.

UNZU, *fearfully.* Is that wife really a c-crane then?

SODO. You fool, be quiet! Don't speak about such a thing, no one can tell, there's no such story.

UNZU. What shall I do? I've cheated Yohyo out of a lot of profit.

SODO. Stop worrying about that. If it's real semba ori we can sell it in the capital for a thousand ryo.

UNZU. What! A thousand ryo!

SODO. Besides you told me that stupid Yohyo had become a little more knowing about money matters recently, didn't you?

UNZU. Um . . . that's as may be.

SODO. Well then, Unzu, we'd better get Yohyo on our side and persuade him to make his wife weave more and quickly too!

UNZU. Um . . . well, perhaps you are right.

SODO. Look out, here he comes!

YOHYO, *walking a little unsteadily and singing.*

Let's cover Grandpa with the eiderdown we sew,
Chin kara kan kara,
Ton, ton, ton. . . .

Why, I completely forgot to get the rice ready for Tsu!

SODO. Oi . . . Yohyo!

YOHYO. What?

SODO. Don't you recognize me? I'm Sodo from the village over there . . . hey, Unzu, you speak to him.

YOHYO. Oh Unzu, worrying about money for me again!

UNZU. Well, yes, if only you would produce that cloth you could make as much money as you wanted.

YOHYO. There's no more cloth.

SODO. Why not?

YOHYO. Tsu says that it's all finished.

UNZU. But why? You could still make a lot of profit out of it.

YOHYO. Um . . . but I love my Tsu dearly.

SODO. You love her dearly, then why not make her weave cloth and so provide money for yourself.

YOHYO. That's all very well, but every time Tsu weaves more cloth she becomes thinner and thinner.

SODO. What! She becomes thinner and thinner? Hey, Yohyo, how and when did she become your bride?

YOHYO. Eh? Oh Tsu! She just appeared one evening when I was going to bed and said she had come to be my wife. He, he, he!

142

SODO. Um . . . hey you . . . did you ever do anything to help a crane?

YOHYO. Eh? A crane? Oh yes, once when I was working in the fields a crane came down wounded by an arrow and in great pain, so I pulled the arrow out and let it fly away.

SODO. What! . . . oh! . . . hey Unzu, if that's true we're beginning to get somewhere at last.

UNZU *is trembling.*

SODO. Then it's true we can still make a lot more money . . . hey Yohyo, that cloth . . . hey, Unzu, you tell him.

UNZU. Um . . . well . . . well, that cloth, if you take it to the capital you can sell it for a thousand. . . .

SODO, *to* UNZU. Fool . . . no, no, no! I say Yohyo, this time you can get hundreds of ryo, so try to make her weave once more.

YOHYO. What did you say? Hundreds of ryo?

SODO. That's what I said, hundreds of ryo!

To UNZU.

That's right, isn't it?

UNZU. Yes, that's right, he can make hundreds of ryo.

YOHYO. Really . . . hundreds of ryo. . . .

SODO. So just ask your wife once again.

He sees TSU *watching them from inside the house.*

Oh, come over here, I want you to listen to what I say!

He pulls YOHYO *into the shadows,* UNZU *also follows.* TSU *comes out peering after them with a wistful look on her face. Before long the* CHILDREN *appear.*

CHILDREN, *one after another.*

Ah, here's Tsu!
Tsu, let's play!
Why did you run away?
Sing a song, Tsu!
Bird in a cage!
Hide and seek!

143

Song!
Ring game!

They surround her.

Tsu, Tsu, oh Tsu!

TSU. Children, it's dark already. That's all for today!

CHILDREN. No, no, Tsu! Play with us, sing us a song!

TSU, *dully.* A song?

CHILDREN. Hide and seek!

TSU. Hide and seek?

CHILDREN. Bird in a cage!

TSU. Bird in a cage?

CHILDREN. Yes, yes! bird in a cage!

They form a ring around TSU, *joining hands and singing while they walk.*

Bird in a cage, bird in a cage,
When, when will you come out?
Swiftly and silently day turns into night,
Who is right behind you, who is right behind you,
Who is right behind you. . . ?
Tsu, Tsu, why don't you put your hand over your eyes?
Crouch down Tsu, crouch down!

TSU, *standing lost in thought, comes to herself.* Eh? Oh. . . .
She crouches and covers her eyes with her hands. The CHILDREN *continue to walk around her singing. The stage is dimmed swiftly, leaving only the figure of* TSU *focused in a ring of light.*

TSU. Yohyo, my dear one, what has happened to you? You are gradually changing. I don't know why, but you are moving away into a world that I can never enter. You are becoming the same as those terrible people whose words I cannot understand and who once wounded me with an arrow. What is the matter with you, how can I really help you? You saved my life. You pulled the arrow out of my back expecting nothing simply because you took pity on me. I came to you as your wife because it gave me such a great joy. I wove that cloth for you and you were as pleased

144

as a child. That's all right if you only care for money. But now you have enough money, and I only want to live alone with you quietly and peacefully in this small house. You are different from the other people. You belong to my world. I wanted our world to be like this for ever, the two of us in the middle of the wide countryside working together and playing with the children . . . but somehow you are going away from me, farther and farther away. What shall I do, oh what shall I do. . . ?

The singing has died away and the CHILDREN *have disappeared long ago. The lights go up and* TSU *suddenly gives a sidelong glance and runs into the house as if pursued.* SODO, UNZU *and* YOHYO *appear.*

SODO. Do you understand? If she says she'll never weave any more cloth for you, threaten to leave her.

YOHYO. He, he, he! That cloth that Tsu wove for me is beautiful stuff, isn't it?

SODO. Because it's such beautiful cloth we can sell it for you at two or three times the price it was before. Understand? Two or three times, so tell your wife that!

YOHYO. What, it will sell for two or three times as much money as before?

SODO. That's right, for hundreds of ryo!

YOHYO. What, hundreds of ryo?

SODO. That's what I said, so you make her weave it right away this evening, eh Unzu?

UNZU. Y-yes right away this very evening.

YOHYO. Um . . . but Tsu said she wouldn't weave any more.

SODO. You fool! If you sell it at a high price and make a lot of profit, your wife will be pleased too!

UNZU. Y-yes your wife will be pleased too.

YOHYO. Um. . . .

SODO. And after that we will take you sight-seeing to the capital. It's a fine city, isn't it, Unzu?

UNZU. Yes, it's a fine place.

YOHYO. It must be a fine town!

SODO. All right, do you understand? You can make a lot of money and go to the capital sight-seeing, as we've just said; you can see all kinds of interesting sights, or perhaps you don't want to go with us, eh?

YOHYO. Of course, I want to go with you.

UNZU. You want money as well, don't you?

YOHYO. Um . . . I want money as well.

SODO, *noticing* TSU *in the house*. Right, we'll get in and see it's woven right away, and if she refuses tell her you'll leave her!

YOHYO. Um . . . .

SODO, *pushing* YOHYO *into the house again*. Good for you, good for you, you're an excellent chap! We'd better hide ourselves, Unzu, until we see what happens.

They hide themselves.

TSU, *springing up to meet* YOHYO *as soon as the others have left*. Yohyo, come along quickly! Oh dear, you're wet through, you mustn't catch cold! Supper's just ready and the soup is hot because you prepared it. Come up nearer to the fire!

YOHYO. Um . . . .

TSU. Now eat your supper!

YOHYO, *eating*. Um . . . .

TSU. What's the matter . . . why are you so lifeless . . . you really shouldn't stay out so late when it is as cold as this. . . . You won't go out again, will you, or talk with strange people any more? Please don't go out!

YOHYO. Um . . . .

TSU. Promise me! Whatever you ask me I'll do for you, now that you have the money you like, whatever you ask me I'll do for you. . . .

YOHYO. Um. . . . I have much money, I keep it in that sack.

146

TSU. Well, now that you have the money, can't we live happily and quietly together, the two of us. Can't we?

YOHYO. Um. . . . I love you, Tsu!

TSU. And I really love you and you will always remain as you are now, won't you?

YOHYO. Um. . . . I really love you, Tsu.

Pause.

TSU. Now have some more . . . what, why not? Why don't you eat, eh?

YOHYO. Oh . . . ah . . . I say, Tsu. . . .

TSU. Well?

YOHYO. Tsu, you're lucky to have been to the capital so often!

TSU. No . . . I only saw it from the sky. . . .

Pulling herself up at her own words.

What's the matter? Why don't you eat some more supper?

YOHYO, *hesitatingly.* Er. . . . I say Tsu. . . .

TSU. Yes?

YOHYO. I say. . . .

Giggling.

I can't say it?

TSU. What? Why? What can't you say. . . ? Shall I try to guess it?

YOHYO. Um . . . please. . . .

TSU. You want griddle cakes again. . . ?

YOHYO. No.

TSU. Wrong guess? Then . . . you want me to sing a song, don't you?

YOHYO. No, I like Tsu's songs, but not today.

TSU. What, still wrong? Then . . . you want me to tell you about the capital . . . yes, that's it, isn't it?

YOHYO, *laughing.* Partly right but partly wrong.

Laughs again.

147

TSU. What, partly right but partly wrong? What is it? Tell me, tell me!

YOHYO. Tsu, you won't be angry?

TSU. Why should I get angry with what you say? Say it please, tell me!

YOHYO. Er . . . well . . . I want to go to the capital.

TSU. What!

YOHYO. I want to go to the capital to make a lot of money so . . . he, he, he! I'll want some more of that cloth. . . .

TSU. What! That cloth? You still. . . .

YOHYO, *quickly hiding his intentions.* Er . . . no . . . it's all right, Tsu, I don't want any more, I don't.

He looks like a scolded child trying with all his might to keep back the tears.

TSU. That cloth. . . . I will never weave again . . . we agreed so faithfully. . . .

YOHYO. Yes, Tsu told me so, so I don't want any more, I don't.

TSU, *with sudden realization.* Oh, I see! It's those men who were here a little while ago. That's it, yes, that's it. Those people are pulling you away from me slowly, slowly. . . .

YOHYO. What? Don't be angry, Tsu!

TSU *only looks at him.*

YOHYO. Oi! . . . Tsu. . . .

TSU, *hollowly.* Money . . . money . . . why do you want it so much. . . ?

YOHYO. You see, if you have money you can buy all kinds of nice things.

TSU. Buy? What's buy? What are nice things? What do you want besides me? I hate money, I hate buying, I hate you unless you love only me, I hate you unless you live with me for ever and ever, only the two of us together.

148

YOHYO. Yes, yes, I want the two of us to be together, Tsu, really I love you.

TSU. Really, really, really?

She embraces YOHYO.

Then, let it always be like this for ever.
Never leave me, never go away from me!

YOHYO. Silly, who wants to leave you, silly, silly Tsu!

TSU. Firmly in your arms like this . . . I think of times past . . . not worried by anything in the broad skies I was carefree. Now I feel as I did then. This is all right, if only we are together I am happy with that. We can always be together, can't we? You won't go to far places, will you?

Pause. Suddenly pushing him away.

You . . . you are still thinking of the capital, you are still thinking about money, aren't you?

YOHYO. But . . . but . . . I am. . . .

TSU. So . . . so. . . .

Suddenly with passion.

No! No! No! Don't go to the capital. You'll never return any more, you'll never come back to me again!

YOHYO. I . . . I will come back, I will come back. I'll go to the capital only to make much money. Yes . . . Tsu . . . let's go together!

Pause.

TSU. You want to go to the capital so much . . . is money such a precious thing to you?

YOHYO. Well yes, everybody wants money.

TSU. You want it so much, you want to go so badly. Why do you like money and the capital better than me? Why, why?

YOHYO. Such . . . such behavior I don't like, Tsu!

TSU. What? You say you don't like me?

YOHYO. I don't like you, I don't like you, I never like you, you're too cross!

149

TSU. What?

YOHYO. Weave the cloth and I'll go to the capital. I'll make money!

TSU. Cruel man, cruel man, what are you saying? How can you . . . ?

YOHYO. Weave the cloth or I'll leave you for good!

TSU. What, leave me for good! Yohyo, what's happened to you? How could you . . . ? You are . . . ?

YOHYO *keeps an obstinate silence.*

TSU, *grasping his shoulder and shaking him.* Yohyo! Yohyo! Yohyo! Are you really . . . Yohyo . . . you . . . you really mean it from the bottom of your heart?

YOHYO. Weave the cloth right away! It will sell for two or three times as much as before. It's worth hundreds of ryo!

TSU, *suddenly aghast and exceedingly confused.* What, what? What did you say just now? . . . Weave the cloth right away, and after that what did you say?

YOHYO. It's worth hundreds of ryo, it will sell for two or three times as much money as it did before!

TSU *looks at him inquiringly, with her head on one side like a bird.*

YOHYO. You see, this time it will sell for two or three times as much as before. . . .

TSU, *crying out.* I cannot understand your words, I cannot understand a word you are saying! Like the people who were her a little while ago with you, I can only see your lips move and hear the sound of your voice, but I cannot understand what you are saying. . . . You . . . at last you have begun to speak the same words that they use, the language of that world I do not understand. . . . Oh, what shall I do, what shall I do, what shall I do?

YOHYO. Hey, what's the matter, Tsu?

TSU. What's the matter, Tsu . . . eh . . . that's what you

said? What's the matter, Tsu, that's what you said to me just now.

YOHYO *only looks at her face in astonishment.*

TSU. Am I wrong? Did you say something different? No? No? Ah! you are slowly going farther and farther away from me, dwindling and dwindling. . . . Oh, what shall I do? Stop it! stop leading Yohyo away.

Goes out of the house.

Please, please, hey, where are you? I beg, I entreat you, please don't lead my Yohyo away.

Calls in every direction.

Please, please, I beg you, I beg you—you are not there? Are you hiding? Do come out . . . you're cowardly . . . unfair . . . unfair. I say . . . I say . . . how hateful, detestable people . . . taking away my Yohyo. Come out . . . now do come out. . . . No . . . please, please. . . . I entreat you, I entreat you, I entreat you. . . .

Gradually her strength fails her and she sinks down in the snow.

YOHYO, *timidly coming out.* Hey . . . Tsu, what's the matter?

He embraces her.

TSU, *recovering.* Oh . . . Yohyo.

YOHYO. Come, let's go back into the house, it's so cold in the snow.

He picks her up and carries her inside. They warm themselves at the fire in silence.

TSU. You want so much to go to the capital?

YOHYO. They say the capital is very beautiful and now the cherry blossoms will be in full bloom.

Pause.

YOHYO, *stretching.* A-h-h I feel sleepy!

He stretches himself out.

There is a pause. TSU *places a covering over him and*

151

gazes at his sleeping face. Suddenly she goes to a corner of the room and brings out a sack; opening it she pours coins into the palm of her hand and allows them to roll away upon the floor. She stares at them without moving. The lights fade swiftly leaving TSU *focused alone with the gold.*

TSU. This is it, this is it . . . everything has happened because of this stuff . . . money . . . money. I only wove that beautiful cloth to give you pleasure . . . only to show you this beautiful cloth . . . only because I was so happy to see you so glad. For that purpose only I wove it and sacrificed my strength and figure. I have no way of keeping you at my side, unless . . . I weave more cloth to allow you to make money. Now . . . except in that way . . . you won't stay by my side? . . . To make money by weaving the cloth . . . except in that way, but . . . but, all right, money . . . if it makes you so happy . . . if you are so glad to see the coins mounting up . . . if you want to go to the capital so badly . . . and if I can prevent your leaving me by doing that myself, if only by doing that you don't leave me . . . just once more, just one more length of cloth I will weave for you. Forgive me, forgive me for doing that, because I think it will probably kill me if I do it again. Forgive me, forgive me that I cannot do it any more for you, you can go to the capital with that cloth. Come back with a lot of money, come back, come back without fail, please come back without fail and then this time we can be together forever, forever together. Promise me, promise me. . . .

The lights go up.

TSU, *shaking* YOHYO. Yohyo, Yohyo!

YOHYO, *yawning.* Mm . . . a-a-ah. . . .

TSU. Listen . . . that . . . that cloth, I'll weave it for you.

YOHYO, *vaguely.* What, what?

TSU. That cloth you wanted . . . I'll weave it for you.

YOHYO. What, that cloth! You'll weave it for me, Tsu?

TSU. Yes. I'll weave one more length only.

YOHYO. Truly? You mean it?

TSU. Truly, yes truly I'll weave it for you so that you can take it with you to the capital and sell it.

YOHYO. Is it true, I can go to the capital? Tr-truly you mean. . . .

TSU. Yes, and bring back a lot of the money you are so fond of. You must come back and then . . . and then. . . .

YOHYO. Oh, you'll weave more cloth for me, you mean it, and I may go to the capital? Oh . . . yes, I'll make a lot of money. Yes, I'll come back with a lot of profit.

TSU, *watching* YOHYO *in his delight*. And now only one more promise as usual, never to look in the weaving room, eh? Absolutely never.

YOHYO. Oh, I won't look in. If only you will weave that cloth.

TSU. Please, this is what I entreat you, you will never, never attempt to peep. . . . If you peep everything will be over between us, remember!

YOHYO. Yes, yes, yes, I won't peep. I'm going to the capital and I'll sell it for two or three times the price before.

TSU. Remember . . . never peep, never peep.

She enters the weaving room.

The sound of a loom is heard, and SODO *rushes from his hiding place followed by* UNZU.

SODO. Good, Unzu, she's begun to weave!

UNZU. Yes, but since watching from over there somehow I feel sorry for his wife.

SODO. You fool! we're here to make money, we've no time to be sorry.

Running into the house he tries to peep into the weaving room.

YOHYO. Hey, you mustn't do that, you mustn't peep!

UNZU. Hey, Sodo, didn't you hear. . . ?

SODO. Oh, don't be such a nuisance! If we don't look how shall we know if it's genuine semba ori or not.

YOHYO. No, no! You mustn't do it! Tsu will be angry! Hey, you!

SODO. Leave me alone, leave me alone I say!

Peeps.

Oh, good lord, good lord!

UNZU. Wh-what is it?

SODO. Hey, look! It's a crane, a crane weaving on the loom!

UNZU. Wh-what? A crane?

Peeps.

Good God, there's no wife there, only a crane weaving!

SODO. Now, Unzu, at last it's certain we shall. . . .

UNZU. Yes. . . .

YOHYO. What's that? What is it? What's going on in there?

SODO. There's something you love in there. I say, Unzu, we can call for the cloth tomorrow morning. Let's go and wait at home!

UNZU. Um. . . .

YOHYO. Hey! What's in there? Isn't Tsu there?

UNZU, *while being led off by* SODO. There's a crane in there, a crane!

The two exit.

YOHYO. Oh, a crane? A crane in there? How I want to see it! No, no, no, Tsu will scold me . . . but what's a crane doing in there? Oh, how I want to see . . . can't I peep in? Oh Tsu, oh Tsu . . . I'll just peep in. . . . No, no, no, Tsu said I mustn't look, didn't you, Tsu. Hey, Tsu . . . Tsu. . . . Oh, what's the matter? How is it with you, Tsu? Hey. . . . What, she keeps silent. I want to see . . . I want to look . . . hey, just a little look. . .

He peeps through at last

Junji Kinoshita

What, there's only a crane in there . . . there's no Tsu.
. . . Why not, what's the matter . . . hey Tsu, Tsu. . . . She
isn't there . . . how can I do . . . there's no Tsu . . . hey
Tsu . . . Tsu . . . Tsu . . . Tsu. . . .

He goes out looking for TSU *on every side. The sound of
the loom continues, the lights dim and a poem is heard
mingled with the sound of the loom.*

Yohyo, Yohyo, where are you going?
Searching vainly for Tsu through the dark snow-
    covered fields.
Tsu yo, Tsu yo, his voice becomes hoarse and the pale
    beams gradually
Illuminate the snow.
Noon comes and still Tsu yo, Tsu yo.
Evening falls and today once more the sky behind the
    house burns red.

*The lights come up reflecting the sunset behind the house.
The sound of the loom continues and* SODO *and* UNZU
appear assisting YOHYO, *whom they have picked up in
the fields.*

UNZU. Hey, bear up, Yohyo!

SODO. Really, you . . . you lying down in the snow, why
did you go so far away?

UNZU. If we hadn't carried you here you'd have been
frozen to death!

YOHYO. Tsu yo . . . Tsu yo!

UNZU. Oh, bear up, Yohyo! You are yourself again. Hey,
Yohyo!

SODO. Hey Yohyo, bear up!

YOHYO. Tsu yo . . . Tsu yo. . . .

Pause.

SODO. And his wife is still weaving cloth all this time!

UNZU. Um . . . usually she weaves all through the night,
but this time it's all through the day as well!

SODO. Well, I'll take another look.

155

He goes over to the weaving room but the noise of the loom suddenly stops.

UNZU. Ah, it's stopped!

SODO. Hey, she's coming out!

Leaving YOHYO, *they go out hurriedly to hide.* TSU *appears carrying two pieces of cloth. She appears to have grown very thin.*

TSU. Yohyo, Yohyo!

She shakes him.

YOHYO. Tsu yo, Tsu yo!

TSU. Oh Yohyo . . . oh Yohyo. . . .

YOHYO. Ah. . . .

He comes to himself.

Oh Tsu yo, oh Tsu yo.

He clings to her and begins to cry.

Tsu yo, Tsu yo, where have you been? Where have you been?

TSU. I'm sorry to have kept you waiting so long. Look the cloth is woven. . . . See . . . hey . . . see, the cloth.

YOHYO. What? Oh . . . you've woven it, oh, oh, oh!

TSU *stares at* YOHYO, *who is transported with joy.*

YOHYO. Oh, this is wonderful! It's beautiful! Why, there are two pieces, aren't there?

TSU. Yes, two pieces, that's why I have been so long. You may take it to the capital now.

YOHYO. Yes, I'll be off right away. You'll come with me of course, Tsu, won't you?

TSU *is weeping.*

YOHYO. Tsu, let's go sight-seeing together, shall we?

TSU. Yohyo . . . you watched me weaving after all!

YOHYO. Ah, I want to be off to the capital quickly now, this is well woven, Tsu!

TSU. After all my entreaties, after all our faithful promises . . . Yohyo, why did you look after all?

YOHYO. Why, why are you crying?

TSU. I wanted to stay with you for ever, for ever but . . . Yohyo, I want you to keep one of these pieces and treasure it because it is woven with my heart!

YOHYO. M-m-m, this is really wonderfully made!

TSU, *holding his shoulder tightly*. Listen, listen, keep it with you, always treasuring it, treasuring it, treasuring it.

YOHYO, *like a child*. Yes, I'll treasure it for ever, I will do whatever you say, Tsu, so Tsu, let's go to the capital together.

TSU. No, I. . . .

She stands up smiling sadly and turns white suddenly.

I have become so thin, I have used all my feathers and now I have only just enough left to fly back with.

YOHYO, *sensing something is wrong*. Hey . . . Tsu. . . .

He tries to hold her but only grasps thin air.

TSU. Yohyo . . . take care of yourself . . . for ever and ever. . . .

The CHILDREN'S *song is heard in the distance.*

> Let's cover Grandpa with the eiderdown we sew,
> Let's cover Grandma with the eiderdown we sew,
> *Chin kara kan kara,*
> *Ton, ton, ton.* . . .

TSU. Ah, I must say farewell to the children too. . . . How often have I played with them and sung songs together. . . . Yohyo, please never forget me, I shall never forget you. It has only been a short time we have spent together, but I have been so happy bound up in your deep love, and singing and playing with the children. I shall never, never forget you wherever I go.

YOHYO. Tsu, where are you going?

TSU. You will never forget me, will you, and you will keep this piece of cloth forever treasuring it in memory of me?

YOHYO. O-oi, Tsu!

TSU. Goodbye . . . goodbye!

YOHYO. Tsu, hey wait, just wait, I'll go with you, hey Tsu, Tsu!

TSU. No, no you cannot come. I can no longer remain a human being, I must go back alone to the skies from whence I came . . . and I can never return. . . . Goodbye . . . may everything go well with you . . . goodbye . . . really goodbye. . . .

She disappears.

YOHYO. Tsu, Tsu, Tsu! Where have you gone? Hey Tsu . . . hey . . . hey . . . Tsu yo, Tsu yo.

He leaves the house roaming about. SODO *and* UNZU *rush from their hiding place to restrain him.*

SODO, *breathlessly to* UNZU. Hey!

UNZU, *out of breath too.* She's really gone!

YOHYO *looks dazed in* UNZU's *arms. The* CHILDREN *appear running.*

CHILDREN, *in unison as though singing.*

Tsu! Tsu! sing us a song!
Tsu! Tsu! come and play with us!
Tsu! Tsu! sing us a song!

All is still and silent.

CHILDREN. Tsu, Tsu, aren't you there? We want you!

To YOHYO.

Hey, where has Tsu gone, when will she come back? Yohyo, Yohyo, tell us, Yohyo!

YOHYO, *going timidly and fearfully into the house.* Tsu yo, the children have come to play. . . . They want you to sing like you always did . . . hey . . . Tsu. . . .

All is still and silent.

ONE OF THE CHILDREN, *suddenly pointing to the sky.* Look! A crane, a crane flying away!

SODO. Oh, a crane!

UNZU. Oh!

158

Junji Kinoshita

THE CHILDREN. A crane, a crane flying away!

They repeat the words while following its flight.

UNZU. Hey Yohyo, see it's a crane!

SODO. It's flying crookedly!

Pause.

SODO, *as if to himself.* Well, now we must be thankful to have got two pieces of cloth!

He tries to take them from YOHYO's *hand, but* YOHYO *clutches them to himself involuntarily.*

UNZU, *following the flight of the crane intently while holding* YOHYO. Ah . . . it's getting smaller and smaller!

YOHYO. Tsu . . . Tsu. . . .

He stumbles forward a step or two as though in the direction of the flying crane and then stands, holding the cloth tightly in both hands. SODO *also goes toward him and the eyes of the three men remain fixed on a distant point in the sky. In the distance the* CHILDREN's *song is carried faintly through the air.*

THE IMMORTAL HUSBAND

James Merrill

to John Bernard Myers

CHARACTERS

ACT I:

MRS. MALLOW
MAID
TITHONUS
GARDENER
LAOMEDON
AURORA

ACT II:

KONSTANTIN
FANYA
TITHONUS
OLGA
AURORA

ACT III:

MARK
AURORA
ENID
MEMNON
TITHONUS
NURSE

The play calls for a cast of six. With the exception of AURORA *and* TITHONUS, *the remaining roles must be doubled or tripled by the same actors in each successive act, in this fashion:*

MRS. MALLOW, OLGA, NURSE
MAID, FANYA, ENID
GARDENER, KONSTANTIN, MARK
LAOMEDON, MEMNON

ACT ONE

England, 1854. A parlor in disarray. Beyond shut French doors, a garden. It is a rainy morning in late spring. MRS. MALLOW, *in black from head to toe, sits mending a dress. The* MAID *packs a trunk with dresses and other clothes that lie here and there about the room. She hums a little tune. A second trunk stands against the wall.* TITHONUS *paces up and down, occasionally pausing to watch the two women.*

MRS. MALLOW. You're standing in my light, dear. It's hard enough to see as it is.

TITHONUS *moves.*

Why you should care to watch us at our dismal task, I can't imagine.

To the MAID.

Is that trunk full now, Jeannie?

MAID. Yes, Mrs. Mallow. I'll call John, shall I?

MRS. MALLOW. Wait. This one can go in on top. I'm nearly done.

MAID. She's a fortunate young lady who'll be getting these lovely clothes.

TITHONUS. Go on, go on! It's the natural thing, to discuss it.

MRS. MALLOW, *handing the dress to the* MAID. Here you are, Jeannie dear.

TITHONUS. And it will be natural for Cousin Aggie to feel grateful—

MRS. MALLOW. What else wants mending?

TITHONUS. —and natural, she being such a plain young woman, for the clothes to be wasted upon her.

MRS. MALLOW. Now hush, Tithonus, it was your mother's wish.

163

MAID, *showing a dress.* There's a tiny tear right here in the hem.

MRS. MALLOW, *taking it.* That won't take a minute.

MAID. Do you know, this is the fifth day of steady rain? John's all upset. He says the rain will wash away the soil from the roots. Rain's not at all good in such quantities, John says.

MRS. MALLOW. Well, John should know, shouldn't he?

TITHONUS. Rain is like sorrow. It exposes our roots.

MRS. MALLOW. And nourishes them.

MAID. I can't recall the mistress ever wearing that dress.

MRS. MALLOW. Oh, this was one of her favorite dresses. A wonder it still holds together. She'd wear it on carriage rides, in midsummer—before you came to us, five, six years ago. After that, she grew so thin, poor soul, she said to me, "Mrs. Mallow,"—when I'd already taken in the seams once or twice—"let's put away that dress, and not try to alter it any more." Now is that trunk firmly shut?

MAID. Yes, Ma'am.

MRS. MALLOW. Then call John, and I shall lock it. Let's see if we can't squeeze these last things into the other trunk. If we're clever we can get both of them on the afternoon coach.

Exit MAID.

TITHONUS. Oh it's wrong, it's wrong! Don't you think it's wrong?

MRS. MALLOW. Do I think what's wrong, dear?

TITHONUS. Life . . . the world . . . death. . . .

MRS. MALLOW. It's not for us to say, Tithonus. Life must go on.

TITHONUS. That's what I hate, to see everybody humming and sewing and bustling about, Father upstairs in a flowered dressing-gown sorting out her jewelry, sending away her clothes, putting everything out of sight, because *she* is out of sight—

164

MRS. MALLOW. You're in my light, dear.

TITHONUS, *moving*. —everything being scrubbed and aired, as if she had done a shameful thing. It's wrong, Mrs. Mallow.

MRS. MALLOW, *biting off a thread*. It's not for us to say.

TITHONUS. Who else will say it, if we don't? It's a small thing to ask, that a time be set aside, that we close our eyes and try to see her as she was,

Touching a bonnet.

dressed to go out, or coming in from a walk. . . .

MRS. MALLOW. You're right, Tithonus. It is a small thing to ask. But did she ask it? No.

Goes to him and strokes his cheek.

She asked only that her clothes go to your cousin Agatha. She asked that I keep her thimble. Look now, how it's begun to shine, and it was badly tarnished this morning when I put it on. Think of it that way, dear.

Goes to trunk and locks it.

Out of sorrow comes beauty. Now where is John?

TITHONUS. She asked nothing of me.

MRS. MALLOW. What can a mother ask of her child, but that he grow strong and virtuous? By doing that, a son shows his love. Not by tears, but by living the way she has taught him to live.

TITHONUS, *with irony*. And by dying the way she has taught him to die?

MRS. MALLOW, *vaguely*. That's right. Now if only John—

TITHONUS *starts out*.

Where are you going, dear?

TITHONUS. I don't know.

MRS. MALLOW. Let me give you some tea and muffins. You didn't touch your breakfast.

TITHONUS, *going out*. I'm not hungry.

MRS. MALLOW, *calling after him.* We must keep up our strength!

Enter MAID *and* GARDENER.

Oh John, there you are. Move that trunk over here.

He does so.

Good. Now Jeannie, I'll let you finish. I'm going up for a word with the master.

MAID. Why, it's stopped raining, look!

MRS. MALLOW, *darkly.* I don't like to think what *that* might mean.

GARDENER. It's good news to me, Mrs. Mallow. Shall I carry the other trunk out to the carriage?

MRS. MALLOW. Yes, do, John. There's scarcely room to walk about. I'll be down presently. And I'll feel like a cup of tea, Jeannie dear, if the kettle's on. And some muffins and jam. We must keep up our strength.

MAID. Certainly, Ma'am.

Exit MRS. MALLOW. *The* GARDENER *moves behind the* MAID *and playfully embraces her.*

Oh John, stop it, do! The poor mistress not cold in her grave!

GARDENER. Ah Jeannie, don't be taken in by all that talk. One fine day you'll be developing a morbid streak.

MAID. If I do, that's my own affair.

Pause.

What kind of streak?

GARDENER. Morbid. It's when you thrive on tragedy, like a vulture.

Pause.

That was a joke, Jeannie. Ah, if you could have seen, the day of the funeral, your cheeks glowing through that black veil! I wanted to kiss them then, right in church. You looked so bright and pretty.

Pause.

166

That was a compliment, Jeannie.

MAID, *preoccupied.* You're a proper poet.

GARDENER. Come now, what is it? Tell John.

MAID. Has Mrs. Mallow got a morbid streak?

GARDENER. I hadn't given the matter much thought.

MAID. I dreamed a dream about her last night.

Remembering it.

I had a little house with a garden and a lake, and everything I wanted. . . .

GARDENER. Was I there?

MAID. I can't recall. . . . No, but all of a sudden, looking up from my knitting, who should I see but Mrs. Mallow, nodding and smiling. "Jeannie dear," she said, "you're turning into the best little housekeeper that ever was." And I looked, and all around me were hundreds of little houses, no bigger than—

Staring into the open trunk.

with somebody in each one. And all the people were dead, and all the houses—I woke up then, I was in such a fright!

GARDENER. That's so like you, Jeannie, to be frightened of a dream.

MAID. What does it mean, do you suppose? Is somebody going to die?

GARDENER, *philosophizing.* We're all of us going to die, so cheer up! It's not so bad!

MAID. Cheer up, John! What a thing to say!

GARDENER. What *is* bad's the way the young master takes it. Mooning and moping—as if that changed anything.

MAID. I think the young master's feeling is beautiful and right.

GARDENER. It's too beautiful. He keeps standing off and admiring it, like he was painting a picture. No,

Looking upward.

he's not the one *she* ought to have.

MAID. And who is the one *she* ought to have? It wouldn't be yourself, would it? And what makes you think Miss Aurora's goddess of the dawn, anyhow? I've never seen her do a single uncommon thing.

GARDENER. Why should she? Of course she doesn't send off fireworks every quarter of an hour. She's not vulgar. But one day, you wait and see—she'll turn herself into a white peacock, like one of them over to the Manor, and stretch her throat and spread her wings and carry off the lover she fancies, just the way it's done in the mythology book!

MAID. See that you don't catch it for educating yourself with the master's books.

GARDENER. I'll catch you first.

He does so.

MAID, *wriggling.* Oh John, enough of your foolishness! I hear them!

GARDENER. I don't.

MRS. MALLOW, *offstage.* We're doing up the last one now. It will go this afternoon.

MAID. She's with the master! Hurry! Don't leave the trunk!

She goes out. The GARDENER *lifts the full trunk. Enter* MRS. MALLOW *and* LAOMEDON.

LAOMEDON. Well, Mrs. Mallow, I don't know what we would do without you. Not only at this time, but all during the past year— Oh John, I'll be wanting the carriage later this morning.

GARDENER. I'll give it a good wash, Sir.

LAOMEDON. If it clears, we'll inspect that broken pump before I go.

GARDENER. There's the apple tree too, Sir, I wish you'd have a look at.

LAOMEDON. Quite so, the apple tree. The whole place

168

has gone to rack and ruin these last weeks. Well, there was a reason for that. . . .

GARDENER. We'll set it to rights before long, Sir.

LAOMEDON. Thank you, John.

Exit GARDENER *with trunk.*

No, Mrs. Mallow, I think we're all very grateful to you.

MRS. MALLOW. It's a pleasure to be useful, Sir.

LAOMEDON. Georgiana said to me, not two weeks ago, "I feel easier, thinking that Mrs. Mallow will be with you." I'll never forget the care you took of her. You seemed to know instinctively whenever she was in pain. The door would open and there you'd be with her medicine, and a kind word, or a little bouquet of spring flowers. . . .

MRS. MALLOW. Oh Sir, you needn't say these things.

LAOMEDON. I shan't go on.

Offering a brooch.

Perhaps this will say what I cannot.

MRS. MALLOW. Her pearl brooch! Oh, I couldn't, Sir! I'm touched, but—it has too many associations. . . .

LAOMEDON. That's one reason we wanted you to have it. I spoke to Tithonus. He shares my feeling.

MRS. MALLOW. Does he now? Well, he's a dear good boy! But it should go to him, for his bride.

LAOMEDON. Between ourselves, I'm not overly sanguine on the subject of Tithonus's bride.

MRS. MALLOW. He'll outgrow that, just wait and see. He's young, Sir.

LAOMEDON. He's no longer a child, but he still acts like one.

Closing her hand over the brooch.

But please. . . .

MRS. MALLOW. I'm at a loss for words. I shall never part with it.

Looking up, sees that TITHONUS *has entered.*

169

Tithonus, dear, your father has told me of your share in this beautiful remembrance.

Kisses him.

TITHONUS. You've given her the pearl brooch?

LAOMEDON. With your permission, if you remember.

TITHONUS. Of course I remember. Keep the brooch, Mrs. Mallow. And the thimble. Why don't you take these clothes, too? Mother's room is empty, move into it. Father, have you ever considered marrying Mrs. Mallow.

MRS. MALLOW. Tithonus! I've lived in this house ten years, and never yet claimed anything that was not my due.

LAOMEDON. We know that, Mrs. Mallow.

To TITHONUS.

The principal use of courtesy is to help others through painful situations. That was not a remark to have made before either Mrs. Mallow or myself.

TITHONUS. I'm sorry, I believe it's wrong not to show what one feels.

LAOMEDON. True, but we do not need to make a display of our feelings.

TITHONUS. It's less of a display than your callousness!

LAOMEDON. Don't imagine, if I try to hide my sorrow, that I feel it less than you. Life is hard, and suffering the common lot.

TITHONUS. Oh Father, stop. . . .

LAOMEDON. As Doctor Johnson said, the hope that we shall meet our loved ones again must support the mind.

TITHONUS. But I don't have that hope. I believe that we shall *never* see her again! Then what supports the mind? What supports *my* mind, Father?

MRS. MALLOW. The boy's idle, Sir. What has he had to do these last weeks but sit about a house all hushed and melancholy?

TITHONUS. I've enjoyed that part of it!

LAOMEDON. You're right, Mrs. Mallow. An idle mind is the Devil's workshop. Of course, he's missed his term at the University. A new one won't begin—

TITHONUS. I don't choose to go back to the University.

LAOMEDON. We'll see about that.

MRS. MALLOW. Tithonus, why? You'd be with friends your own age.

TITHONUS. I hate people my own age.

LAOMEDON. I can't blame you. What is your age? Nineteen?

TITHONUS. Not yet! Not till August!

LAOMEDON. Old enough in any event to conduct yourself with dignity. What supports your mind is youth, with all the virtues and vices of youth. Purity and energy on one hand, arrogance and idleness on the other. Times have certainly changed! At your age I had lived through three battles. I was the youngest Englishman to witness the signing of the Treaty of Amiens.

TITHONUS, *slowly and gently.* Perhaps when I am old I shall no longer feel what I feel now. I hope I shan't. Because I feel that you, both of you, *don't* feel anything. You're dry inside, dry and old, and that's somehow far worse than dying. *You* want even her memory to die. Soon nothing will be left that was hers.

Pause.

LAOMEDON, *hurt.* Well, we mustn't stand about all morning. There are a hundred and one things waiting to be done. It's turning into a fine day. I'm going upstairs to dress.

MAID, *entering.* Cook's just back from the village, Sir, and brought the newspaper.

Gives it to him.

Oh Mrs. Mallow, I clean forgot your tea!

MRS. MALLOW. I'll have it in the kitchen, Jeannie, presently.

Exit MAID.

LAOMEDON, *reading.* Ha! It seems we are now connected with Ireland, by submarine telegraph.

MRS. MALLOW. What will they think of next?

LAOMEDON. A year ago it was France. Well, to work. I slept last night like a child.

He goes out.

MRS. MALLOW. Shame on you, Tithonus, for talking so to your father, with all the sorrow in his heart.

Opening the trunk.

I can't think what's got into you. You used to be such a sweet, considerate boy. You'd come running to show me things you'd found, a caterpillar, an odd stone. . . .

TITHONUS. I've made a decision, Mrs. Mallow. I can't stay at home any longer. I don't belong here.

MRS. MALLOW, *bustling about, not quite listening.* Now if you're going to take up my precious time with nonsense— Not belong here, indeed!

TITHONUS. Everything's changed, yet everything's the same. You heard Father—pompous, callous, as ever before. In a strange way I'm relieved that Mother's dead.

MRS. MALLOW. I understand that, dear. She suffered greatly, and now she's no longer in pain.

TITHONUS. No. I'm relieved for *my* sake. I'm not bound by her love. It will be easier to go away.

MRS. MALLOW. And where had you thought of going, may I ask?

Pointedly.

And with whom?

TITHONUS. Anywhere. Italy, Africa, Sweden, Constantinople. If Father were dead, it would be easier yet!

MRS. MALLOW, *shocked.* Hush now! As if easiness were all we looked for!

TITHONUS. And if *you* were dead, too, I could walk out

that door, through the orchard, whistling a song. Don't mistake me, I mean it tenderly!

MRS. MALLOW. Enough, Tithonus! Life and death are sacred things. We do not make jokes about them.

TITHONUS. I don't want anybody dead. But I don't want to die myself—I'm too young! So much is expected of me. I've done nothing yet to make my name endure, to give me immortality. . . .

MRS. MALLOW. There are other ways to make your name endure. For instance, when you have children of your own—

TITHONUS. I never want to have children. It's too cruel, that a child should suffer as it does!

Pause.

MRS. MALLOW. Tithonus, dear, believe me, this spell of terrible loneliness is at an end. I've been lonely, too, sitting by that bed in silence.

Taking a shawl which TITHONUS *has picked up, and placing it in the trunk.*

I may not be a woman of much learning, but I've learned about life. I've sat by many a deathbed.

Warmly.

Oh, I have such hopes for you, Tithonus! You're turning into such a fine, clever young man!

TITHONUS. But I don't want to *turn* into anything! Change is what I've always hated—to see people, like leaves on fire, twisted and crumpled by life. . . .

MRS. MALLOW. No. There is no such violence. At times the eyes remain open, and must be shut.

More softly.

Dying is part of life, Tithonus. It happens to us from day to day.

TITHONUS. That's the terrible compromise you make! You let it happen!

MRS. MALLOW. Yes. We let it happen.

Holding out her arms in a motherly gesture.

Dear child, dear indignant child, we have no choice!

Pause. TITHONUS *appears to falter, then slowly draws away from her and goes out. After a moment,* MRS. MALLOW *resumes her packing. A burst of sunlight on the stage, which has been gradually brightening. Grieg "Morning" music.* MRS. MALLOW *looks up fatalistically.*

I might have known, it never rains but it pours.

AURORA, *offstage.* Tithonus! Lazy one!

The French doors part. AURORA *stands on the threshold, a young girl of the period, wearing a pale, flowered dress, her hair in a Grecian knot.*

Oh! He's not here? It's true, he wasn't expecting me this week, but—

Laughing, advancing.

You weren't expecting me either, judging from your expression. It's been ages since I've seen you. You're always somewhere else when I come. But I daresay you keep up with me through Tithonus.

MRS. MALLOW. Hardly. He never speaks of you, Aurora.

AURORA. Perhaps not to you. Oh, look at all the clothes! Whose are they?

Holds up a dress, which MRS. MALLOW *takes and places in the trunk.*

Where is Tithonus?

MRS. MALLOW. I couldn't say. Look for him, why don't you?

AURORA, *starting out.* Thank you, I shall.

MRS. MALLOW. Aurora, I have this to say, and then I shall leave you. Take care of what you're doing to the boy. Your influence upon him is a pernicious one. I'm sure you don't mean it so, but the truth is, you stand in his way, in the way of his maturity. You encourage Tithonus to stay a child. I don't know what else you could do, being so much a child yourself. A lovely child, yes, that's what you are.

AURORA *begins to giggle.*

I hadn't hoped to provide entertainment for you.

AURORA. Have you ever been told that your mouth works in a most killing way when you talk, as though you were eating something? I'm sorry, I'm not really laughing at that. Isn't it a beautiful day? You feel that you want to laugh on a day like this!

Inspecting a cloak.

What a pretty cloak! I love other people's clothes, don't you?

MRS. MALLOW. Is it necessary to stand on it in order to admire it?

AURORA *wanders about.*

You're beyond your depth with Tithonus. What's right for you isn't right for him.

AURORA *tries on a bonnet.*

Kindly put that down!

AURORA. You're wrong about Tithonus, you know. He has a very special sensibility—more like one of *us.* You don't do justice to him. I do.

MRS. MALLOW. Call it justice if you like. I don't.

AURORA. Tell me something—oh, it's no concern of mine—but why do you wear black? Granted it *does* express the real you, still it's not becoming. Besides, Tithonus is very handsome, don't you agree?

MRS. MALLOW. Goodbye, Aurora. One day you will recognize my usefulness, my good influence, and understand—

AURORA. I understand enough to know sour grapes when I smell them. We even have *that* up there!

MRS. MALLOW. You have not only the comprehension but the cruelty of a child. One day *he* will understand that.

She goes out.

AURORA, *to herself*. Small wonder the English climate is what it is. What do they ever do to *make* the sun shine?

Sees the GARDENER *in the garden.*

You there! Joseph? James?

GARDENER *starts, then, blushing with pleasure, crosses the threshold.* Oh, it's you, Miss! Lovely morning, Miss.

AURORA. Why, thank you!

GARDENER. I had a feeling you'd be coming, soon as the sky cleared.

AURORA. Well, here I am. Have you seen Tithonus?

GARDENER. Yes, Miss. He just now walked out the front door and settled himself by the apple tree. Wrapped in thought.

AURORA. Tell him I've come, will you please?

GARDENER. Yes, Miss.

AURORA, *seeing that he does not go*. What is it?

GARDENER. Oh, Miss, I—I can't explain. No offense meant.

AURORA. I shall never be offended by those who find me beautiful, Joseph.

GARDENER. John, Miss.

AURORA. John. Now will you call Tithonus?

GARDENER. Right away, Miss.

Exit. AURORA, *alone, tries on the cloak and bonnet before a mirror, humming to herself.* TITHONUS *enters from the garden and stops, unable to choose between laughter and tears.*

TITHONUS. Is it you?

AURORA, *turning*. I couldn't wait. I know you didn't—

TITHONUS. What are you doing?

AURORA. Doing? Oh,

Laughing.

I was seeing if I could look mortal—do I?

TITHONUS. Yes.

176

AURORA. You didn't want to see me today, you're sorry I came—but, my darling, it's been five days!

TITHONUS. Aurora! You've never looked more beautiful! Your beautiful eyes, your throat. . . . I've missed you, Aurora, I've needed you. . . .

AURORA. But you told me not to come! You never say what you mean.

TITHONUS. But you're here! You always do the right thing, whatever I say.

AURORA. I hope I always shall. Even so, darling, you must *tell* me what you feel and what you need. Don't let's have any confusion. This is love, this is love for the first time, and often I'm on pins and needles. I'm so frightfully unsound— ethically? is that the word?

Starts to take off the bonnet.

TITHONUS. No, stay as you are for a moment! Aurora, I've never loved you so much!

AURORA. For myself, I know what I need—the sense of its having put forth leaves, our love, like the apple tree out there, where I saw you first, through the blossoms, reading, with a blossom in your mouth. "I want that," I said to myself. *Now* look at our tree—greener and golder and growing stronger. I feel all this has happened because of me, and I am proud of the loveliness around me, for being equal to the love within me. Whose clothes are these?

TITHONUS. My mother's.

AURORA. I like her so much, you know. Is she going away?

Remembers.

Oh, of course, she's— That was why you told me not to come.

Instinctively removes bonnet and cloak, placing them in the trunk.

I imagine you loved her very dearly. A pity you haven't a really good photograph of her.

177

Embarrassed.

Photography—it's rather a new thing I've been learning about. I'd thought of taking it up as a hobby. . . . Oh, will I *ever* know what to say at such moments?

TITHONUS. Now father's sending away her clothes.

AURORA. Very sensible of him!

TITHONUS. That was *not* the thing to say.

AURORA. You've had a row with him? Another one?

LAOMEDON, *offstage.* Tithonus!

AURORA. Here he is!

TITHONUS *groans.*

Well, don't let him get the better of you!

LAOMEDON *enters, fully dressed.* Tithonus, I was thinking —oh, excuse me, Aurora. Have you succeeded in cheering up your young friend?

AURORA. Oh, how much you disapprove of me!

LAOMEDON. You have never heard me say so.

AURORA. Precisely! If you *had,* I'd have felt some grudging fondness, some weak little seed of liking, for me to warm into flower. It's unnatural of you! I *am* likable!

LAOMEDON. I'm pleased to have it from your own mouth.

AURORA. What's more, Laomedon, I don't like to be disliked.

LAOMEDON. Who does? That must be your human side.
To TITHONUS.

I came to ask if you cared to go with me to the village in about an hour.

TITHONUS. I think not, Father, thank you.

LAOMEDON. My thought was to find some occupation for you, until you return to the University. Mr. Hobbs, for instance, might let you work in his office, if only to oblige me. That would be a most valuable experience.

TITHONUS. I've told you, Father, that I don't intend to return to the University.

178

LAOMEDON. And I replied that we would see about that.

TITHONUS. And I don't intend to be embalmed in a lawyer's office.

LAOMEDON. Perhaps you have some alternative of your own.

TITHONUS. My alternative is to do exactly as I do.

LAOMEDON. In that case I have something to say to you.

AURORA. I'll be on my way. . . .

TITHONUS. Oh stay, please!

AURORA. Really, I can't bear scenes!

LAOMEDON. In my opinion, young lady, it might be a good thing for you to hear what I have to say.

AURORA. Aren't you forgetting as usual who I am?

LAOMEDON. I know who you are. And I know my place. But since you have condescended to meddle with human affairs, and with my son's life in particular, it wouldn't hurt you to learn how sensible people think down here—whatever the thinking processes may be where you come from.

AURORA, *gaily*. Oh, we never think!

LAOMEDON. I thought as much.

AURORA. And even with people, Laomedon, I never feel the really brilliant ones think at all!

TITHONUS. Neither do I!

AURORA. Besides, Tithonus is teaching me about people.

LAOMEDON. You see me as an old bore, don't you?

TITHONUS. Of course not, Father.

AURORA. Or at least, a very distinguished one.

LAOMEDON. No matter. That is how I saw my father at your age, and how your son will see you. Nature is very economical.

AURORA. An example to us all!

LAOMEDON. I am a soldier, a simple man who has worked hard. And what *you* can't believe is that I've enjoyed it.

There's nothing finer than to live through every difficulty that comes your way.

TITHONUS. It may have been so in your own life. But if, as you say, you're a simple person who enjoys the difficulty of living, why can't I be a difficult person who doesn't enjoy it? Because I don't!

AURORA. Neither do I!

TITHONUS. I'm wasting my youth, is that what you think? And wilful waste makes woeful want?

LAOMEDON. You may scoff at your father's maxims, as I once did. That will not make them less true. They are convenient expressions of profound human laws. I have proven them by bitter experience.

AURORA. Experience isn't always bitter, you know.

LAOMEDON. I don't speak of *your* experience, Aurora.

She giggles. LAOMEDON *turns to go.*

We'll have our talk later. I see I've chosen a bad time.

AURORA, *whispering to* TITHONUS. Go on! Stand up to him!

TITHONUS. All right, Father. Tell me plainly what you expect me to do.

LAOMEDON. Tell me first what you *do* do.

A silence.

AURORA. He reads!

TITHONUS. Yes! I spent much of yesterday reading. Didn't you see me?

LAOMEDON. I saw you on the sofa with some books.

TITHONUS. Well, I was reading.

LAOMEDON. May I know which authors you were reading?

TITHONUS. Different ones. Ovid. Ossian. Mrs. Browning.

LAOMEDON. Go on.

TITHONUS. I'm—ah—about to begin a large painting. The canvas isn't quite prepared, but I have a whole notebook of sketches.

LAOMEDON. What is to be the subject of your painting?

TITHONUS. I haven't altogether decided. Possibly a *Massacre of the Innocents*—or else a pastoral scene of some sort, *Pan among Nymphs*, you know. . . .

AURORA. Oh, do let me pose for you! The way I look on the ceiling at the Rospigliosi's—well, it's just not *me!*

LAOMEDON, *to* TITHONUS. What else?

TITHONUS. At the moment, there's nothing else.

LAOMEDON. Thank you. You have answered my question.

TITHONUS. If anything, I'm ashamed there should be so much, at such a time.

LAOMEDON. I shall now answer yours. I notice that your mother's death does not keep you from agreeable society.

AURORA. But he's so young! You must make allowances!

LAOMEDON, *cheerfully*. I do. Since he is unfit to take charge of his own life, I shall have to do it for him. That's the allowance I make for his youth.

To TITHONUS.

Believe me, I have your interest at heart. I merely expect you to do something serious and responsible, Tithonus. Don't look as if it were the end of the world!

Pause.

Tell me, have you a genuine distaste for work? Or do you reject as a matter of course whatever *I* recommend?

TITHONUS. There is one thing I can do, Father, that might satisfy you.

LAOMEDON. I'm very easy to please, you know. I had a reputation for it throughout my regiment.

TITHONUS. I told Mrs. Mallow this morning, I've decided to leave home.

AURORA. Tithonus, how wonderful! You'll come with me!

He nods. AURORA *turns to* LAOMEDON.

You can't imagine—I've been asking him for months! He needs to travel, it's so broadening!

LAOMEDON, *after a pause.* Do as you wish, Tithonus. You may one day regret—no, I have nothing more to say.

TITHONUS. Father, wait, I want you to understand!

LAOMEDON. I want to understand. But not now.

With faint irony.

Will you be leaving before lunch?

TITHONUS. No, I needn't. . . .

LAOMEDON. Splendid! Perhaps you can spare a moment or two then, in private.

TITHONUS. Certainly, Father.

Exit LAOMEDON.

AURORA. He is rather pompous, even for one's father. I suppose it's the result of a military career. Ho hum, what shall we do until lunch?

Eagerly.

We could make love!

TITHONUS. Really, Aurora! If somebody came in—

AURORA. All right! It was only an idea!

Aside.

Modesty, modesty!

To TITHONUS.

Well, then, on with my education! Last time we took up—let me see, was it pain? Sportsmanship? One's brother-hood to the ape?

TITHONUS. You remember perfectly well—we talked about religion.

AURORA. Ah yes, religion! I was fascinated—to see oneself through the eyes of others! Couldn't we go on with that?

TITHONUS. You're disappointed, aren't you, that I'm not leaving with you until after I've talked to Father?

AURORA. No, not at all.

TITHONUS. Well, *I* would be—having to wait even a few hours.

182

James Merrill

AURORA. But you see, I have no sense of time. You're giving me what I wanted. A few hours or a few days sooner or later, what difference does it make?

TITHONUS. It would make a difference to me. I *need* time. Some days I choke on my food. I feel I can't keep up with life.

AURORA. Really? Why I could sit for days over a meal, even a dull meal.

TITHONUS. Or else I don't try at all. I lie down. I sleep.

AURORA. Now this interests me very much. Oh darling, you see why I love you! You show me what people feel. In no time at all I'll be having the same feelings myself! Go on!

TITHONUS. Aurora, I've tried to put it out of my head, but I can't. You don't *really* understand what I say, do you?

AURORA, *biting her lip.* No, I don't.

He turns away. She giggles.

But tell me—darling, I'm serious now—why should I understand?

TITHONUS. You're forever smiling!

AURORA. I *am* she who smiles. I am the rosy-fingered one. What do you mean by understanding?

TITHONUS. You see!

AURORA. I *do* see. I see what is shown to me, my dear. When I go into a room and find, say, a book lying on the table, it is not my way to open it. I've never held letters to the light in order to read what might be inside. If the book lies open, if the letter has been dropped, open, to the floor— why then, I do read it. I feel it has been left for me to read. I mean, I never see the hidden side of things. That must always be most unpleasant. If people are unhappy, I don't want to know about it. I'll do anything—I'll even lie to them!—in order to keep them smiling. I can't bear to know what people do in the dark.

TITHONUS. But you do know.

183

AURORA. With you, I don't think of it as being in the dark. . . .

TITHONUS, *taking her face in his hands*. And what do you see now?

AURORA. I see that you're handsome and full of life. When I get my camera I shall photograph only you. I see that your ear is translucent. The capillaries fan out like twigs against a sunset—

Frightened.

You're hurting me! I see what's *there!* I see light and love!

TITHONUS. You see your own light and your own love!

AURORA. Darling!

TITHONUS. I don't mean that. Aurora, I love you. But to see only what is shown to us isn't understanding. Understanding is when we see in the dark, the way a cat does. Some part of me is dark and sad, invisible in your brightness. Understanding will be the day you come to me suffering, or with a capacity for suffering. Understanding has more to do with tears than with smiling. And you've never wept.

AURORA. No. Would I enjoy that?

Pause.

Be reasonable! If gloom and murkiness are what you want, there are plenty who'll be delighted to oblige you. Just don't ask—

Striking her brow.

Oh, silly me! I *have* something that will cheer you up!

TITHONUS. That's not what I need!

AURORA. But I have! I'm not the goddess of the dawn for nothing. Ah, now you're interested!

TITHONUS. Tell me then.

AURORA. Perhaps now I won't, you've been so horrid.

TITHONUS. Ah, don't play with me! Tell me or not, as you please, but don't play these games!

James Merrill

AURORA. I've brought a little gift. Oh, promise you'll like it!

TITHONUS. What is it?

AURORA. Nothing at all, really. Something you once said you wanted. . . .

TITHONUS. Aurora! It isn't—

AURORA, *nodding.* Are you pleased?

TITHONUS. Oh my angel! You're sure? There's no mistake?

AURORA. Mistake! Oh really now!

TITHONUS. Forgive me. But tell me yourself, then, what it is.

AURORA. You're such a baby! You *know* what it is!

TITHONUS. But say it!

AURORA. One doesn't put these things into words. . . . Must I?

TITHONUS. You're playing with me again!

AURORA, *annoyed.* But I love to play! All right. Henceforth you are immortal. There!

TITHONUS. Say it again!

AURORA. Henceforth you are immortal.

TITHONUS. I'll never die?

AURORA. Never.

TITHONUS. Can it be that simple? Don't I need to do something?

AURORA. No. You may kiss me if you like.

TITHONUS. I can't believe it! And I said you didn't understand! Do you know what it means?

AURORA. So very much? *I'm* glad, too. To me it means that I shall have you always. Didn't you want to kiss me?

TITHONUS. Oh, I love you! Aurora—thank you!

AURORA. You're welcome, I'm sure.

TITHONUS. But how—I'm sorry, I want to know everything. How did you go about it?

185

AURORA. Well, let me see. You expressed the wish—mercy, it must have been a month ago. I didn't think too much about it at first. Then I began to rack my brains. I wanted you to have some little thing from me, something small and useful that you would always have to remember me by. And it came to me! Just the thing, I said to myself.

TITHONUS. There's nobody like you!

AURORA. Well, after that I had to wait. Every day I'd ask if he was in a good humor.

TITHONUS. He?

AURORA, *pointing upward*. He's fearfully bad-tempered, or can be. It's quite proverbial. And while it was little enough to ask, since everybody's entitled to *one* gift, I didn't want to be refused. Well, to make a long story short, yesterday evening I was given the sign. I slipped right in and spoke my piece, rather prettily, I must say.

TITHONUS. Just like that!

AURORA. No. No, you don't understand at all. There's a whole etiquette involved. You have to sort of crouch beside him, with your left hand on his knees and your right hand fiddling with his beard—like Thetis in that Ingres painting. I was the slightest bit nervous, having never done it before. But, you know—it worked!

TITHONUS. It sounds so easy, how can you be sure?

AURORA. Don't *worry!* What's the matter with you? You keep complaining about how you hate difficult things, and now that something perfectly simple happens, you're not satisfied!

TITHONUS. I am, I am! It's all I've ever wanted. I just don't feel any change yet. I guess it takes a certain time.

AURORA. I wouldn't know. Probably it does. Oh, you *mustn't* frown, I feel responsible for you! Tell me I've made you happy!

TITHONUS. You've made me infinitely happy. *Now* I think I'm beginning to feel it. Yes. My heart is beating quietly and happily. It will never stop. Look at this hand. It will be mine always.

AURORA, *taking his hand.* It will be *mine* always.

They kiss.

TITHONUS. I'm hungry! Should I be?

AURORA. Did you have your breakfast?

TITHONUS. No. But I mean, does one *get* hungry, now that. . . ?

AURORA, *laughing.* Now that one's immortal? Yes, my darling, one does!

TITHONUS, *ringing a bell.* How glorious the world is! Look at those flowers glowing, look at the grain of this wood! I feel such excitement, a tingling in me, as if I were never again to be tired or bored, an energy that will never exhaust itself!

Enter MAID.

Jeannie, bring me some muffins and jam, will you please?

To AURORA.

Would you care for something?

AURORA. I couldn't really. I've had my ambrosia.

TITHONUS. Just the muffins and jam, then. Oh, and a cup of tea might taste good.

MAID. Right away, Sir. The water's boiling already.

TITHONUS. And Jeannie, what's my father up to?

MAID. He's out talking to John, Sir. About the mistletoe. It's killing that beautiful apple tree, Sir.

TITHONUS, *peering into the garden.* Good. Here they come.

Playfully.

Now that Jeannie's under the spell of the new gardener, she'll talk of nothing but trees and flowers.

MAID. La, Sir, you're such a tease!

Exit.

AURORA. You're going to tell your father?

TITHONUS. He'll have to know. Besides, here's the real alternative to Mr. Hobbs!

LAOMEDON *and* GARDENER *are seen through the French doors.*

AURORA. Oh, I suppose it would be, wouldn't it?

GARDENER. You mark my words, Sir, that whole fine branch will be dead inside of a year.

TITHONUS. Father, have you a moment?

LAOMEDON. My wife loved the mistletoe. . . .

GARDENER. I don't say it's not pretty to look at, like a little cluster of pearls. But it's a parasite, Sir.

LAOMEDON. I'm tempted to let it grow, just the same.

AURORA. I've always heard that mistletoe was something one got kissed under.

GARDENER. So it is, Miss.

AURORA, *to* TITHONUS. You see, your father's quite a sentimentalist.

LAOMEDON. Very well, go ahead with it. And, John, that trunk looks ready. Ask Mrs. Mallow if she will be good enough to lock it. Then you can take it to the carriage.

GARDENER. Right you are, Sir.

Exit.

TITHONUS. It's odd, I felt such a pang a while ago, looking at that trunk. I don't feel it any more.

LAOMEDON, *stepping into the room.* Well, Son, what is it?

TITHONUS. Father—

LAOMEDON. You had something to say to me?

TITHONUS. Father, I'm sorry. I shouldn't have spoken that way to you.

LAOMEDON. Is that all you have to say?

TITHONUS. No. . . .

LAOMEDON. Then out with it! Time is money.

Enter MRS. MALLOW, *followed by* GARDENER.

TITHONUS. When I say I'm sorry, I don't mean only for that. I'm sorry for *you*, also.

LAOMEDON. Ah. And how have I come to deserve your pity?

TITHONUS. I don't mean to be impertinent. I feel so full of warmth and compassion—towards everything and everybody! Mrs. Mallow, I haven't made things easy for you, either.

LAOMEDON, *to* AURORA. And what part have *you* played in this worthy transformation?

AURORA. Oh it's so trivial! I simply—

TITHONUS. Father, you are going to die!

Pause. LAOMEDON *and* AURORA *share a moment of irrepressible gaiety.*

LAOMEDON, *to* TITHONUS. Not this morning, I trust, unless someone has prompted you to do away with me.

TITHONUS. Can't you listen to me? You're going to die and—I'm not!

MAID *enters with tea things on a tray.*

LAOMEDON. Don't talk nonsense! You're wasting my time.

TITHONUS. Listen to me! I'm never going to die! Aurora has given me immortal life!

AURORA. It's true. I have given Tithonus immortal life.

MRS. MALLOW. For shame, Aurora!

MAID. Immortal life!

GARDENER. I don't know as how I'd enjoy *that!*

LAOMEDON, *to them.* That will do, both of you.

Takes the tray from the MAID.

Not a word of this in the kitchen, you understand.

MAID *and* GARDENER *nod dumbly and go out.*

TITHONUS. I don't see why you both should act as if something shameful had happened.

189

MRS. MALLOW. The less said about it, the better, dear.

LAOMEDON. Did you mean for me to congratulate you?

TITHONUS, *to* MRS. MALLOW. I thought he'd be pleased for my sake. For his own sake, too, if it comes to that. He needn't worry about me now.

To LAOMEDON.

Or are you envious?

LAOMEDON. No. Here, take this tray from me.

TITHONUS. You can just hold the tray for a bit! Selfish, pompous old man! Must we learn that suffering is the common lot? When you say that, you mean one thing only— that you want me to suffer!

LAOMEDON. I have never wanted you to suffer—until perhaps this instant.

TITHONUS. Stop lying to me! All those warnings, all those homilies! We let it happen, do we, Mrs. Mallow? We have no choice? You'll let it happen, you've made your compromise! Oh Father, even if you live another ten, another twenty years, even if you were my age—you'll dry up and die, each year older and sicker, and your mind gone! And I'll be as I am now, strong, young, a hundred years, a thousand, after you're in your grave!

LAMEDON, *handing the tray to* MRS. MALLOW *who puts it down*. That's enough. Live if you can. I'm glad neither I nor your mother will be here to see what you make of your life. Those are the last words I shall ever speak to you.

Turns to go.

AURORA. Oh wait! Please!

LAOMEDON. I have nothing to say to *you*.

AURORA. No, it's not that! Oh, please—

To TITHONUS.

Darling, I'm frightened. You said something just now. . . . Darling, there's nothing in it about not growing old!

TITHONUS, *not understanding*. What?

James Merrill

AURORA. Perhaps it doesn't matter. I hope it doesn't matter, but—you know, you won't stay young. You'll never die, but—well, you'll grow old, naturally, the way people *do*.

MRS. MALLOW, *to herself*. Yes.

TITHONUS, *aghast*. But that's the whole point!

AURORA. You didn't ask for that! You never said you wanted to stay young!

TITHONUS. Then you've *never* understood!

AURORA. *You* never bothered to explain!

TITHONUS. I knew it was too simple! I said so, didn't I? But you smiled and— You can have it changed, you can ask again!

AURORA. No . . . I'm afraid not. . . .

TITHONUS. But you must!

AURORA. I can't. Once only. . . .

TITHONUS. But what will become of *me*?

AURORA. Oh my dearest, my only love—what can I say? That it's my fault—does that help? It's a terrible thing, I suppose, but it doesn't change *us*! I don't see that it does! I'm yours, entirely, eternally. . . .

TITHONUS. Don't say that! Think what I'll be in— Oh God, less than a hundred years! A horrible old man, drooling, deaf!

AURORA. You needn't be! I've seen some very beautiful old men!

TITHONUS. But I *will* be! And you won't love me then—wait and see!

AURORA. I'll love you always, I think.

TITHONUS. Ah, now you're thinking! It's high time.

AURORA. My youth, when your own is gone, shall be yours—not yours, but at your disposal. Till the end of time.

TITHONUS, *closing his eyes*. And there *is* no end. . . .

MRS. MALLOW. It may be only the threat of dying presses us to live, and he is luckier than he knows.

AURORA. How?

MRS. MALLOW. Old age is a kind of death, Aurora. It may be one will do as well as the other.

TITHONUS *turns to her for comfort, like a child. She strokes his hair.*

Ah but Tithonus, what you have feared is not death so much as—

AURORA, *wonderingly.* Life! Fear life? But one's not *meant* to do that!

With a new tenderness.

Tithonus!

TITHONUS. Let me be!

AURORA. I want to come close to you. You asked me to come to you suffering— I'm suffering now. Something hurts, here. . . . Try to imagine how *I* feel, knowing what I've done.

TITHONUS. You've never felt anything but sunlight and pleasure! I have to be by myself now. Can't you understand even that?

AURORA. Ah don't!

TITHONUS, *through his teeth.* I'll be back. Don't forget, we have an eternity ahead of us, all to ourselves!

He starts out. But the GARDENER *enters with an armful of mistletoe.*

GARDENER. Here you are, Sir, look! That tree will live forever now, just like you, Miss, and the young—

He falls silent. TITHONUS *snatches the mistletoe from him and goes out. A long pause.* AURORA *is weeping silently.* LAOMEDON *and* MRS. MALLOW *turn to go.*

AURORA, *suddenly looking at her hands, puzzled.* What is it? My eyes are full of water!

LAOMEDON. Those are tears, Aurora.

192

Russia, 1894. A grove on the slope of a mountain. A tree stump, scattered leaves. It is a lovely afternoon in early autumn. TITHONUS, *nearly sixty, sits at an easel, painting. His clothes suggest the dilettante rather than the bohemian. Laughter offstage. Enter the young lovers,* FANYA *followed by* KONSTANTIN. *The latter carries a rug and a large picnic basket. They do not at first see* TITHONUS.

KONSTANTIN. Laugh all you wish, and run, but I am carrying this basket. Can we Russians go nowhere without a samovar? In ten years I shall have instigated reforms. Tea will be drunk only in the parlor.

FANYA. But let us stop here then! I'm overheated myself, and here there's a breeze. . . .

KONSTANTIN *puts down his burden and embraces her.*

Kostya, Kostya. Where is Olga Vassilyevna? Can we have left her so far behind?

KONSTANTIN. Don't think of her. Fanya, my soul, my life!

FANYA. Sick people have such a power. I'd be afraid not to obey her.

KONSTANTIN. Come!

FANYA. She will tell Mamma we ran away together.

KONSTANTIN. That will be my first reform—the abolition of the chaperon. They'll be herded out in their black dresses and shot like turkeys, if they don't recant.

FANYA. You're terrible!

KONSTANTIN. So come with me! We'll leave the basket in this clearing, where she will be sure to stumble on it. She'll decide we've gone only a bit farther, to look at the view.

FANYA. You know we can't!

KONSTANTIN. Fanya, she refuses to acknowledge her illness, and you've seen how it vexes her whenever *we* do.

193

Come! She will want to doze off after her climb, like any self-respecting person. While

> "Deep in the greenwood who shall spy
>   Where I and my beloved lie,
>   Unless the nightingale—"

FANYA. The wood isn't green. Why aren't you silly more often?

KONSTANTIN. I? Silly?

FANYA. The nightingales have gone.

KONSTANTIN. They have flown into your throat and make their music there.

FANYA, *seeing* TITHONUS. Oh! We didn't know—

As TITHONUS *does not respond, she exchanges a look of puzzled amusement with* KONSTANTIN, *then moves forward gaily into* TITHONUS's *line of vision.*

Forgive us, please, for interrupting your work.

TITHONUS. Not at all, Mademoiselle, I stopped listening almost at once.

FANYA. You are an artist!

KONSTANTIN. Fanya Alexandrovna, let us move on. We are intruding upon a rich mind at work.

FANYA. I am passionately fond of nature. What a satisfaction for you! And what application! Did you climb from the village? Think, Kostya, isn't it inspiring? I must find out from Nurse what became of my sketch-book. I remember doing some rather pretty things, even last year. But now. . . .

KONSTANTIN. Now you are busy with clothes and carriage-rides.

FANYA. And with you, Kostya, with you! But when we are married I shall do a water color every day!

To TITHONUS.

Imagine, we are to be married next year! Mamma thinks I am too young. I can't agree with her, and yet I don't mind waiting. I am so happy! If you knew him as I do—!

KONSTANTIN. There are few who would have her patience in that respect. Come, Fanya.

In an undertone.

Do try to avoid subjects you know nothing about.

To TITHONUS.

Good day, Sir.

TITHONUS. Good day.

FANYA. But we haven't seen his painting!

KONSTANTIN. Whoever told you that he wanted us to see it?

FANYA. Ah, you don't understand artists! It used to give me extreme pleasure to have somebody look over my shoulder.

To TITHONUS.

Mayn't we see it?

TITHONUS *gestures indifferently that they may, and they do.*

What exquisite colors! Oh, it's much better than *mine!*

KONSTANTIN. Have you given it a title?

TITHONUS. Not really. As you see, it's no more than a view of the village.

KONSTANTIN. Ah! That's the *village* down in there . . . .?

FANYA. Of course that's the village! Kostya, I'm ashamed of you.

KONSTANTIN. You must understand I know nothing about painting. I should never have thought that was the village, though.

TITHONUS. The village seen through leaves.

KONSTANTIN. Interesting. . . .

FANYA. Well, *I* think it's truly lovely.

TITHONUS. I don't ask for flattery.

FANYA. No, it is!

KONSTANTIN. Can you tell me your purpose in painting such a picture?

TITHONUS. My purpose? All the young men are talking about purpose nowadays. It may be I did so myself as a young man, but I have forgotten. Yes. And having forgotten, I cannot regret. I am what I am, and it is soothing to know that. The pain that comes from wishing to be what we are not! As for this picture, I'm afraid I had no purpose. Is that old-fashioned of me?

KONSTANTIN. Far from it, unfortunately. Yet it's curious. Here you have given yourself the bother of a long climb, with your easel on your back—in order to paint the village. And look! The village has vanished! There are only the dimmest traces left on your canvas—a few odd shapes, a few drab colors, like a village destroyed by fire, seen a week later, through a mass of red-gold foliage. . . .

TITHONUS. Perhaps my purpose was precisely that.

KONSTANTIN. But why, then?

TITHONUS. I don't understand you.

FANYA. Neither do I!

KONSTANTIN. The village is real! There is an inn and a blacksmith, there are dogs, men, living, dying! All this is hidden away—behind leaves!

TITHONUS. The leaves are real as well.

KONSTANTIN, *shouting*. Very good! Paint leaves then!

FANYA. Kostya!

KONSTANTIN. Excuse me. I don't like to see a village hidden by leaves, that's all. I didn't mean to offend you.

FANYA. You see, he does have very good manners. Most of the time you'd never dream he was a Nihilist.

KONSTANTIN *glares at her*.

Oh dear, it slipped out! We haven't yet told my parents.

TITHONUS. Told them?

FANYA, *proudly*. That Konstantin Stepanovitch is a Nihilist. They would surely be opposed to the match. And yet

ne's so brilliant! His professors at the Medical School cannot
find words to praise him. He has such ideas, so new, so
fascinating!

TITHONUS. Is it possible we have advanced to an age in
which men are praised for new ideas? In my day we had
our Nihilism. We called it that.

KONSTANTIN. I believe in mankind. Nihilism is only a
name, a negative belief.

Pause.

Have you ever seen a man's hand cut off at the wrist?
The blood leaps out, the man's eyes roll backwards, his
cries are—

FANYA, *grasping her wrist.* Oh stop!

TITHONUS *listens unmoved.*

KONSTANTIN. Even to hear it described is painful. We
cannot help thinking of our own mutilation. Isn't this proof
of a deep human sympathy that binds all men together?
Kuvshenko would agree with me.

TITHONUS, *bored.* Ah.

KONSTANTIN. You are objecting, "But does he overlook a
man's environment?" I do not. It is the source of every
individual mannerism. Take yourself. Already I can tell—
what?—that you are a foreigner. How do I know? By observ-
ing that you repress your curiosity. Perhaps curiosity isn't
the word. One sees that you have traveled much, and
reflected. . . .

TITHONUS. You are right. I have no curiosity.

KONSTANTIN, *taken aback.* We all have curiosity. No, I
mean rather a kind of outward-goingness, a very Russian
trait. We are constantly wanting to know about others—
their forebears, their professions, their lives. The Germans
and the English intellectualize their curiosity. The French
restrict it to their private sensations. Our Russian curiosity is
human. We are forever inquiring into our own destinies.

TITHONUS. That is strange. Our destiny is one of the few
matters revealed to us.

KONSTANTIN. But revelation comes to those who seek it!

TITHONUS. Perhaps.

FANYA. I know what he means, Kostya. There have been hours when I've seen my whole life ahead of me, like a sunlit valley. I used not to be able to imagine myself living past the age of nineteen. But now that I *am* nineteen—

OLGA, *who has entered unnoticed.* You can see all the way to thirty-nine?

They turn, surprised. She is out of breath and dressed in gray or black with touches of white.

And when, dear, you have passed *that* milestone, you will be able to see yourself at a hundred and three, as I do now after this brutal climb!

KONSTANTIN. Welcome, Olga Vassilyevna!

FANYA. We've been wondering what became of you.

OLGA. Have you? I doubt it. Spread out the rug for me, Konstantin. I can't walk another step.

She struggles to catch her breath. FANYA *touches her arm.*
It's nothing.

Vivaciously.

We'll have our tea here, shall we? If this gentleman will pardon us.

TITHONUS. Please! Don't think of me!

OLGA. We come opportunely, perhaps?

TITHONUS. You do, after a lonely day.

FANYA. He is an artist!

OLGA. So I see. Well, I shall not embarrass him by looking at his picture. Artists hate that. Besides, I should have nothing good to say of it, I warn you, Monsieur.

FANYA. You should, though! It's very well done.

OLGA. No doubt it is. But today I am out for air and exercise. I can look at pictures all winter if I choose. And in a few weeks these colors will be gone, these wonderful dying leaves. . . .

TITHONUS, *to* KONSTANTIN. The real leaves.

KONSTANTIN, *with a shrug and a smile.* The real leaves.

OLGA, *to* TITHONUS, *while unpacking the basket.* You'll join our little feast, I hope?

TITHONUS. Thank you. I should enjoy a glass of tea.

OLGA. Ah, you're not the glutton I am! I can do without tea, but not without my smoked meats and preserves.

To the others.

But my dear friends! Where is the water?

FANYA. Oh, the water!

OLGA. Haven't you found the spring yet? What have you been *doing?* Our guest is thirsting for his tea.

To TITHONUS.

We call this *our* mountainside. We come here every year.

To KONSTANTIN, *giving him a flask.*

Don't you remember where it was?

KONSTANTIN, *patiently.* Yes, of course.

OLGA. Then find it!

To FANYA, *who makes to follow him.*

Stay with us, *chérie,* it will bring him back sooner.

KONSTANTIN *runs out.*

Where is your embroidery? A young girl should always be doing something with her hands.

To TITHONUS.

You're a stranger here. Do you plan to stay long?

TITHONUS. It's not likely. For years we have had, my wife and I, no fixed home. A *pied-à-terre* in Paris, nothing more. But now we are at the age—or rather *I* am at the age, for my wife is still young—when a home becomes a necessity. I am no longer thrilled by restaurants.

FANYA. You've never had a home?

TITHONUS. As a child only. In latter years I have traveled.

FANYA. And I have lived all my life here—isn't it strange?—a few miles from the village, in my father's big dark house.

OLGA. Don't boast, dear.

FANYA. Was I? I'm sorry. Miss Mannering—she teaches me—wrote in my album for my name-day: "Though we travel the world over in search of the beautiful, we must carry it with us, or we find it not."

TITHONUS. I don't think that saying has any truth in it at all. "Carry it with us"—as if we were turtles! We carry ourselves, that's more than enough.

FANYA. But I should like to travel, just the same.

OLGA. I too have never had a home, since early childhood. Schools and convents, positions in genteel families, not altogether a servant, never quite a friend. I married a schoolmaster, an older man, honest, proud of his uniform. He is dead, there were no children. I began to pay long visits, then very long visits—isn't it so, Fanya? As a widow, I had rank of a sort. I knew how to make myself useful. People seemed to appreciate me.

FANYA. Appreciate! They adore you!

OLGA. It is a life, in short.

TITHONUS. Better than some.

OLGA. Poorer than others.

FANYA. Have you been to Italy, then?

TITHONUS. Italy, Africa, Sweden, Constantinople. . . .

FANYA. How I envy you! Tell us about Constantinople!

TITHONUS. A fascinating city, but fearful, too. Swarming with life! This ring I wear comes from the Bazaar in Constantinople. A serpent, you see, with its tail in its mouth.

FANYA. It makes me shiver.

TITHONUS. It is a symbol of eternity and of wisdom.

OLGA. Also of evil, I've been told.

KONSTANTIN, *entering with the filled flask*. Come quickly! The spring's not a hundred steps from here! There's a waterfall—at this season!—and ferns taller than Fanya Alexandrovna!

FANYA. Oh, let's see it!

OLGA. Later, perhaps.

KONSTANTIN. The light's on it now—it won't wait!

OLGA, *laughing.* And there are a dozen little rainbows, and snails, and gnats. I know. Run along then, drink it all in.

KONSTANTIN *puts down the flask and goes out with* FANYA.

And now that *we're* unchaperoned, let us have a quiet tea.

TITHONUS. How lazy one is, not to have a look at something beautiful, only a few steps away. . . .

OLGA. How old one is, you mean. *We* should see nothing remarkable, you and I.

TITHONUS. That young man—

OLGA. Konstantin? He's my godson.

TITHONUS. He appears full of ideals.

OLGA. He picked a quarrel with you, didn't he? Do you enjoy that?

TITHONUS. Quarreling with people? No. I despise quarrels. Yet I have known others—my own father—who, out of some insane zest for experience, seemed almost to revel in it. Your godson will never permit himself to compromise. I admire that.

OLGA. Never to compromise? But you pass up a great blessing! Compromise is to our souls what sleep is to our bodies. And who would choose never to sleep? It is the compromise of the body with death, a delicious thing! We don't agree. . . .

All at once she stiffens with pain, her hand at her throat. The spasm passes unremarked by TITHONUS.

Konstantin Stepanovitch has a good mind, a trifle pedantic still, but clever, resourceful. . . . He is entering into a match with that child whose principal charm is an enormous dowry.

TITHONUS. Pardon me, isn't the girl very much in love with him?

OLGA. True. What bearing has that upon her charm?

TITHONUS. It is charming to be loved.

OLGA, *impatiently*. Well, of course, if one is a child or an invalid. . . .

Laughing.

My godson once had me read a pamphlet by a psychologist, proposing love as a cure for all kinds of illnesses.

TITHONUS. Now that is rubbish!

OLGA. Ah well, he gave it to me as a joke. I told him, anyhow—"There's nothing comic," I said, "in having grown so old and so poor that nobody who comes along will look twice at you."

TITHONUS. You're right. There is nothing comic in such a thought.

OLGA, *making the best of an unexpected answer*. It takes an unusual man to understand that. I'd never met one, till now, who didn't resort to a lot of idiotic compliments. "Why, Olga Vassilyevna, what nonsense! You're hardly out of your cradle!" At least I know better than to believe them.

TITHONUS. How indelicate of me! You mustn't think I meant—

OLGA. There, there! I'm teasing you!

TITHONUS. Teasing me? Why should you want to tease *me*?

OLGA, *deciding to ignore this*. As for Fanya, she'll be married, that's the main thing. What if in five years her husband chooses to regret his freedom? He'll never leave her—unless he *truly* refuses to compromise. And then—well, I ask only that Konstantin not make a silly mistake.

TITHONUS. You oughtn't to look so much on the dark side! Why, he struck me as caring for her so deeply, so passionately—

202

OLGA. Ah, you've forgotten! A young man cares for *everybody* passionately. What's more, you don't know poverty! I should myself care passionately for any pliable person who would not only provide me with absolute material comfort but bring about my advancement in the world.

To the samovar.

Boil, why don't you?

TITHONUS. A watched pot. . . .

They laugh together.

No! What shocking things you say! Material comfort! Advancement in the world! Am I to believe that all that has any hold over a person such as yourself?

OLGA. Are we talking seriously?

In a dramatic whisper.

Yes! All that *has* a hold over me! I am the soul of worldliness!

The look on his face sends her into a burst of laughter.

Come, my friend, I like you! I shall brew you a glass of tea and draw you out.

TITHONUS. Am I so innocent?

OLGA. Pristine. Don't frown!

TITHONUS. Do I frown?

OLGA. Or are you one of those innocent men who turn out to be the ruin of us all?

TITHONUS *is embarrassed.*

Dear friend, forgive me. It's as if we had known each other before, in a different life. Think of me as laughing for joy, to have found you once again.

Gives him her hand.

TITHONUS. Yes, it is so. . . . I have no defenses. I feel an extraordinary ease, as though something clogged had been set running again, a stopped watch shaken and set running. . . .

OLGA, *alert to something else.* Do you hear? the cry of a strange bird. . . .

TITHONUS. For years something has gone untouched, a spring inside me. . . . What you said just now—reverberates. There is a stirring, as of roots at the end of winter. Yes. When I turned and saw you standing there, I knew that I . . . had not had a happy life. Forgive me.

OLGA. One can say anything to a stranger.

TITHONUS, *excited.* But in all fairness to yourself, you must know—I am not free.

OLGA. Few of us are!

TITHONUS. I mean, I told you earlier—I am married.

OLGA, *as if that had anything to do with it.* Married!

TITHONUS. Yes. To Au—

OLGA. Hush, ridiculous man! Married! What do you take me for? On an acquaintance of ten minutes!

TITHONUS. But you said—! Forgive me, I am a fool. I have never understood the motives of others.

OLGA, *laughing.* I should say you have not! I feel like La Fontaine's dolphin, who thought to save a man from drowning only to discover it was a monkey—and just in time!

TITHONUS. I beg you—

OLGA. Back into the sea he went, poor ape! What a fiasco! "But you said—!"

More gently.

What did I say? I proposed an orgy of conversation, the only kind permitted to strangers who have reached the age of discretion.

TITHONUS *smiles with her, unwittingly relieved.*

Come now! Let us forget this unfortunate passage. It is behind us and casts an amusing light, quite as if we had *had* the miserable liaison, after all. Nothing draws people closer than a misunderstanding.

TITHONUS. How true that is! In my own life, at perhaps the very moment that determined my life—

He is interrupted by renewed laughter.

Now why are you laughing?

OLGA. What an egotist you are! First you imagine that I want you to make love to me, next that I want to hear about your life! Haven't you understood? I *know* your life, I know it without your telling me.

TITHONUS. What then do you want from me?

OLGA, *with sad intensity*. Want! Want! Mightn't it be enough to live and breathe? Must one always—?

She is overcome by a second spell of illness.

TITHONUS, *rising in alarm*. What is it? You're not well!

OLGA, *choking*. No! Leave me!

TITHONUS. Leave you! No! Never!

OLGA, *recovering*. It is of no importance whatsoever.

He helps her to her feet.

There, you see, it's over. The laughter brought it on. Last year, it is true, I was ailing. But now I am well, remarkably well. You see, I know my own life, also. . . . Listen, the water's boiling. . . .

She brews tea.

TITHONUS, *humorously scolding*. You know, you frightened me!

Producing a sheaf of photographs.

Ha! These might interest you. My wife is an amateur photographer.

Showing them.

Here is a remarkable view of her family's home—see how clearly you distinguish the mountaintop. It was taken from the temple below. . . . Here am I, only last year, in the Alps . . . again in Burgos . . . in Amsterdam. A heavenly effect of light there on the canal. She develops all her own photographs. I wonder sometimes if she's ever really happy outside of her little darkroom. . . . Ah! here is one of her early efforts. That is myself, in the first year of our marriage. Forty years ago.

OLGA, *who by now has given up trying*. You were very handsome.

TITHONUS. Yes. I was young.

A pause.

You spoke just now of wanting. At that age I wanted—oh, scandalous, impossible things. Since then, I have learned that we can alter our wants.

OLGA. No. We can uproot them, as I have done. Where I had planted an alley of chrysanthemums there is now a little row of herbs.

Pouring tea.

Be honest now, haven't you done the same?

TITHONUS. I? I have done nothing. And I want nothing.

Pause.

But I would accept, if pressed, a glass of tea.

OLGA, *handing it to him*. Sugar? Cream? Rum?

TITHONUS. Nothing.

OLGA. No turkey? Not a single tart? They're all for me. . . . I was thinking of an old woman who read tea leaves, old Varya—she's dead, poor soul. . . .

TITHONUS, *after a pause*. How agreeable this moment is! If only it would not pass away. . . .

OLGA. Agreeable things *do* pass away. That is how we distinguish them from disagreeable things. They pass away and they reappear, the seasons, the lovers in the landscape. Sometimes the very faces seem to be repeating themselves, faces from long ago.

TITHONUS. The leaves are falling, but they will return. We read their meaning as in the bottom of a glass of tea. One must be content to sit, to let it run its course.

Pause.

You look at me with—what is it?—mockery? impatience?

OLGA. Drink your tea, my friend.

TITHONUS. Do not fear, I shall not launch into a tedious account of my life, my little daily miseries. Why should one speak of these things? One is never understood. Many of your Russian writers succumb to this—shall we say, gossip of the soul?—and go their way, poor men, without ever achieving that refinement we look for in an enduring life.

Pause.

An enduring work, I meant to say. At every turning, now, what does one hear but the cries of men whose feelings are too overwhelming to be contained? Feelings indeed! If only they knew what it meant to have a fountain in the breast, flowing, quenching, musical—where I have only a stone! I cannot feel! My heart is dry as dust! You see, I laugh at it, yet . . . I have a wife, I have an unborn child! The deeds we do in the name of love!—not love, for I feel nothing. My wife, do you understand?—dressed in a Chinese robe of the clearest blue! "Husband," she said, "is it I who have failed you? What have I done," she said, "to deserve your reproach?"—I who cannot even feel reproach!—And taking my hand, she laid it below her heart where through the silk and her young flesh I might feel that other heart, the heart of my own child. I felt it, yes, but felt nothing else, not even envy of the child who will never give up the blessing I—I cannot even reproach myself! She rose from the table, upsetting her cup of chocolate. It shattered to the floor, staining us both, a piece of miraculous Sèvres given her by Lady Hamilton. She took my face between her hands, passionately, then pressed her chin against my skull—but not before I had seen her own face wet and bright as a spring dawn.

No longer looking at OLGA, *but holding before him the photograph of himself as a young man.*

A dawn, an everlasting dawn!—but for me, no night, no tempest, no cause to rejoice in it. I long for that night in which things lose themselves, the dark negative of my soul, my mild, trivial, terrible soul.

Slowly, almost tenderly, TITHONUS *begins to tear up the photograph.*

I have remembered everything and experienced nothing. Sunlight in cities, brilliance of theaters, the phosphorescence of names and places in the mind bent on darkness—nothing but light, light, light! It is not to be borne.

He scatters the destroyed photograph.

Forgive me. If I talk as I have, senselessly, you must understand that I had glimpsed in your face something, a darkness, a mortality. Olga Vassilyevna, whoever you are, break the spell!

Softly.

Oh, in my heart I feel you have already done so! Have you already done so? I dare not look. Am I free? Will it end?

He turns. OLGA *has risen and stands swaying, one hand over her eyes.*

You *are* ill! Good God!

OLGA. Yes, I am ill. The doctors say I am dying. I want so much not to.

Too late, TITHONUS *makes a move towards her.*

Stay where you are. It will pass.

She goes out.

TITHONUS, *spent and bewildered, mechanically tastes his tea.* Cold . . . disgusting. . .

He puts down his glass, crosses to the easel and begins to dismount it. Enter FANYA *and* KOSTANTIN, *dreamily oblivious of him.*

FANYA. But shan't we perhaps one day go to Sorrento?

KOSTANTIN. No.

FANYA. To China? To California?

KOSTANTIN. Never.

FANYA, *scattering leaves.* Not even if I should wish it?

208

James Merrill

KONSTANTIN. There will be no need to travel. My heart is so full. Fanya! All of life will be wherever we are!

FANYA. But Italy won't.

KONSTANTIN. So much bad painting!

FANYA. Not even when we're rich?

KONSTANTIN. We shall never be richer than we are now.

FANYA. My dearest. . . . Look at the village! How short the days are now. . . .

KONSTANTIN, *suddenly.* Fanya, do you see?

FANYA. What?

KONSTANTIN, *pointing.* A woman—down there! It's not the path we came by. . . . No, right below us!

FANYA. Oh! Isn't she wonderfully pretty! I've never seen such hair—and her clothes! Who could she be?

Half-serious.

On second thought, Kostya, I don't think it's at all nice of you to look. She's *too* pretty!

TITHONUS *looks down, rises, waves his hand.*

KONSTANTIN. She sees us, look! she's smiling! She's waving her hand!

FANYA. Do you *know* her?

OLGA *enters.* KONSTANTIN *waves to the approaching figure.* Kostya!

KONSTANTIN. It's so silly of you to be jealous. Look, she's out of sight.

FANYA. Who *is* she? You waved to her!

TITHONUS. You have just seen my wife, who has charmingly taken it upon herself to join us here.

FANYA, *turning.* Oh, it's our friend! We keep not seeing you!

KONSTANTIN. Your wife, truly?

TITHONUS. Why should you notice an old man? Yes, Sir, my wife.

209

OLGA. Children, our excursion is over, come!

KONSTANTIN. But we mustn't leave now!

OLGA. Indeed we must. The carriage will be waiting. Put those things in the basket.

FANYA. Olga Vassilyevna, what is wrong?

OLGA. Nothing, I assure you.

To TITHONUS.

What devotion to come this distance on foot, in her condition! One sees that you are a good husband, a happy man. . . . Hurry, Fanya!

To KONSTANTIN.

Help her, why don't you?

To TITHONUS.

You're pouting, aren't you?—because I would not receive your confidences. Well, I forgive you.

TITHONUS. To forgive is to forget.

OLGA. As you wish. I don't forgive you, then.

TITHONUS. Nor I you.

Offering the serpent ring.

But would you accept, as a remembrance, this?

OLGA. How could I rob you of your only—I meant to say, your most unusual treasure?

TITHONUS. One likes to offer something with associations.

OLGA. Then keep it. I don't doubt there's a story behind it.

Turning.

Are we ready, Fanya?

FANYA. Nearly.

KONSTANTIN. I don't see that we have to hurry away.

AURORA, *offstage, calling.* Where are you, darling?

FANYA, *closing the basket.* There!

TITHONUS, *calling.* This way!

To OLGA.

I should be most happy to present you to my wife.

OLGA. Pray, make her our excuses.

To FANYA.

Lead the way down the mountainside, *chérie.*

FANYA. I think we have everything. . . .

To TITHONUS, *sweetly.*

Perhaps we'll meet again. Mamma lets me have *my* friends to tea on Tuesdays. If you're staying nearby—

OLGA, *warningly.* Fanya!

FANYA, *to* OLGA. Oh, shouldn't I have . . . ? I'm sorry.

Giving TITHONUS *her hand.*

Goodbye.

To KONSTANTIN.

Don't leave the basket, Kostya!

She goes out, carrying the rug.

KONSTANTIN. Olga Vassilyevna, I suspect you of a discourtesy!

OLGA. How they talk, these young people! Take care of your own manners, Konstantin, and offer a sick old woman your arm. I must have the eyes of a cat, I can see nothing in this light.

She gives TITHONUS *her hand. He kisses it.*

Au revoir, Monsieur.

Turning.

Now where is Fanya, gone on ahead? Well, we shall have many things to tell the others, safe in the parlor, tonight. . . .

OLGA *and* KONSTANTIN *go, leaving the basket.*

AURORA, *offstage, closer.* Tithonus!

TITHONUS. I'm here! Are you all right?

AURORA. Of course! I just wanted to see you!

TITHONUS. I'll pack my paints and join you down there!

AURORA. Stay where you are! I'm not a bit out of breath!

TITHONUS. You shouldn't be climbing about!

AURORA. What?

TITHONUS. Nothing!

AURORA. Who are you with?

TITHONUS. Nobody!

AURORA. I saw them!

TITHONUS. I don't know who they were! They've gone, anyhow!

AURORA, *very close*. Why? They were charming! They waved to me!

KONSTANTIN, *re-entering*. I left the basket after all. I hope I'm not—

He stops. AURORA *enters, visibly pregnant and flushed.*

TITHONUS, *to* KONSTANTIN. She tries to do too much. It's not right.

KONSTANTIN. No, it's not right. . .

AURORA, *to* TITHONUS. Oh, what a climb! But here I am!

TITHONUS, *kissing her hand*. Yes, here you are, at last.

AURORA. But what a pretty spot! And you told me your friends had left!

To KONSTANTIN.

Good afternoon.

To TITHONUS.

I believe I have not met this gentleman.

TITHONUS. I must confess, I—

KONSTANTIN. Konstantin Stepanovitch Tschudin, at your service.

AURORA, *giving him her hand*. I'm delighted. You'll excuse my appearance. I was ordered—

TITHONUS. You were ordered to confine yourself to the morning-room.

AURORA, *in high spirits*. Quite so, the morning-room,

212

where I belong, if I may have my little joke. But there were too many plants, the air was damp and green with them, and before I knew it I was out of doors. As I walked through the village, a dozen wise old women with rosy wrinkled cheeks pressed round me, stroking me, kissing me, showing me the way. . . .

Her tone changes.

I'm all at once extraordinarily tired.

KONSTANTIN, *opening the basket.* I'm certain we have a drop of cognac here.

TITHONUS. I trust it's not the sight of me that has tired you.

AURORA. Darling, you're peevish—why?

She picks up one or two bits of the torn photograph, vaguely puzzled.

Tell me what you've done today.

TITHONUS. Oh, nothing, you know. . . .

KONSTANTIN. A very interesting picture.

AURORA. I'm so glad! May I see it?

TITHONUS, *coldly.* I'd rather you didn't. It's unfinished, and I don't know if I care enough to make the necessary changes.

Taking up his easel, paintbox, etc.

Shall we be on our way?

AURORA, *accepting a glass from* KONSTANTIN. Yes, I feel— oh, thank you, you've very kind—quite at the end of my strength. It is a new feeling—

TITHONUS, *petulant.* Aurora!

AURORA. —and a curiously pleasant one . . .

She drinks, returns the glass, and picks up TITHONUS's *campstool.*

. . . part of the great human adventure. . . .

She follows TITHONUS *out.*

213

ACT THREE

America, 1954. A garden adjoining the house of AURORA *and* TITHONUS. *There is a reclining lawn chair among other pieces of garden furniture, a trellis and a neglected plot of geraniums. One feels that no other houses are nearby. It is early morning.*

AURORA *sits smoking. She is carelessly and unbecomingly dressed, without make-up. Within reach are gardening tools. After a moment* MARK *enters. He wears slacks and a white polo shirt.*

MARK. Lovely morning, isn't it?

AURORA, *squinting.* Who's that? Oh. No, it isn't lovely, since you ask.

MARK. Perhaps you haven't had your coffee.

AURORA. I have, though. And a filthy egg. And don't expect me to talk about it. My mind is a Black Hole.

He touches her neck.

And don't make love to me!

MARK. In that case I'll help you with the flowers.

AURORA. Flowers! They're a simple scandal. I don't want to weed them, I want to wring their necks. Get away from them, do, they'll smear you from head to foot. I know.

MARK, *laughing.* All right. What has happened?

AURORA. Nothing that hasn't happened for the last hundred years. It's like the water-drop torture, it keeps accumulating. I ought at least to be thankful that the boy has come. The boy! He's three times your age. Old enough to give his poor mother some advice. It's clear that *I* can't think any more.

MARK. But that's wonderful news! I thought I saw a strange car in the drive. When did he come?

AURORA. At the crack of dawn. For his father's birthday.

MARK. You should be tremendously relieved.

AURORA. How so?

MARK. Why, just that he'll take his share of the responsibility. He's retired, he's come home, hasn't he? You'll have a certain freedom to lead your own life, after these years of strain.

AURORA. I don't believe he's staying.

MARK. He's not staying?

AURORA. I can't blame him. What did Tithonus and I ever do for him? That's what he said to me, his own mother, who cooked his breakfast! But he was right.

MARK. I don't think I'm going to like Memnon.

AURORA. He is awfully pompous to be one's son. I suppose it's the result of a military career. His father's father was the same way.

MARK. It wouldn't hurt him to take over for a little while.

AURORA. No, it wouldn't. Oh, I never dreamed I'd feel so worn, so old—!

MARK. *You* will never be old.

AURORA. Don't tell me, my sweet. Hand me the shears. No, I meant the trowel. I may *look* the same, but listen to me. I sound like Madeleine Usher.

MARK. I get angry hearing you make fun of yourself. The beautiful way you bear this situation—

AURORA, *stabbing at the flowers.* It's not beautiful the way *I* bear it. It's your precious little wife, *she's* the marvel. She sits and holds his hand and changes his linen and at the right interval shouts the right word in his ear, or what he appears to take for the right word. Five days of this! It's too mortifying, meeting you so casually, having you for a month in the country, and letting her do so much. You didn't know us when we still could do things stylishly. But the servants today won't put up with it, and he can't be left alone. I'd hoped that Memnon—ah, well, *speriamo!*

MARK. Tithonus isn't the one who needs caring for.

AURORA. It's quite hopeless, you know, trying to care for others. But she appears to enjoy it.

MARK. She likes to feel helpful. I don't know what she enjoys.

AURORA. She's really too perfect, an authentic *jeune fille,* the kind that used to read Goldsmith and play the harp, the kind that nowadays—listen to me, please! I talk, I swear, like a vampire at a cotillion. Next, I'll hear myself ask you for a fig newton and a cup of Moxie!

MARK. Aurora, stop this! I know that you're baffled and worried and hurt. You insult me by the tone you take.

AURORA. Rot. I'm simply indulging myself. Must you take away my last amusement?

MARK. It's no amusement, either for you or for anyone who has watched you these days.

AURORA. Have you watched me?

MARK. You know I have.

AURORA. It is always amusing to give in to one's baser sentiments.

MARK. You have no base sentiments, try as you may.

AURORA. Believe me, I do.

MARK. Then confess to me the basest of them.

AURORA, *stalling.* My basest sentiment? How Victorian that sounds! Well, it is a Victorian sentiment.

Serious.

It is that I find you a very handsome and estimable man. And my most elevated sentiment is my love for Tithonus. You see, I can say anything.

MARK. Aurora!

AURORA. And I shall never leave him. And I am not unhappy.

MARK. You *are* unhappy, you're miserable! You took him as a lover, in all good faith. Well—you loved him, didn't you?

216

AURORA. You don't know!

MARK. Then why be all nervous and guilty because you've changed? What is your change compared to his?

AURORA. I'm kinder to Tithonus than you are to that poor patient child—who, after all, supports you, doesn't she?

MARK. If Enid wants to support me, that's her own affair.

AURORA. Don't be so touchy.

MARK. I'm ashamed of the whole situation, if you must know. But I'm only human. Shame doesn't become a creature like yourself.

AURORA. Because I'm *not* human, you mean? You needn't rub it in, Mark.

MARK. Now who's being touchy?

AURORA. I know I'm not human. It's not for lack of trying. I've wanted to suffer! I've shed tears, I've borne a child. I've been faithful to Tithonus, not that I've *had* to be by any means. But I wanted to go through what *people* go through. I haven't wanted to snap my fingers and fly off in a glittering machine. I've done my best, but it hasn't really worked. I haven't suffered enough, I suppose.

MARK. It isn't suffering that makes us human, to begin with. And it certainly isn't living with Tithonus.

AURORA. It *must* be suffering! If that doesn't make you human, what does?

MARK. I've always thought it was something you were born with.

AURORA. Flippancy's not going to help me!

MARK. Oh Aurora, you're so lovely and young, you can't *not* be all of that, even to please your lover. Of course you talk like an old woman. He wants you old and dim, he wants to drag you down with him into some kind of horrible endless twilight. Don't you see? You're in danger!

AURORA. Danger . . . ?

MARK. Think of him. He has hardly a mind and hardly a body, but he has twined himself about you like mistletoe.

You're forever draining yourself dry in order to replenish him. How could he die?

AURORA, *bursting into tears*. Mistletoe!

MARK, *taking her in his arms*. Oh my lovely. That's it. There.

AURORA. Do you know, can you imagine, what it means, after so long, to feel that somebody watches you, and knows, and cares, quietly, gently cares and understands? He has never wanted to know what *I* was feeling. He has never known, it has always been *himself*. . . .

MARK. Leave him. Forget him. You can if you want to. Oh Aurora, come with me. I love you. Tell me you love me. Don't tell me then, I *know*.

AURORA. Enid loves you.

MARK. Yes. And what a poor thing it is, to *be* loved! I don't want that. I need to feel it myself, and I do!

AURORA. Do you mean that you would leave your wife?

MARK. I would leave her for you.

A long pause.

AURORA. There *might* be a way. . . .

Controlling herself.

You should not have made me weep. Tears are moral. When I've finished weeping, I've finished caring for myself. The sun shines after a little tempest, it's like that. My sense of obligation is revived.

MARK. But we're both weary to death of obligations!

AURORA. Are we? Darling, yes, I love you. There it is and there it ends. I am weary of obligations, but not to death. Thank you for these moments. I feel young and strong suddenly, and I love you. And that is all you shall ever have from me. That and this.

Kisses him.

MARK. I don't understand. I want only you.

AURORA. There, enough! I *must* get at those flowers. Is it my turn now to comfort you? You're not cross with me?

My voice sounds so fresh and happy, I can't think why. . . .
Am I happy? I must be, yes I am, deliciously so, for no
good reason. Poor poor dear dear young man!

ENID, *entering from the house.* Good morning.

AURORA, *blandly.* And dear lovely good creature that *you*
are! We've been talking about you. I was saying, if you
knew what it does for me, for all of us, to have you here.
I may be a goddess, but you are a saint. I'm afraid it's
telling on you, though.

ENID. No, I'm fine, really. I enjoy sitting with him. It's
an education, just listening.

AURORA. I simply meant you look a trifle worn.

ENID. That's my hay fever. I have it every summer. My
eyes swell up.

AURORA. I want you to rest today, just the same. Read,
go down to the lake, do whatever you feel like doing.
Memnon will want to be with his father, and I shall
want to—

Grimacing.

be with Memnon. He's only here for the day.

ENID. I know. He told me.

AURORA. Oh, you've met then. Doesn't he strike you as
rather bourgeois?

ENID. Oh, I couldn't tell. I met him just now in the hall.
Tithonus was awake and had called for you.

AURORA. And Memnon's with him now?

ENID. I don't know. I told him he could go in, but he
said he thought he would—

AURORA. Don't tell me what he thought. I don't want
to know.

MARK. Should Tithonus be left alone?

ENID. Good heavens, I wasn't thinking!

Starts off, distressed.

AURORA. No no no no *no*, dear. Let *me* go. Does he know
it's his birthday?

ENID. I don't think so. I had a present for him, but it didn't seem to register.

AURORA. Aren't you an angel! What did you give him?

ENID. He complains so of the cold, I've been knitting a little scarf. Rather, it *began* as a little scarf, but if anything, it's too long now.

AURORA. I'm sure it's perfect. When he gets used to it, he'll love it. It takes a few days, you know, with new things. Well. . . .

Starts away.

MARK. Aurora, think about what I've said.

AURORA *goes out. A pause.*

ENID. I think I *shall* go down to the lake. Will you come? I love to look over the side of a boat. You can see your face in the water if it's calm and you're turned away from the sun. Not a reflection really, a kind of dark transparency, and through it, below, the grasses moving, something white, one or two fish. . . .

Covering her eyes.

These unbroken shining days! How does she manage them?

Pause.

I don't want to pry, but tell me—what is Aurora to think about?

MARK. I suggested we might all go off one of these days, with a picnic. There are some fascinating things not far away, churches, antique shops. You know better than I, after reading the guidebook.

ENID. I didn't know you enjoyed sight-seeing.

MARK. Whatever made you think I didn't? Once in a while, it's very pleasant. I didn't know you had hay fever.

ENID. Whatever makes you think I do? And how about Tithonus? You know he can't be moved.

MARK, *lighting a cigarette.* Strange. I didn't think of that.

ENID. Didn't she?

MARK. Didn't she what?

ENID. See that as an objection to your plan?

MARK. Yes—so she did.

ENID, *faintly.* Then why, if the whole thing is impossible, did you ask her to think about it?

MARK. You'll have to speak louder if you want me to hear you.

ENID, *doing so.* Or did you intend for me to stay with Tithonus while you and she go off together?

MARK. No, certainly not. I'm sure she can get someone from the village. We might offer to pay for whoever comes. We can afford it, and it would be a nice gesture.

ENID. It has to be someone he knows!

Pause.

Oh dearest, all I mean is that I *don't* take much pleasure in sitting with him the better part of the day and night.

MARK, *losing his temper.* Then why do it, if you don't enjoy it?

ENID. Don't be cross.

MARK. Don't be pathetic.

ENID. I'm surprised you have any preference in the matter.

MARK. What matter?

ENID. The matter of how you want me to be.

MARK, *politely.* I'm sorry. Be just as you are.

ENID. Just as I am! With my eyes swollen and my heart sick? If that's how I am—oh Mark, make me stop! I don't want to talk this way, I'm beginning to feel at home in this unhappiness. In another moment I'll start *liking* it!

MARK. That's so typical of you, Enid, to find the silver lining of an imaginary cloud.

ENID. What's the matter with us? It's like being in an earthquake. The ground slips from under you, but silently, and in bright sunlight.

MEMNON *enters from the house. He is dressed in a double-breasted business suit, with loud tie and steel-rimmed glasses. He carries a briefcase and before long will light a cigar.*

MEMNON. Morning!

MARK. This will be Memnon.

Turning.

Good morning.

MEMNON. Just looking around, thanks. Don't believe you and I have met. I'm the old man's son, retired myself now.

MARK, *shaking hands.* How are you? I think you already know my wife.

MEMNON. Can't say I've had that pleasure—

Recognizing ENID.

Why sure! Isn't that the limit? Why, I thought you were the nurse! No offense, I hope?

ENID. None whatever. I *am* the nurse.

MEMNON, *to* MARK. What outfit were you in?

MARK. Excuse me?

ENID. What outfit were you in, dear?

MARK. I was thirteen when the war ended.

ENID, *smoothing it over, to* MEMNON. How do you think your father looks?

MEMNON. Oh, pretty much the same, I guess.

ENID. He *is* remarkable, isn't he?

MEMNON. Remarkable's the word, all right. Between you and me, though, we never had too much to say to each other, Dad and I.

ENID. I suppose he always *was* so much older, wasn't he? But you must be very close to your mother.

MEMNON. Not really. She was always so much younger. They used to look on me like some kind of freak, you know, being human and all. Been sensitive ever since to people making fun of me.

ENID. I hope you're here for a nice leisurely visit.

MEMNON. Afraid not. Like to stay but got to get back. Just down to wish Dad many happy returns.

ENID. What a pity! Really must you? I'd think, now you're retired from active duty, your time would be your own.

MEMNON. That's what *I* thought till I spoke to my agent last week. He told me I'd have to buckle down hard if I wanted my book to get *published* even, let alone *sell*.

ENID. Your book?

MEMNON. My war journal. But like you say, war's over, *has* been for a number of years. Public's beginning to lose interest. My agent said to me, we can't go on living in a fool's paradise.

ENID, *after a pause*. But that's perfectly thrilling!

MARK. Does it have a title?

MEMNON. Not yet. Wanted to call it *Old Soldiers Never Die*, but then I started to wonder how Dad would take it. Seemed a bit inappropriate.

MARK. How about *From Ranks to Riches?*

MEMNON *jots it down*.

ENID. You must tell your father about it. He has so many wonderful reminiscences of his own. But gracious, if you have work to do, I couldn't imagine a more perfect atmosphere than right here. That west porch, facing the water!

MARK. Probably the General wants to be within reach of documents and newspaper files.

MEMNON. Between ourselves, that's the whole point. I could kick myself for not having made some kind of notes at the time. A line a day would have done it. But man! we were in combat! Also, you can't go into seclusion just to write a book. You've got to keep in the public eye! They want your opinions on national affairs. You go after honorary degrees, you lay cornerstones! Show them you're still full of beans!

AURORA, *entering.* What under the sun are you talking about?

She is now beautifully groomed and carries a large straw purse.

ENID. Don't you look lovely!

MEMNON, *whom* AURORA *kisses on the forehead.* More like my daughter than my mother.

MARK. We've had a little talk about literature.

AURORA. How elevating!

ENID, *to* MEMNON. Have you a family?

MEMNON. No. Never got around to it. Never regretted it, either.

AURORA, *to* MARK. I've had such a curious few minutes on the telephone.

MARK. With whom?

AURORA. Somebody I'd forgotten all about.

MEMNON, *to* ENID. You know, the example of Mother and Dad did a lot to discourage me from having a family of my own.

AURORA, *to* MARK, *hushed but excited.* I've changed my mind!

MARK, *eagerly.* What do you mean?

AURORA, *aloud.* I mean— we might bring Tithonus out into the garden. It's such a beautiful mild day, it would be a little treat for him.

ENID. I'll get him ready.

AURORA. He *is* ready. And we have two grown men to work for us, so just sit down with me, my sweet. This is your day of rest.

To the others.

Will you fetch him, please? One of you can carry him, the other bring his covers.

MEMNON. Is he much of a load?

AURORA. Light as a feather. You've lifted him, Mark. It's the same as picking up a baby, you just want to be careful the head doesn't drop off.

MEMNON *and* MARK *go out. A pause.*

Oh living, living. . . . Don't you sometimes feel you'd like to run away, put it all behind you, all the effort, all the pretense?

ENID. Do you pretend, Aurora?

AURORA. I never used to. But now I feel I'm constantly pretending, contriving little lies with my face and voice. I try to appear light and calm, to keep something twirling in my hand. . . .

ENID. Perhaps you simply pretend to be pretending.

AURORA. Perhaps. What would you say?

ENID. I would say that you were quite truly happy. I envy you.

AURORA. Hush! You mustn't, you needn't. . . .

Pause.

What a child you are!

ENID. If only I were beautiful!

AURORA. Appearances aren't everything. Besides, you're lovely!

ENID. But they *are*, and I'm *not!* It's unfair, the things we were told—by our beautiful mothers, our beautiful sisters, even our beautiful husbands! They made us believe that a sweet disposition meant more than a good figure. They told us that if we were generous and patient and truthful, nobody would care about our not having red-gold hair and gray-gold eyes and wonderful useless hands. I suppose it was sheer human pity on their part, and yet if they *had* told the truth I might have learned to bear it, by now. I try. I sit at the mirror and stare at my face. I say to myself aloud, over and over, "Appearances *are* everything!" It's like dipping my heart in brine!

AURORA. Are you fond of me, Enid? Sometimes I wonder if you like me at all.

ENID. Oh, how hard I've tried not to! But I am, I do, so very much! You can't know the thoughts I've had.

AURORA. Can't I? You have seen me as a young wife tired of her husband. You have imagined me in search of a handsome lover. You have wept all night out of jealousy and helplessness. Isn't it so?

ENID *bows her head.*

Well, I have known all of that. And I have had to smile, thinking how little cause for tears I should have if I were in your position.

ENID. How good you are! Can you guess what a relief—? I'd thought—I hadn't dared think! Then none of it is true?

AURORA, *lying but radiant.* None of it!

ENID. There was no reason for me to have—?

AURORA. No reason!

ENID. He really and truly—

AURORA. With all his heart!

ENID. —loves me?

AURORA, *tears in her eyes.* Loves you!

Squeezing ENID's *hand.*

They'll be coming. Where's your handkerchief?

ENID *gives it to her.* AURORA *blows her nose.*

We must never lose faith in those who love us.

ENID. Tell me one thing. What was he saying to you, earlier?

AURORA. You *still* don't believe me!

ENID. I do, I want to! But please—

AURORA, *glowing.* It was a secret. He particularly didn't want you to know about it. But you will, I promise, and soon.

Voices offstage.

226

MEMNON. Old enough to know better, ha ha ha!

TITHONUS, *cross*. Aurora! How old is the boy?

AURORA. I haven't the faintest notion.

To MEMNON.

How old *are* you?

MEMNON, *dignified*. I'm sixty-one.

TITHONUS. How old?

AURORA. Memnon says he's sixty-one, darling.

To MEMNON.

Are you really? I should have thought younger. . . .

TITHONUS, *cackling with mirth*. Sixty-one! Getting along in years, is he not? Not much time left to enjoy life at sixty-one! Tell him, tell him his father says to enjoy it while he can! He can't take it with him!

MEMNON. The old buzzard!

AURORA. Hush, he's your father, Memnon.

TITHONUS. Sixty-one!

ENID, *to* MEMNON. Don't take it that way.

MARK, *to* AURORA. With children you have to keep changing their pants. When they're old it's their mouths they can't control.

AURORA. You will be old some day.

MARK. But I shall have lived. It won't matter.

TITHONUS. Now, when *I* was sixty-one, or thereabouts—what a difference!

AURORA, *to* MARK. What can have put it into your head that you are finer than Tithonus? No matter what he may be now, he has had an extraordinary life.

MARK. I don't believe it!

AURORA. What you say reflects very prettily on *me*.

MARK. I can't help that.

TITHONUS. When I think of all I have seen, people I have known—but intimately, all their lives long!

AURORA. I don't mean to be snappish. Something's wrong with me today.

MARK. Come. We have to talk.

He leads her to one side. They remain visible and their voices can be heard murmuring in the background.

MEMNON. Must be the old man gets on her nerves. He like this all the time?

TITHONUS. London! The parties!

ENID, *to* MEMNON. All the time.

TITHONUS. None of the postwar gatherings, so artfully informal, could match in brilliance those contrived and permeated by that proud and generous spirit, Mrs. Dickinson Davin, born Lady Milly Rapping. Aurora, do you remember? Aurora!

ENID, *trying to imitate* AURORA. Yes, darling!

TITHONUS. Moving idly through the high hushed rooms, pausing, not wholly for effect, beneath an *Emily* Mandible needlepoint, to the informed eye so much more of a piece than the glib if popular designs of her ill-fated niece, only a newcomer—of which but one or two were admitted every season—would have been taken aback at the sight of Field Marshal Pellet in lively banter with Mrs. Mock, the American ambassadress, from whose grandfather I still treasure a handful of mosaic picked up as a very young man in Hagia Sofia. . . . Where am I?

ENID. Mrs. Mock.

TITHONUS. The American ambassadress, quite so, from whose grandmother I still treasure a handful of mosaic given her by an urchin, who knew not what it was; or Greta Stempel-Ross, fresh from her native . . . her native . . . oh, how it irritates me! Fresh from her native. . . .

AURORA, *softly to* MARK. She had splendid references and a very impressive telephone manner.

MARK. Then it's all settled!

TITHONUS. Well, no matter—and only the following season

to take by storm the small but lofty citadel of Taste—
What do I want with Venice? Lady Milly used to ask. I
have my own Campanile here! And she would tap her
forehead—that even in those uncertain days before the war,
no, after the war, before the *other* war, yes, still shone
gallantly in our midst, not only by her singing of Krank and
Claude Delice, but by her revelation of the folk melodies
of her native . . . the folk melodies of her native . . .
Aurora!

MEMNON. I couldn't take *that* for very long.

AURORA, *to* MARK. It was odd, though—as if she'd been
waiting for the call.

TITHONUS. Aurora! Aurora!

AURORA, *to* MARK. Excuse me.

ENID, *to* MEMNON. Aurora's wonderful.

AURORA, *to* TITHONUS. What is it, my darling?

TITHONUS. I can't remember, I can't remember! If you
knew how it exasperates me to forget!

AURORA, *tenderly*. What have you forgotten?

TITHONUS. Now I've even lost the name. That singer.
You've heard the name hundreds of times. I said it only a
moment ago.

AURORA. Emmy Destinn?

To the others.

He loved Emmy Destinn.

TITHONUS. No, no, no! Not Emmy Destinn. Do you suppose I would ever forget that voice? Now, somebody said
of *her*—what was it? We were sitting at supper, there were
lanterns. . . . Well, no matter. I have it all stored away
somewhere. Waste not, want not.

Whimpering.

No, I mean that girl, that girl in London before, *after*
the war. Greta! Greta something-or-other—you know who
I mean. Where was she from?

AURORA. Greta Stempel-Ross! I'd forgotten all about her. *To the others.*

Really, she did have a heavenly voice, heavenly.

TITHONUS. But where was she from?

AURORA. Roumania.

TITHONUS. Of course. Her native Roumania.

MEMNON. Well, that's settled!

AURORA. What time can it be? I must fly to the village, isn't that a bore?

MEMNON *looks at his watch, then listens, but it has stopped.*

AURORA *turns to* ENID.

Mark said he would go with me—it's what we've been plotting—if you'll let me borrow him?

ENID, *smiling.* Just bring him back.

AURORA. Actually I'd go alone, if it were something I could do by myself. But it's a surprise for Tithonus, a rather *big* surprise, which wasn't to have been ready until today.

ENID. So many surprises. . . .

AURORA, *beaming, her finger to her lips.* My dear, I hate to ask, but for these hours, two at the most, *could* you—?

She indicates TITHONUS.

ENID. I'd love to. Are you leaving at once?

AURORA. Virtually.

MEMNON. Virtuously? Ha ha ha!

ENID. Let me just run upstairs and fetch my knitting.

AURORA, *to* MARK. You're quite sure you don't mind coming?

MEMNON. Where are you going, Mother?

MARK. Quite sure.

AURORA, *to* MEMNON. I have to run down to the village for something I had forgotten.

232

James Merrill

TITHONUS. I'm chilly. The way they treat me here! Handsome is as handsome does, I always say.

MEMNON, *pulling himself together*. You know, really think I might be—

AURORA. Memnon, be a lamb, run to my room. You'll find an extra blanket in the bottom drawer of the bureau.

MEMNON. Was thinking, I might as well be shoving off myself. Long drive ahead of me.

AURORA, *fierily*. You will stay here until we return. I've never heard of such utter rudeness, walking out on your father's birthday! It's not as though you had celebrated *all* of them with him! Do I make myself clear? Now kindly fetch that blanket.

MEMNON *goes out*.

TITHONUS. I'm cold, cold. . . . I could freeze before any-one. . . . Not even in Portugal, that February. . . .

AURORA *smooths his brow, absently*.

Aurora, is the summer over? I shall come begging for grain, like the grasshopper. . . .

MARK. It hurts to sever ties. Once we're away—

AURORA. Oh my dear, beware of me. Beware of my facility. It's too easy, everything I do.

MARK. Those years with Tithonus weren't easy.

AURORA. Oh, they *were*, now that they're over! I feel myself shaking them off, uncontrollably! I couldn't turn back if I wanted to.

MARK. But think who you are! If you can't easily rid yourself of a problem, who can?

AURORA. My problem now is you. All too easily I see you as a way out, a little staircase of flesh by which to climb again into the open air. Have I the right? Do I love you that much?

MARK. Yes. But I don't matter. What matters is that you fulfil your destiny.

233

AURORA. I have no destiny, you know.

MARK. You do, though. You need to live by pleasure and light, anyone who sees you knows. And as long as you love me, I shall help make all that more vivid.

AURORA, *touched*. Mark, Mark—what can I give you, to show you all the things I feel?

MARK. Nothing unusual, nothing costly. Just let me keep my own mortality, which you will have made precious.

AURORA. Your own mortality? Do you mean that you *want* to die?

MARK. No. Not for a moment. But it won't matter. You can't understand, and why should you?

AURORA, *kissing him*. You're charming and you're right. Why should I understand?

MARK. What time are we picking up the nurse?

AURORA. I told her we'd be leaving almost at once.

MARK. Then let's go!

MEMNON, *entering with the blanket*. If *this* doesn't keep him warm enough. . . . Is he asleep?

AURORA. His eyes are shut. Look, he has thrown his covers off.

To MARK, *as she begins to arrange them.*

Help me.

TITHONUS, *shrinking from* MARK. Aurora, they're hurting me! Their hands are rough!

AURORA, *to* MARK. I'll do it, then. I thought he knew your touch.

She continues to enfold him, like something wrapped away for winter. Enter ENID *with her knitting.*

MEMNON. Wouldn't have thought he'd care so much.

ENID. When does one ever finish caring?

TITHONUS. Aurora, keep me warm. . . . I fear the winter. . . . Soon the winds will be upon us, roaring. . . .

AURORA. Sleep now, Tithonus.

He shuts his eyes.

ENID. There is such a sadness in his face, as though he knew. . . .

AURORA. Knew what, my dear?

ENID. That you were leaving, if only for an hour or two.

MARK. That cover has the look of a cocoon.

AURORA, *her task finished.* It does. Goodbye. And if by noon we shouldn't have returned, give him some food—a cup of broth, or tea. He needs so little. . . . So.

ENID. Mark—do you have some money with you?

MARK. No.

To AURORA.

Do I need money?

AURORA. Perhaps she wants something from the village.

To ENID.

Can we bring you something from the village?

ENID. No.

AURORA. Then shall we go?

Starts out.

Oh wait! Before the light fails, so as not to forget—!

She takes a camera from her purse, gets into position, focuses.

Smile, everybody! Let's remember this day always!

Snaps picture.

There! Be good!

AURORA *and* MARK *leave. A long pause.* MEMNON *starts to smooth out a wrinkle in* TITHONUS's *cover.*

TITHONUS, *waking refreshed.* Ah! Have I slept? Yes, I think I have had a nice nap. Aurora! Something is not as it should be. I have an uncanny instinct in such matters. I once took it upon myself to warn a young friend of mine, the poet Clarence Boiler DeKay, on the eve of his marriage. Forty years later he confessed to me privately that I had been right. A stitch in time saves nine. My mind swarms with interesting observations. I am never bored. I have lived longer than anybody, and acquired a profound experience of the human heart. It is too late to pretend otherwise. You can't teach an old dog new tricks. The pot calls the kettle black.

MEMNON. He used to tell me *I* talked in clichés!

TITHONUS. An idle mind is the Devil's workshop.

MEMNON, *hemming and hawing*. You know, think I'd better be shoving off myself now, if you'll excuse me. Got a long drive ahead of me. Mother wanted me to hang around till they checked in, but if I know her, once she starts whipping out that camera she's gone for the whole day. Guess I don't need to tell you how she appreciates what you're doing. She told me this morning that until you came she hadn't had a holiday for she didn't know how long, years I guess.

ENID *is silent*.

You know, it's funny—this place always gave me the creeps. Folks say, home is where you hang your hat. Closer to truth, it's where you hang your*self*. If you'd like me to stay till they come back, I'd be glad to, really would.

ENID *shakes her head, forcing a smile*.

She didn't want me to stay either, if you ask me. Just trying to be polite, being my mother and all.

TITHONUS. Wilful waste makes woeful want. Nothing succeeds like success. I have learned all this through bitter experience.

MEMNON. Can't see that it's much fun for you, sitting with him.

ENID, *tonelessly*. I don't mind. More and more it appears we have interests in common.

MEMNON. How do you mean?

TITHONUS. I feel a storm approaching. That is not as it should be.

236

MEMNON. Oh, I get it! His wife, your husband, you mean? *Laughs weakly.*

That's pretty good! Well, I guess you don't have anything to worry about *there!*

TITHONUS. I am still remarkably sensitive to everything around me.

ENID. I believe a storm *is* coming. You'd best be on your way.

TITHONUS, *dropping off to sleep.* Though we travel the world over in search of the beautiful, we must carry it with us or we find it not.

MEMNON. Well, if you're sure there's nothing, I'll say goodbye.

ENID, *giving him her hand.* Goodbye.

MEMNON. Au revoir, I guess I mean.

ENID. Goodbye.

MEMNON. Goodbye, Dad.

Shouts.

Goodbye, Father!

Shrugs.

ENID. I wish you success with your book.

MEMNON. Oh, thank you! I'll send you an autographed copy.

Exit, waving his briefcase. A silence.

TITHONUS, *dreaming.* My love, my love, was it a dream . . . ?

ENID, *stroking his brow.* Be still. It *is* a dream.

She rests her head on her arm. It is conceivable that she and TITHONUS *dream this final scene.* AURORA *enters upstage with the* NURSE. *The latter is dressed entirely in white—cap, veil, shoes, stockings, etc.*

AURORA, *whispering.* There he is. I can't stay, the car's waiting. We must be off at once.

NURSE, *moving about, tidying things up.* It seems we are hand in glove with one another. You don't want it known that you've sent for me. I have my pride, too. I'm not the sort of woman one sends for.

AURORA. Oh, I didn't mean—

NURSE. I am not hired by the hour.

AURORA. When I needed you I called. I never meant to imply—

NURSE. Don't try to apologize. You don't know how. You've made your decision, Aurora. Henceforth, if I'm to care for him, I'll do it in my own way. Your way, to judge from the results, has failed.

AURORA. You will be good to him? You won't try to disillusion him when you talk about me?

NURSE. We shall never talk about you.

AURORA. They're both asleep. I think I shall just tiptoe over and kiss him lightly once, on the forehead. . . .

NURSE. No.

AURORA. Is it so much to ask?

NURSE. If you have any fondness left for him, leave him to me. Go. Go now.

AURORA, *after a pause, smiling brilliantly.* Yes, of course! What *could* I have been thinking of?

NURSE. Goodbye, Aurora.

AURORA. Goodbye! Oh, do you *know* what it's like, to feel love, to feel love for the first time? Bless you!

She blows a kiss and runs out. An uneasy twilight falls.

NURSE, *to* ENID. You need watch no longer.

ENID, *starting.* Oh!

NURSE. I have come to sit with him.

ENID. Oh, yes of course—no, I don't mean that. I'm sorry, I can't think. Did Aurora send you? Have they been delayed?

NURSE, *as if she had never heard the name.* Aurora?

ENID. Well, she's not here. I'm sitting with him. This is

Aurora's husband. I'm her guest. . . . I must still be half asleep. . . .

NURSE. I know.

ENID. She ought to be back any moment, there are her flowers. They went off, Aurora and—*my* husband, for only an hour or so, to the village. You must have come from there. Perhaps you saw the car? I couldn't describe it, never having kept a journal, but it's Aurora's car, there's no mistaking it.

NURSE. I have not come from the village. Is there a village here?

ENID. Well, I don't want to pry. . . . Do sit down, won't you anyhow?

NURSE. Yes, I have come to sit with him.

ENID. Not on my account, I hope. I enjoy sitting with him, really I do. It's an education in itself.

NURSE. I have not come on your account. He knows why I have come.

ENID. Oh, you're *his* friend!

NURSE. He wanted me. I know how to make myself useful.

A pause.

Thank you.

ENID. What?

NURSE. I am here. He will not need you any more.

ENID, *starting out reluctantly, then stopping.* I—have nowhere else to go.

NURSE. Are you sure? Isn't it more that you really want to stay?

ENID. Yes. I want to stay.

NURSE. Then do. We shan't mind. Yes, by all means, stay. Now that I look at you, I can see that you are very tired.

ENID, *nervously.* That's my hay fever. Every summer. My eyes swell up.

239

NURSE. Do whatever you please. Sit in that chair, why
don't you? Knit him a scarf if you enjoy doing things with
your hands. You need time, my child, time in which to
think about time, to think of it no longer as a packed bright
space entered and left behind, to think of it rather as a
gray wind, a soft thread wound, endlessly, about you. . . .

ENID, *as if struggling to wake*. But that isn't true! Time
does end!

NURSE, *gently restraining her*. For some of us perhaps.

ENID. It does! It must!

NURSE. Not for him, whom we are here to care for.

ENID. But we'll be caring for him all our lives!

NURSE, *radiantly*. Yes!

ENID. He'll never die!

TITHONUS, *opening his eyes and looking meaningfully
from one to the other*. A watched pot never boils.

NURSE, *sweetly, to* ENID. You see? You see?

TITHONUS *chuckles on and on*. ENID *crumples obediently
into her chair and begins to unravel some yarn. The*
NURSE, *with many smiles of encouragement, takes up her
position by the lawn chair.*

A LEAK IN THE UNIVERSE

I. A. Richards

CAIN. But the thing had a demon?

LUCIFER.   He but woke one
In those he spoke to with his forky tongue.

~

                That must be our cure—
To be no more; sad cure; for who would lose
Though full of pain, this intellectual being,
Those thoughts that wander through eternity,
To perish rather, swallowed up and lost
In the wide womb of uncreated Night,
Devoid of sense and motion? And who knows,
Let this be good, whether our angry Foe
Can give it, or will ever? How he can
Is doubtful. . . .

~

. . . an Emptiness ready to receive all things.
Tao abides in the Emptiness,
The Emptiness is the Fast of the Mind.

CHARACTERS

THE CONJUROR
DR. BALTSCHIEDER KLAUS, *Physicist*
MRS. NEMO, *Medium*
DR. HERMANN ZOCCA
DR. OMORI, *a Buddhist*
VOICES

Most of the scenes take place at the Institution for Advancing Studies.

PROLOGUE

Spoken by the CONJUROR *in traditional frock coat, etc. He has a small gray imperial. Behind him on a table is something covered by a golden cloth. This is lit, but otherwise the room is dark.*

Yes, fellow Conjurors. May these few scenes,
    The spirits too, fetched here through such queer
      places
(Yourselves not least) be the regardful means
    By which the play may win for you new graces.

Though all be cheat (unless you make it sound)
    Each idol clay (unless your breath it merit)
The phantom seed seeks being in your ground;
    Rootless as yet, it would your blood inherit.

What is conceived without an alien aid?
    What concept grows without transfiguration,
Unrecognizably turned inside out and made
    Responsive to a foregone destination?

This play's about itself, and so are you:
    Stalking yourselves and studying what you lost,
What to give up for what and what to do
    With what is left to you and at what cost.

Resolve and re-resolve you as you may
    The image cannot be the god; though he,
The god invoked, sustain throughout the play
    Each instrument through which you strain to see.

You see what you deserve to see, no less;
    Though maybe more. What you may make of this
Is yours. It can no more than guess
    What moves you in it to applaud or hiss.

A LEAK IN THE UNIVERSE   *Prologue*

What this may tender tenders yet the void
   However you replenish: no substance lent
The vacant forms that all your life employed
   When nothing yielded naught and nothing meant.

244

Scene One

The Conjuror steps to the table, takes up his wand and removes the cloth showing the box. Points to it with his wand.

CONJUROR.

Just the thing for a conjuror
No illusion whatever.

Takes it up with both hands ceremoniously.

A perfectly authentic box
As you see.
No double walls;
No false lid or bottom.
Made . . . ? Made, if you like, of box.

Lightly tapping it and turning it.

Boxwood, you know,
The very wood for boxes.

Shall we start with this box?
At the back of the shop,
In the dusk, on the shelf,
Gray with the dust on it.

Blowing dust away, flicking it, shaking it and opening it.

Wordless when shaken,
When open, empty!
Simple . . . room for the ashes.
Just the right size;
Many times wider
Than any than,
Longer beyond measure,
Deeper beyond compare.
There it was and we were
In the lost and found.

Puts it back on the table again ceremoniously, spreading the cloth for it.

245

Just the thing for a conjuror. I had
A pretty, slight device—Quies, I called it—
Whalebone, wire and silk and something.
Put it in a box;
Then put your change, your keys, your glasses. . . .
With Quies cosy in the box and shake it.

Shakes an imaginary box by his ear.

Silence! No rattle. Not a click, not a scratch. . . .
They might as well have not been there;
You'd say they were not. But they were.
Shake it—not a sound—by your ear.
Quies might have had quite a career!

The thing then was to find a worthy box.
I found it.
There it was, on the shelf, waiting for me.
I liked the yellow gleam on it, like the evening sky in
rain.

Takes box in hands again.
Opens it.

Inside no box was emptier. Nothing seen
Of any speck of dust or mothy grain.
The corners like a whistle were so clean;
The hinge so firm, wide-morticed, free and sane,
All so aboveboard, comforting and true,
It did you good to see it so well made,
Without a crack or cranny. Soothing too—
To hear the soft snap as the lid came to.

Shuts box.

After putting box on table, conjuror *stands behind it as
if performing a trick in fullest view of audience. He goes
through the motions of the acts he describes.*

Took my find home, I did,
Lifted its smooth, sweet lid,
Slipt in my pretty toy,
My Quies, deft and coy,

246

I. A. Richards

Dropped in my fountain pen,
Added my watch and chain,
And my latch key;
Shut down the lid again.

Lightly I took it up
Gently I shook it up
Listened with glee
Soundless each jerk I gave
Silent as any grave.
Not any throb or thud
Not even a wabble heard.

Shaking box hard.

Not the most violent shake
Would the least rumour wake
Shift, slide, slip or quake
Inside could be.
Satisfied, content,
Hither and thither
I waved it. No quiver,
Not even a shiver!

Was any man ever
Contenter than me!

I lifted up the lid.

Inside no box was emptier;
The whole thing like a whistle was so clean.

Steps forward from the table.

Stand still, Space-time, and if you have a track
Turn round on it and instantly come back.
You cannot? You are trackless? Gone is gone!
And nothing's left me here to work upon.
Nothing but nothing. For me, at least, who know
Only too well, none better, the whole show:

What can be done and cannot in this trade,
Any every illusion magic ever made.
I whom no magic circle could put out,
Prince conjuror confirmed beyond all doubt,
Grand master atheist of the inmost rings,
Eyes and hands cauterized by secret things
I who know every turn of all the tricks
Am not tricked here, and there is no way *not*
To see and believe and tremble. No way out.

Out into nowhere! As well have time turn round!
What would it turn in? Travel back through what?
And where could nothing be, when start or end?
My watch, which while I slept worked out my hours—
No overtime or leisure still for watches—
Gone now, no-whither! And all my time gone with it!
My overfaithful pen that, as I wrote
The books which died just now, has served me right,
Gone too. My key gone too. Shut out and homeless!
Gone too to nowhere my young joker, Quies!
A symbol that's become too good a symbol,
And lost itself and me. That vanisher
Has vanished me. And now where is the master
To bring back all in triumph for a finish?
Finish indeed! I rather think *I'm* finished.

Knock at the door. CONJUROR *switches on light, and his
room with bookcases, etc., appears.*

Come in!

Enter DR. BALTSCHIEDER KLAUS.

KLAUS. Hello, Professor, what's up now? At it again!

CONJUROR. No, but you're . . . perhaps, the very man I
need.

KLAUS. Anything for an audience!

CONJUROR. The other way about. *I* have a problem for
you.

KLAUS. I don't know a thing about conjuring.

CONJUROR. And I know very little physics. This isn't conjuring. I think it is physics.

KLAUS. Probably not; but still what is it? I'm rather good at explaining.

CONJUROR. You see the box. Is there anything odd about it?

KLAUS, *taking the box up and examining it.*

No, except that it is a nice box and *very* well made. I suppose there is a trick about it?

CONJUROR.

If there is, it's no trick I have ever heard of.

KLAUS.

Is that so? Well then, what's wrong with the box? I'd be glad to keep my cigars in it.

CONJUROR.

I don't think you would! Not for long! See here, What shall we put in it? Black diamonds?

Taking little bits of coal from scuttle.

Bits of the ancient forests? Some of yesterday's forests?

Takes up newspaper, tears it and puts in bits of twisted-up paper.

There is a touch of the forest, I think, about this box. What else? Some coins. Put the price of a newspaper in.

KLAUS. I haven't a nickel. Here's a dollar bill.

CONJUROR. So now we shut it.

KLAUS. That is a good line of patter you have.

CONJUROR. It isn't patter.

KLAUS. Isn't it? Well, you ought to know. What happens now?

CONJUROR. You take the box and shake it. Do you hear the coal rattling around in it? Do you hear the paper rustling?

KLAUS. I don't hear anything.

249

*Shakes it at one ear then shakes it at the other. Puts a
finger in the other ear.*

I'm rather good at hearing things too.

Tries his wrist watch at his ear.

I can hear my wrist watch tick two feet away. I can't
hear anything moving in the box though.

CONJUROR. I know you can't. There is nothing there to
hear.

KLAUS. It's a damn smart box if there isn't!

CONJUROR. I'd give what I call my soul to hear it rattle.

KLAUS. Do you mean they aren't there?

CONJUROR. They aren't there.

KLAUS. You didn't put them in!

CONJUROR. I did. Yes, I really put them in. If anything is
real, I really put them in.

KLAUS. Well then, you'll have to eat them if they aren't
there.

Opens the box, looks inside, and smiles.

Congratulations! That's the best trick and the best build-
up you've had yet.

CONJUROR. It wasn't a trick and it wasn't a build-up.

KLAUS. Look here! Something's upset you. I knew it the
moment I came in. You aren't well. You're upset.

CONJUROR. How did you know that?

KLAUS. You didn't rise when I called you "Professor."
That always gets you. I'm rather good at getting rises.

CONJUROR. Oh, I took that for just a Nobel Prize winner's
joke. But I *am* upset. This box, you know, there's not a bit
of trick about it. It does just what you saw and heard it do.
I mean what you didn't hear and didn't see.

KLAUS.

   Quite impossible! It must have double sides or some-
      thing.

I. A. Richards

CONJUROR.

    Quite impossible! I know my business, thank you!
    That box quite simply makes things go out of existence.

KLAUS.

    Nonsense! You just don't know what you are saying.

CONJUROR. I am saying there is no trick in the world can do what it does. That coal, that newspaper and your dollar *were*. Now they're not.

KLAUS. That won't do at all! They must be somewhere.

CONJUROR.

    Why shouldn't they be nowhere? Why not sheer
    Nothingness? An instantaneous utter lack of being?

KLAUS.

    You don't know what you are talking about.

CONJUROR.

    I very seldom do. But you, you physicists,
    You are the folk who should know what we can talk of!
    That is why I think this is your problem.
    I can only tell you it is no conjuring trick.
    Why can't you think that a something becomes nothing?

KLAUS. For a thousand reasons. I'll spare you the thermodynamics. And the nuclear ground—you wouldn't understand them. But take pressure merely. If this box really went empty, you wouldn't be able to open it. There'd be a perfect vacuum. I doubt if it would be able to take the pressure. It's not too strong. I believe I could push it in with my thumbs. I'm rather strong with my thumbs.

Makes as if to try.

CONJUROR, *snatching the box from him.*

    Give it me. I may not know what I'm saying;
    But you don't know what you are doing.
    Suppose it spread?

KLAUS.

    What?

251

CONJUROR.

The property the box has.

KLAUS.

What property?

CONJUROR.

The gift it has to turn a thing to nothing:
You, for example.

KLAUS.

That won't do, you know. Energy, matter
Can't—doesn't—just go out of existence
However, this property you say the box has:

CONJUROR.

Let's say the box sets up a boundary
A limit to the volume within which things vanish.
It stops things getting inside that volume,
Otherwise. . . .

KLAUS.

The whole world would go pushing in.

CONJUROR.

Like the rush-hour crowds into the subway!
Who goes home?

KLAUS.

But what's home?

CONJUROR.

Nowhere.

KLAUS. Bah! This doesn't make any sort of sense whatsoever. Say it's the inner surfaces are those limits.

CONJUROR *hands him the box again.*

KLAUS. It's certainly very clean inside and smooth too. See here! I'll write my name inside the lid here; And we'll see what it does with that little pattern of graphite!

Penciling and closing box. Little snap audible. Then opens it, looks inside and stares very hard at CONJUROR.

CONJUROR. Swept and garnished! Swept but not garnished!

KLAUS. Completely erased! No that's not it. I'm pretty sure this surface hasn't been rubbed. This must be another box. But I had it in my hands here, all the time.

CONJUROR. It is the same box, and the same surface.

KLAUS. But surfaces aren't as simple as you think they are! They are more like clouds you walk into. It may look like a wall but it isn't. Some of my graphite ought to be here still. But I don't see any trace of it. This must be another box.

CONJUROR.
No. That isn't the answer.

KLAUS.
You don't see what a question this brings up;
The limits of a volume. The geometry of it's fearful.
You say that everything *inside* vanishes. But
What's inside? It's like all the Welsh in Liverpool
Absconding along with the Welsh in Wales. Too funny!
And when does this vanishing happen? When the lid
Snaps to, or as it opens, or sometime in between?

CONJUROR.
It might not be instantaneous, might be gradual.
That would take some of the strain off the box.

KLAUS.
You haven't found anything half-gone, have you?
I'd like to see what my dollar bill, half-gone, looks like!
Besides we ought to hear air oozing into the vacuum.

Listening.

O, it's all nonsense. I'm going bats myself.
If I had this box in my lab I'd weigh it
Open, with a gram weight in it, and then shut,
With the weight vanished. We'd photograph
This vanishing trick with X-rays. No, it's too much!
It's preposterous. A Leak in the Universe! What a laugh!
I knew very well all along this wouldn't be physics.
Own up! It's the cleverest thing I've ever heard of!
How do you do it?

253

CONJUROR.

> I don't do it. The box does it. I don't know how.

KLAUS.

> But I thought you knew all there is to know
> About the conjuring world.

CONJUROR.

> This isn't conjuring.

KLAUS.

> O, so somebody has got ahead of you, has he?
> Conjuring is an Advancing Study after all, it seems.
> You're been writing away at your *Theory of Illusion,*
> Your *Social Conditions of Observation* and the rest of
>   them
> And not getting out into the field. . . . When you learn
> How it's done, give the man my congratulations, will
>   you?

CONJUROR.

> When you are President of the Royal Society
> Tell them about this, will you?

KLAUS.

> Of course! And don't look so queer. I've seen it happen
> Again and again in Physics: head of the field
> Suddenly says the new stuff won't hold water.
> It only means he hasn't been doing his homework
> Or he's getting old, or something. Cheer up.
> The best of luck. So long!

Exit KLAUS.

CONJUROR.

> You make me see there had to be such a box.

Turning to box.

> But you! Which of my worlds do you fit into?
> The magician's? The Illusionist's? The Wonder-worker's!
> Or the historian's—the historian of illusions?
> My Lord! You've done your work too well on him!

*Bows to the box and goes off and falls on a couch, lying
on it stiff and outstretched.*

254

Won't you swell a bit, if I wait? I'm flexible.
You need not be anything like six feet long!

Crawls across the box, kneeling by it.

I can tuck myself into less space than anyone dreams of.
Houdini taught me and I've improved on him.
A waste-paper basket does for me or a trash can.

Getting on his feet again.

No, no.

Taking up the box gently.

I know! That's not what you are here for.
That wasn't, really, our idea of supernature.
But how much idea of it have we after all?
With all our ideas of it gone now into nothing.
Back into nothingness! Don't I know the art
Of making something, any amount of it, out of nothing?
Why not learn the obverse, round it out!

But is there no one to ask? No one anywhere?
No one to ask about nothing? No one?
Perhaps I do know such a no-one.

Takes up telephone and dials.

May I speak to Mrs. Nemo?
O, that you, Mary?
O, I've been going along as usual.
Are you doing very much just now? Really! Did you?
Would you have time for a little problem of mine?
You may be able to tell me something about a box
    I've picked up—
Just a nice box with something about it.
I'll bring it round.

Scene Two

MRS. NEMO, *the medium, admirably turned out, sleek, blond cover-girl, mannequin type, very beautiful and candid, in a neat modest room. She is sitting in a tall straight-backed arm chair. On a table at her side is a large parrot cage with a silk cloth draped over it. Enter* CONJUROR, *carrying a despatch case.*

MRS. NEMO.

You haven't been very long in coming.

CONJUROR.

I didn't want to lose any time.

MRS. NEMO.

It's something you are pretty serious about?

CONJUROR.

Well, you know me, Mary, I'm curious.

MRS. NEMO.

That's just what you are! You won't leave well alone. But what can I do for you now? It's nothing *physical*, is it?

CONJUROR.

Physical?

MRS. NEMO.

I mean ectoplasm. You are not expecting me to produce something.

CONJUROR.

I'm rather hoping for some information.

MRS. NEMO.

You said something about a box. You don't want me to put something in it, do you?

CONJUROR.

No, not at all!

MRS. NEMO.

Thank goodness. You know, I'm rather suspicious of conjurors.

They are always trying to catch the medium out
And you never know what at! Last time there was a
box. . . .
O it was dreadful. Surgical examinations. You can't
imagine. . . .

CONJUROR.

Stomach pumps and regurgitations!
I don't doubt I can.

MRS. NEMO.

O you! But, you know, what with Captain Nemo being
So much at sea and all that, a girl has to look out.

CONJUROR.

I've often wondered why you go in for the mediumship
business.

MRS. NEMO.

Why, when a person has certain gifts, she ought to
Use them, oughtn't she? And, besides, there is
Helping people, isn't there? I'm going to try to help
you.

CONJUROR.

Thank you. I hope you will.

MRS. NEMO.

And with Captain Nemo away, I think all this business,
As *you* call it, keeps me out of mischief.

CONJUROR.

You mean: "Satan finds some mischief still
                    For idle hands to do!"?

MRS. NEMO.

That's it. But I wasn't thinking of my hands.
I don't do very much with my hands.
I was thinking more of me,
Myself, you know.

CONJUROR.

I do know. Well, here is this box.

MRS. NEMO.

What a beautiful box!

257

CONJUROR.

It is, isn't it?

MRS. NEMO.

What sort of a box is that?

CONJUROR.

I was rather hoping you would be able to tell me.

MRS. NEMO. Well I'll try. But there's something very odd about trances. You never know. They may or they may not. One thing? There's no funny stuff about this box, is there?

CONJUROR. Funny stuff?

MRS. NEMO. The other day they brought me a man's collar to clairvoy and, would you think, it was that man's collar—the one who murdered the six women! I had an awful time.

CONJUROR. You must have had. But there is nothing of that sort about this box, I'm sure.

MRS. NEMO. It doesn't look like a murderer's box, does it? But you can't be certain, can you? They brought me a lovely crystal goblet and it gave me such shakes in my trance that I dropped it.

CONJUROR. Broken?

MRS. NEMO. Uh huh! In a thousand pieces. Such a pity.

CONJUROR. Oh! Do you have to have the thing you are clairvoying—Do you have to have it actually in your hands as you clairvoy it?

MRS. NEMO. Oh no, that isn't necessary. It can be on the table in front of me. And, another thing. You know, don't you, that you mustn't wake me up. Don't, *whatever you do*, wake me up. I mean I must wake up of my own accord. If you wake me, I'll be ill for days. Promise.

CONJUROR. I promise.

MRS. NEMO. And don't go into a trance yourself while you are waiting for the voices to speak! I had that happen, yesterday. It was dreadful. I woke up feeling all washed up (you generally do, you know) and there was my client as stiff as the poker and bleating out the most awful gibberish— in verse it was too. But then he is a poet, so I suppose that's all right?

CONJUROR. Most embarrassing. Who is he?

MRS. NEMO. I oughtn't to tell you. But you don't talk, do you? It was Sir Glendoveer Pearks. He often comes to me for inspiration.

CONJUROR. Does he indeed! How long did this go on for?

MRS. NEMO. Do you know, I had to wake him up. I expect he's feeling pretty poorly now. But I simply had to wake him. I had to go out and I couldn't leave him there raving. He's rather sweet, you know. Do you know what I did? I wanted to wake him up gently. You won't tell anyone, will you? I gave him a kiss and what do you think he did? He snatched up his hat and ran. I thought that rather funny. Don't you?

CONJUROR. Very! You won't find *me* going off into any trances.

MRS. NEMO. I suppose I had better get started. We'll just put the box here. I'll relax and look at it and you just sit quiet and do nothing.

CONJUROR. Can't I take notes?

MRS. NEMO, *putting on a veil.* Oh yes, of course. You may as well. I don't always know what they say till later. A good thing, too, sometimes. . . .

Pause. When the medium speaks again, it is in a man's resonant voice, speaking more and more slowly.

VOICE.
How could I choose,
    Or it choose me,
To save the world
    Or let it be?

259

Black on the cliff-face,
　　Glide the streams;
Seep and ooze
　　From deluding dreams.

Where would he lead them,
　　The baffled king?
Why would they heed *him*
　　In anything?

Tearless, my eyes;
　　Hopeless, my heart.
Is this my place;
　　Was that my part?

Wrying the Load!
　　Am I no friend,
To let all down
　　And make an end?

*Medium stretches, rubs her eyes and starts talking in her
own voice.*

MRS. NEMO. It's a funny thing. I said I didn't usually hear
what the voices said. But I did then. Poetry. What next!
I remember too that chap in the cave. He was proud, proud
as the Devil. He didn't see me. I wasn't there, really, of
course; but he wouldn't have seen me anyhow if I had
been there. He was that sort. Not so much proud, though,
as looking down his nose at everything—himself included.
I've never seen anything like it.

CONJUROR. What was he dressed in?

MRS. NEMO. Something yellow, thick and yellow. But he'd
put it off his shoulders. It was all in folds round his middle.
He had the box in his hands on his lap and his feet tucked
in under him.

CONJUROR. Was the box open or shut?

MRS. NEMO. Shut.

260

CONJUROR. Do you remember how he held it?

MRS. NEMO. Yes, I noticed that. It was so queer. He'd got the backs of his hands towards himself and the box resting on his thumbs, like this.

Picks up the box and sits, on her feet, on the floor with the box so held. Suddenly puts it on a chair and scrambles up.

I don't know why, but I didn't like that. It felt funny.

Gets back in her tall chair.

CONJUROR. What was the cave like?

MRS. NEMO. Just an overhanging rock. It was all open in front—and what a drop! I'd have thought he'd get giddy sitting there so near the edge. I've seen mountains and precipices. Captain Nemo took me down the Gemmi on our honeymoon. But this was something different. I don't believe those mountains are anywhere.

CONJUROR. Perhaps not. The voice didn't seem to think these mountains real either:

O the mind, mind has mountains
Cliffs of fall, frightful, sheer, no man fathomed.

MRS. NEMO. That wasn't what it said.

CONJUROR. I know it wasn't. That was Hopkins.

MRS. NEMO. Oh! Well, it was rather like it. Do you want to hear it again?

CONJUROR. I would indeed. But how?

MRS. NEMO. Perfectly easy. I have it all on tape.

CONJUROR. You have it all on tape?

MRS. NEMO. Yes. I have to. It wouldn't do at all to have these seances without a proper record of what goes on. It's much safer to have the evidence all clear. Sometimes I tell the client beforehand and sometimes I don't. They say mediums in trances are suggestible, you see.

CONJUROR. I do see indeed! But where is the mike?

MRS. NEMO. Here.

Lifts cloth off the parrot's cage.

And I've a switch here under the arm of my chair. I show it you because a Conjuror like you would spot it anyway in no time.

CONJUROR. Well, well, well. . . . What I've missed!

MRS. NEMO. I'll have to wind back.

Stream of high-speed reverse squeakings from the tape. She stops it.

That ought to be about the place.

Switches forwards.

A new voice, strongly Welsh, speaks.

VOICE.

Then voluble and bold, now hid, now seen. . . .
Voluble box, will you do for my center?

CONJUROR. Great Cadwallader! What's this?

MRS. NEMO, *stopping tape.* I wound it back too far. That is Sir Glendoveer in his trance.

CONJUROR. Let's hear a bit more.

MRS. NEMO *winds back and restarts.*

VOICE.

Then voluble and bold, now hid, now seen. . . .
Voluble box will you do for my centre—
That still point all things turn on, all things seek?
That centre lay betwixt
Our Satan's haunches fixt
While all the spheres swept round the shaggy Sleek.

Fallen fallen light renew?
Fallen from Paradise too
Our glassy essence clouded
Beautiful then. . . .
Lifting his brow
Against his Maker
Erect amidst his circling spires
That on the grass floated.

262

Ah, whirling boxwood,
What lash
Sends you spinning hither?
What snake beguiles us now?
What Lethe channels
Wind upward from this cavern?

Pause.

Many times wider
Than any than
Longer beyond measure
Deeper beyond compare
There it was and we were
In the lost and found.

Pause.

CONJUROR.
Keep on still.

VOICE.
Figure upon figure
Echo, reminder.
What is lost but the loss?
What found but the finder?

Shall we start with this box
In the dusk, on the shelf?

Pause and vague noise on tape. MRS. NEMO *switches off and stares at* CONJUROR.

MRS. NEMO. Did you ever? It was talking about your box.

CONJUROR. It seems so.

MRS. NEMO. A pity I woke him up! But it doesn't make much sense, does it?

CONJUROR. I'm not quite sure. It's talking about my box and my box doesn't make much sense either.

MRS. NEMO. It all seems to me to be gibberish.

CONJUROR. It certainly isn't very good. But Sir Glendoveer was in a trance you know. And there are bits in it that don't sound too bad. I'll look into it. I tell you what. I'll make a transcript and a recording and get one of the Institute pundits to do an analysis on it. Will that be all right?

MRS. NEMO. You can do what you like if you won't let on what it is. Don't give me or Sir Glendoveer away.

CONJUROR. I promise. I won't tell a soul. Well, priestess. Thank you very much. You've been most helpful. Given me a lot. Though what it is you've given me I don't know yet. But that's as an oracle should be. Goodbye, Pythoness!

Exit CONJUROR.

264

Scene Three

CONJUROR's *room as before but without the box*. CON-
JUROR *stands with his back to the audience looking out
of the window. Knock at the door.*

CONJUROR. Come in.

Enter PROFESSOR HERMANN ZOCCA *with a bag.*

CONJUROR. This is very good of you to take the time.

ZOCCA. Not at all. I'm really obliged to you for letting me
look into the rubbish. Don't you agree that rubbish can be
much more rewarding than the merely meritorious?

CONJUROR. You remember Chesterton? "Next to authentic
goodness in a work we require a certain rich badness."

ZOCCA. I *don't* remember Chesterton. He was a weakness
of the years before I went to college. Did Chesterton say
that?

CONJUROR. He wrote it somewhere.

ZOCCA. It's not bad at all. "A certain rich badness," that's
just it. I was thinking something of the sort about these
lines as I came across through the garden. They are—as you
no doubt see—a kind of compost heap. I don't want to deny
gardening virtues for compost. I merely mean that these
lines are just decontexed handfuls of the decaying literature
of the past heaped up anyhow. Detached leaves, as it were,
rotting together.

CONJUROR. They seemed to me to have a familiar odor.

ZOCCA. They are a mix-up—by an unscholarly person—of
three of the most familiar texts of European literature—
with touches at two points of something a little different.
I brought round the texts in case you didn't have an *Aeneid*,
a *Divine Comedy*, a *Paradise Lost* and a Blake at hand.
I take it you'd like the details—for diagnostic purposes,
perhaps?

CONJUROR. Just what I do want.

ZOCCA. Very well. May I expound?

CONJUROR. By all means. Pray begin.

ZOCCA *reads verses with immense emphasis and clarity but with no expression and in a fixed sort of chant.*

"Then voluble and bold, now hid, now seen," *Paradise Lost,* Book Nine, line 436

It's Satan approaching Eve before the temptation. He has entered into the serpent, you remember, and here he is on his way to her. "Voluble" is rather an odd word, not very successful here. It doesn't mean, as you might think, "talkative," but something like "spinning."

CONJUROR. Spinning.

ZOCCA. Spinning.

Milton took it from Virgil (*Aeneid,* Book Seven, line 379), and somehow this poetaster has used, in the next line, a mistranslation of Virgil's phrase: "voluble box."

"Voluble box, will you do for my centre?" I won't worry you with the Latin, but *volubile buxum* refers to a top—or rather to Queen Amata who is being sent spinning by the Fury Allecto. *Buxum,* of course, is boxwood. Roman tops were turned from boxwood. I don't know why the writer thought that a box could be a centre. However, he takes it up with a quote from T. S. Eliot in the next line:

"That still point all things turn on, all thinks seek."

CONJUROR. Did you ever notice how *thing* and *think* sound the same?

ZOCCA. The Eliot line is

"At the still point of the turning world"

If I recall aright Eliot uses this phrase "still point" in several places; but you won't want to bother about that. It's just one of the bits of fashionable flotsam and jetsam that our author here would have in mind.

"That all things turn on?" They turn on it because it's the centre of the Universe.

"All things seek." That's Aristotle's or Dante's centre, the point things move toward by gravitation. Now we come to Dante:

"That centre lay betwixt
Our Satan's haunches fixt."

That's an odd way of putting it, but it is the case that, in
the last book of the *Inferno*, that is where the central point
of the universe is to be found. Virgil and Dante have to
pass by it to get out of Hell. They dive in between Satan's
flapping wings. (He's buried to mid-chest, you remember,
in the ice of the bottom ring of Hell) and climb somehow
or other down Satan, hanging onto the hair on him, till
they come—here's the line in the Wickstead version—

"to where the thigh revolves just on the swelling of
the haunch."

I must say it seems an odd place to put the centre of the
universe but then Dante was an odd person.

"While all the spheres swept round the shaggy Sleek"
The spheres revolve on that point and the "shaggy Sleek,"
I suppose, is Satan again. "Sleek" is a word Milton uses of
the tempter. Here are the lines from Dante—

"I caught hold of the hair of the evil Worm which
pierces through the world."

CONJUROR. It is queer! Virgil and Dante crawling like
lice through Satan's pelt, past such a centre!

ZOCCA. That's it. Is this the sort of thing you want?

CONJUROR. Very much so. You know it does sort of fit
together in a way.

ZOCCA. Philosophically, I suppose everything fits together
in a way.

CONJUROR. O! No, no, no, not *that* way. Just as plain
information.

ZOCCA. I'm glad it seems so to you. It's a matter of taste.
I'm only identifying the ingredients in the cocktail. I drink
wine myself.

CONJUROR. You are very wise. Well, what comes next?

ZOCCA. A bit of Blake:

"Fallen, fallen light renew"

267

CONJUROR. Of course, that's from his "Hear the Voice of the Bard."

Taking up and opening the Blake. Reads.

Hear the Voice of the Bard!
Who Present, Past and Future, sees;
Whose ears have heard
The Holy Word
That walked among the ancient trees.
Calling the Lapsed Soul,
And weeping in the evening dew;
That might control
The starry pole
And fallen, fallen light renew!

ZOCCA. You can please yourself whether it is the *Voice of the Bard*, or the *Holy Word* or the *dew* which does the controlling!

CONJUROR. I suppose there might be some connection between the starry pole and the still point? And the restoring of Satan to his former brightness?

ZOCCA. There might if you wanted enough to make one.

CONJUROR. How do you read the next line:
"Fallen from Paradise too."
Has Satan had two falls? Fallen from Paradise as well as from Heaven? You remember he very nearly got converted by the sight of Eve in her garden.

ZOCCA. Aren't you exaggerating a little?

CONJUROR. On the other hand there is Isaiah, isn't there?
"How art thou fallen from Heaven, O Lucifer, son of the morning!"

ZOCCA. But *that*, you should know, has nothing whatever to do with Satan. It's about the conquest of Babylon by Cyrus.

CONJUROR. Maybe, maybe: but it talks to me about Satan.

ZOCCA. Well now, to get on . . .
"Beautiful then . . .

268

Lifting his brow
Against his Maker"
That's the last book of the *Inferno* again, lines 34-36.
   "If he was once as beautiful as he is ugly now
   And lifted up his brow against his Maker
   Well may all affliction stem from him."

CONJUROR.
   Well may all affliction stem from him.
   The rot set in at the top.

ZOCCA. Eh? I beg your pardon?

CONJUROR. That is why it is so deadly.

ZOCCA. I don't follow you.

CONJUROR. Lilies that fester smell far worse than weeds.

ZOCCA. Do they? Anyhow there aren't any lilies in this compost heap.

CONJUROR. No Shakespeare?

ZOCCA. I don't think so: but there is some more Milton:
   "Erect amid his circling spires
   That on the grass floated"

CONJUROR. "Erect amid*st*" Milton had it. Makes it more snakey, doesn't it?

ZOCCA. It's possible. "Spire" is an obsolete word for a coil.

CONJUROR. Thank you.

ZOCCA. Now we go back to the *Aeneid*. Same passage. Our author has just lighted on three passages which have some sort of common theme and mixed them. Much too easy a way of composing.

CONJUROR. But what's happening there in the *Aeneid*?

ZOCCA. There is a war being started. An unnecessary war. Aeneas and Latinus are going to get on perfectly together, but suddenly Juno set on the Fury, Allecto, to stir up a war. Like whipping a top. Of course, it doesn't make any difference. It all comes right in the end. What it mainly does is drag out the action . . . add the second half, the last six books, to the *Aeneid*.

269

CONJUROR. I see. What's this Lethe doing here?

ZOCCA. O, Virgil and Dante climb on up to Purgatory through a long kind of cave or tunnel worn out by a rivulet. Somewhere in the *Purgatorio* this stream is called Lethe.

I suppose Dante must have visited a limestone cave sometime, been down a pothole.

CONJUROR. Why of course, I forgot, you are a potholer, aren't you?

ZOCCA, *getting up.* I'm very fond of exploring caverns. It's the analog, I often think, of literary studies.

Starts packing his books into his bag.

CONJUROR. I wouldn't have dared say that. Well I'm more grateful than I can say.

ZOCCA, *with the* Iliad *in his hand.* Oh, but we nearly forgot the other verses.

Opens the Iliad *where there is a sheet of paper in it.*

Derivative slop again, of course. What was that in *Anna Livia Plurabelle?* "A side strain from the main drain." That's about it! The second and third verses here are out of the *Iliad.* It's from the opening of Book Nine. Agememnon, you recall, has about lost the war and he tells the Greek host so. Here it is: "And Agamemnon stood up weeping like unto a fountain of dark water that from a beetling cliff poureth down its black stream." I suppose the speaker here might be Achilles, who thinks a few pages later (very out of character it is) of giving up the whole thing.

CONJUROR. That's interesting too. Well thank you again!

ZOCCA. Only too glad. What's the point of this Institute if we can't all put our special knowledge at one another's disposal?

CONJUROR. I can't think you'll ever want any of my stuff? However. . . .

ZOCCA. You never know, do you? Anything I can do. Any time?

Exit.

I. A. Richards

CONJUROR, *looking at the closing door.*

How our achievements mock us!

Opens a drawer and takes out the box.

Where does this thing lead now?
That it should come to me, this . . . box. The one man
Who could be sure it had no Quies by it.
That I should take it to the Nemo and be given
These two voices

To box.

What are you trying to do?
And why with me? Why try to suck me down?
Zocca, of course, and Klaus too, for that matter,
They are far enough down, spinning away,
Fast enough caught in the throat of the vortex already,
Gone most of the way to nonentity on their own,
And proud of it! You need not bother with them!
But me? Why come after me?
The voices don't say what you're up to—
But let's hear them again!

*Puts box back in drawer which he locks. Looks ironically
at key and pockets it. Switches on tape.*

TAPE.

How could I choose,
   Or it choose me,
To save the world
   Or let it be?

Black on the cliff-face
   Glide the streams:
Seep and ooze
   From deluding dreams.

Where would he lead them,
   The baffled king?
Why would they heed *him*
   In anything?

Tearless, my eyes:
  Hopeless, my heart.
Is this my place;
  Was that my part?

Wrying the Load.
  Am I no friend,
To let all down
  And make an end?

CONJUROR.

"Let all down"?
Why should I . . . and how?

Holds the box on top of his head in both hands.

That's him, himself, maybe?
What follows is a more oblique description
I wish I knew where from?

Tape repeats.

TAPE.

Then voluble and bold, now hid, now seen. . . .
Voluble box will you do for my centre—
That still point all things turn on, all things seek?
That centre lay betwixt
Our Satan's haunches fixt
While all the spheres swept round the shaggy Sleek.

Fallen fallen light renew?
Fallen from Paradise too
Our glassy essence clouded
Beautiful then. . . .
Lifting his brow
Against his Maker,
Erect amidst his circling spires
That on the grass floated.

Ah, whirling boxwood,
What lash

Sends you spinning hither?
What snake beguiles us now?
What Lethe channels
Wind upward from this cavern?

CONJUROR. "Cavern" indeed. I must say I feel a bit near the edge. What was it Nemo said? "You'd think he'd get giddy sitting there so near it"—the giddy verge. Giddy! I suppose I am that? Voluble top, indeed! Why should a thing of this size come after *me?* Am *I* fit to cope with miracles? Maybe you are though! As a miracle yourself think nothing alien to you but the natural.

Knock at door. CONJUROR *jumps violently, stares as if anything might enter.*

CONJUROR. Come in!

Enter BALTSCHIEDER KLAUS *looking worried.*

KLAUS. I thought you'd like to have my report from the Lab.

CONJUROR. From the Lab? Er. Oh! Yes?

KLAUS. There is something very remarkable. . . .

CONJUROR. Is there?

KLAUS. By the way, we are alone, aren't we?

CONJUROR. There's no one within earshot.

KLAUS. You have the box, haven't you?

CONJUROR. The box! O you're quite safe; it can't overhear you. And I don't suppose it understands English. Besides it doesn't need to. It can read thoughts, I'm sure.

KLAUS. Where is it?

CONJUROR. It's safe. In fact, it's in a safe deposit.

KLAUS. That's a wise precaution, because actually it may be very important to physics.

CONJUROR. To physics? It belongs to physics now does it? I thought it was only a conjuring gadget.

KLAUS. Let me tell you. . . . Those photographs you let us take. . . .

273

CONJUROR. Yes?

KLAUS. They are disturbing. I might say they are crucial.

CONJUROR. O?

KLAUS. Though, of course, it's just about what we would have expected.

CONJUROR. What is?

KLAUS. Why, the result. It is a new confirmation of one of the most fundamental conventions of modern physics: the equivalence of matter and energy.

CONJUROR. You mean you didn't get a photo?

KLAUS, *with some emphasis.* I mean that the energy of the X-rays disappears just as my dollar bill did.

CONJUROR. And the result's a blank!

KLAUS. It's a very positive result indeed. And it confirms my other results perfectly. The loss of weight, the magnetic and radiation results and others.

CONJUROR. I didn't know you'd done so much on it.

KLAUS. I've almost enough—perhaps I've got quite enough —for a paper! It will be rather nice to do something for the Institute. Bit of luck, the box turning up here. To tell you the truth, people don't think what they did of the Institute. There's an impression that too many of the people here aren't *really* first class. Advertisers and stick-in-the-muds. Got fixed ideas and closed minds and all that. This will do the Institute a lot of good.

CONJUROR. On the other hand it could do it quite a lot of damage.

KLAUS. You mean. . . .

CONJUROR. If the box really weren't what you now think it is.

KLAUS. I don't make you out. You seem to have a very unusual attitude to research. Altogether, I suppose you are mixed up with a lot of rather shady people in your field. . . .

274

CONJUROR. O yes.

KLAUS. Ambiguous situations and all that?

CONJUROR. Very.

KLAUS. If you don't mind my saying so, you are being a bit ambiguous yourself.

CONJUROR. I grant that. I can't help it.

KLAUS. You can't help it. But it's so very different from the scientific spirit, and indeed the spirit of the Institute as a whole.

CONJUROR. I can't help that either. You see, it's the box. I'm acting for the box.

KLAUS. The box belongs to science. It's most important that it should be properly investigated.

CONJUROR. Of course I agree to the last. But as to its belonging to science, if you mean that literally, I'm afraid I regard myself as its keeper.

KLAUS. Is that really the position you are going to take?

CONJUROR. For the time being at any rate. And if I were you, Klaus, I'd dump that paper and those photos in the waste-paper basket. The box could be the very devil.

KLAUS. So, you've found out how it's done, have you—what you didn't know before—unless you were deceiving me?

CONJUROR. I wasn't deceiving you. I do know rather more now. There is more to the box than physics.

KLAUS. Can there be?

CONJUROR. An ideal physics someday might reach everything. I'm not denying it. But meanwhile, Klaus, the box won't help contemporary research. I can't explain, but I do know just enough to be sure of that.

KLAUS. That's your last word, I take it?

CONJUROR. Almost. The last word might be this: in the narrow sense of trick, the box isn't a trick; but it *is* in the biggest. I don't want it to betray you. So you'd do best to think of it as a trick—a trick you escaped.

KLAUS. I'm glad to hear you say that. In fact I'm very much relieved! Do you know I had begun to wonder if we might not have political problems to face. Headlines! ANNIHILATOR IN OUR MIDST. NEW THREAT FROM SCIENCE. "Is the government aware that a secret device, an annihilator, is at present located next door to a vital strategic centre?" Can't you hear them? But I've been sure there was something wrong somewhere. Really there are things which are unthinkable. The questions we've been putting about that box really were, you know, unthinkable! Unthinkable! As Forte-piano pointed out, you remember: we can't think of nothing. The concept doesn't occur. Therefore, the whole thing was nonsense. It's good you've come round to that.

CONJUROR. I'm not sure I have. "X has pointed out" usually means: "Just now for some funny reason I feel like agreeing with X" and funny probably means phony. However. . . .

KLAUS. Let's drop it, then! By all means! I believe I'd say "Thank you very much!" if I knew what for.

Exit.

CONJUROR *goes meditatively to his desk, unlocks the drawer, takes out the box, looks at it for a little and then puts it in his despatch case. Then takes up telephone and dials Operator.*

CONJUROR. Operator! Will you suspend service from now on? Have me disconnected. I just haven't a telephone any longer. No calls whatever. Yes, that's right.

Puts telephone down.

Now for the moral issues. I don't want it to betray me either.

Scene Four

Another room at the Institute. PROFESSOR OMORI, *a little old Japanese in a black robe, is sitting beside a card table with four candles on it, the only lighting of the room.* CONJUROR *sits opposite him. The box on the table between them.*

OMORI.

Yes, candles only still, though my eyes are old;
I need the shadows to see by. Too much light's
Like too much noise.

CONJUROR.

Like being run by others?

OMORI.

Like any insistence. This toy of yours
Smells to me like an overweening bit of insistence
From one of the world's most willful. At the same
   time, it
Might be like many rebellions. This teaser of yours
Might be, you know, some sort of a cosmic joke
None the worse for being somewhat fearsome.
And the man who made it might not have known it
   was so.
It could well be a joke on him.

CONJUROR.

The man who made it? Can you go beyond him?

OMORI.

Don't we always?

CONJUROR.

But do we know, then, where we are going?

OMORI.

We don't, but something else may, maybe the same
That asked that question in you. *That* could know that.

CONJUROR.

How many of these interior experts have I?

OMORI.

I wouldn't try to count them. Who'd be counting?

CONJUROR.

This man who made the box, what was he?

OMORI.

Not was but is. He is the box you know.
The artist is his work. He has put himself and his power
    in it.
But he's Achilles too. He's the same thing:
Again and again, whenever, wherever, it comes.
Achilles suddenly seeing what war is and wanting
To be done with it.
Anyone wanting a divorce, or a death, or a war, or
Anything else to be out of it all forever,
Anyone looking for a way out, a forever.
But the contriver of THIS
Let's call him a Waker, someone who has started
Out from the dreaming we call living, and gained
Some of the Waker's powers. The WAKE, you know,
The fully enlightened Buddha, has or is ALL.

CONJUROR.

I've read so, but I need to wake myself
Before I take that in. But this one
Was, or is, if you like, no Buddha?

OMORI.

As your Satan, your Prometheus, is no Christ.

CONJUROR.

A rebel?

OMORI.

The Rebel. Or, as the voices said, *The Serpent.*

CONJUROR.

Voices are rather like anonymous letters;
We needn't take them too seriously.

OMORI.

And yet we do. They have oracular status:
As though not having an author gave them authority.

278

Still, it's not what the voices said about this
But what it does that makes us shiver.

Pointing to the box.

CONJUROR.

Yes, but apart from tricks what does it do?

OMORI.

It teaches.

CONJUROR.

But what is its teaching?

OMORI.

Like all the greatest.

CONJUROR.

What does it teach?

OMORI.

You cannot say. And yet. . . .

CONJUROR.

It changes us.

OMORI.

We wake a little.

CONJUROR.

But if the teaching is poison. . . .

OMORI.

This is. No doubt of it! It is *The* poison.
It would, if it could, put its end to everything.

CONJUROR.

Yes, I see that.

OMORI.

But does it?

CONJUROR.

I don't know yet.

OMORI.

Not, of course, the evanishment of sundry oddments
But the analog in you: your hopes and wishes?
Does it make you want to drop all of them into the box

Along with all you ever wrote or thought or did?
And then hop in along with them to be together?

CONJUROR.

I don't know yet. What does it do to you?

OMORI.

It makes me want to giggle. Ah, the contrast
Between the design and the outcome! Between what
   he meant
And what he has done. That's why I called it a joke.
Not his joke but a joke on him.

CONJUROR.

He meant to kill?

OMORI.

And brought to life!

CONJUROR.

Not seldom. . . .
"The way down is the way up." We make it up:
Why shouldn't we unmake it? My Nobel Prize winner
Complained of ambiguity. . . . Where are we?

OMORI.

Near the heart of it. Our teacher:
Let's say he simply took this box and taught it
This trick we can't conceive.

CONJUROR.

Or we conceive it
In too many ways and cannot choose between them!

OMORI.

It's still a cannot!

CONJUROR.

And yet an invitation: the kind of invitation
The magnet offers to the filings. Sometimes, I think. . . .
I think I see how it works.
Maybe no more
Than a little switch of attention, a lifted stress
A break in a circuit, a shift of love . . . and then
I think I too see how to do it.

OMORI.
> And feel like doing it?

CONJUROR.
> Like shutting up the whole shop!

OMORI.
> What will you do then. Open a new station
> In the Underground? *Nihilist's Haven.*
> I can think of some fancy posters,
> And quotes too:
> *Vestigia nulla retrorsum! Ne plus ultra!*
> "Ah Love! Could you and I with Him conspire
> To grasp this sorry scheme of things entire
>   Would we not shatter it to bits. . . ."

Pointing to box.

> Did you ever notice who the HIM is
> In that bit of Fitzgerald?
> It's HIM.
> But there's no "Then" for HIM—no "Then
> Remold it nearer to the heart's desire!"

CONJUROR.
> No! We'd be putting an end to the show for good!

OMORI. And stay on behind knowing you'd done that?

CONJUROR.
> I think I'm somewhat used to that already.
> It's the magician's, the illusionist's, predicament.
> And I wasn't, as a psychologist, born yesterday.
> What between the behaviorists and the scholars
> We've spirited a good deal away in our time too.
> But not the craving to push on out through the dream
>   wrack
> Into the unlivable void.

OMORI, *pointing to box.* Look at it now, I think it's smiling!

Box has opened a little. CONJUROR *and* OMORI *nod at one another.*

CONJUROR.

> You see what I see. That's all it does though.
> I've sometimes thought it's its way of saying "SHUT UP."

Puts his left hand out to OMORI *who takes it. Then with his right hand shuts the box.*

> I'm happier when it's shut somehow. It has less of a pull then.
> Do you feel that?

OMORI.

> It's why we sit here talking on about nothing!
> I'm not underrating the hurl and spin of the vortex.

CONJUROR.

> I think to get it he gave up the other modes of action
> The words, the miracles, the other symbols.
> The loss piles up the urge behind the searching:
> The trough sucks on the wave.

OMORI.

> And this was costly.

CONJUROR.

> Another San Graal!

OMORI.

> The obverse. For that had ALL to offer
> And this has. . . .

CONJUROR.

> NOTHING. *Nothing*, Nothing, nothing, nothing.

OMORI.

> How pathetically like a bottle of gin!
> What an ambition! What a way of becoming the ALL!

CONJUROR.

> What a sacrifice though, too! The box itself would be left in being.

OMORI.

> We called it a learner. Couldn't it learn. . . .

282

CONJUROR.

    The trick it teaches? "Physician heal thyself.
    He saved others; himself he could not save."
    What do you think? There are plenty of sick doctors
    Killing themselves to keep other people alive,
    This vanishing business would be just the opposite.

OMORI.

    The box is a sort of sketch, I take it.

CONJUROR.

    A sketch?

OMORI.

    A sketch, a diagram, an active symbol.
    And what it stands for. . . .

CONJUROR.

    What does it stand for?

OMORI.

    You remember there are two sorts of Buddhas:
    Those that enter at once into Nirvana
    And others who forgo, who wait without
    Till each least wandering ant shall have found its
        freedom
    Turning the power from their renouncement on us.

CONJUROR.

    The box is a renouncer too. It waits.

OMORI.

    Waits as a symbol for all the world to pass
    Out through its gateway.

CONJUROR.

    Saved from being.

OMORI.

    From being.

CONJUROR.

    Meanwhile, the world endures. And if it cries,
    Cries out in languages beyond our hearing.

Only the new-born, as it first draws breath,
Cries out loud what we know about this being.

OMORI.

That's what the box would say. Are you its prophet?
Maybe we'd do well to watch out?

CONJUROR.

What? You too?

OMORI *nods.*

OMORI.

There is such a thing as possession. You're not **Mrs.
Nemo.**

Pause. CONJUROR *walks about.*

Maybe the Buddha had a pun in mind
In the command: "Seek nothing—to gain all."
To seek nothing for nothing's sake is heresy.
Contempt, disdain, a pride outdoing Satan's,
Annihilation masking as Nirvana.
Simpler and in some moods much more alluring.
To say Nirvana is a way of living
Is false, is ignorance: but to make it *Ceasing*
Is worse; the worst: knowledge destroying itself.
Knowledge consuming knowledge.

CONJUROR.

Cannibalism, in fact
Like that munching thing in Dante.
So this is the Ultimate Rebel?

OMORI.

Yes, it's the Arch-fiend, all right, for Buddhism.
Yet, who'd think it. It seems such a pretty toy.

CONJUROR.

Toy!

OMORI.

You miss your watch, no doubt.
A toy, a joke. . . .

284

CONJUROR.

    Can I ask you a really naïve and innocent question?

OMORI.

    Don't I know them!

CONJUROR.

    They are not too easy to ask either
    But how far do you go, yourself, along with the box
    Don't you want to puncture the balloon as much **as**
      it does?

OMORI.

    The balloon?

CONJUROR.

    Yes, the great round bag of illusion
    This smoothy of a universe we ride in.

OMORI.

    A balloon, yes, it is, but one of Montgolfier's sort
    Kept up by hot air from a fire we have burning
    A fire we won't put out. This fellow here,

Tapping the box gently.

    This rebel, wants to set the whole affair alight
    And go out in a rushing downfall.

CONJUROR.

    Whereas you?

OMORI.

    We try to put the fire out. Cool our hearts
    Too low to go on burning.

CONJUROR, *shouting.*

    You've no more use
    For the balloon, for BEING itself, than we have!

OMORI.

    O but we have! It's our perch while we go on trying
    To cool down. Rebelling is only raging, only casting
    Another armful of straw on the old, old fire.

Telephone rings, off.

285

CONJUROR.
Damn!

OMORI.
May I?
Goes out.

CONJUROR, *walking up and down impatiently.*
Why should it linger. . . . Why not, if there's a way—
And there is, I see it, thanks be to the Box, I see it—
Why not pull that switch . . . and let it,
With every star in every galaxy, go right out.
And be alone without? Why I'm that already!

OMORI, *returning.*
It's your Mrs. Nemo. She wants to talk to you
It sounds terribly like a message from our impatient
friend.

CONJUROR *goes out.*

OMORI, *to box.*
A warning? A threat?
A sort of an ultimatum is it?

286

CONJUROR, *coming back with a slip of paper in his hand.* It's a bit startling. I must say I understand Mary Nemo's agitation. Nuisance for her in a way. To have a seance burst in on in this sort of fashion. However, she isn't as frail as she looks!

OMORI. What happened?

CONJUROR. She says she was trying to help her client (I think it's Sir Glendoveer back again) when suddenly a voice spoke through her: not a nice sort of voice. She gave it to me from the tape. Wouldn't say it herself—not her waking self. Here you are!

Offers OMORI *the paper to look at. Both regard it.*

OMORI. Ahem! Here we are, as you say! I don't blame her for not wanting to read *that* out. Lucky she had the tape. What happened to the client?

CONJUROR. She thinks he's left for the Continent. Awful nuisance for her, poor girl. I wouldn't want to say it out aloud myself for that matter either. Still, here we have it.

Puts slip down on the table. Both turn, first CONJUROR, *then* OMORI, *to regard the box.*

Who would have thought it?

OMORI. "Tell that what's its name and that other such and such what's coming to them." Isn't that about the substance?

CONJUROR.
    Not very diplomatic. Vain, hateful, cruel, disappointed,
    Devilish: "As beautiful then as he is ugly now
    Well may all affliction stem from him."
    Just at the moment when we were giving it
    Such sympathetic consideration. . . .

OMORI.
    Probably *that* was what did it.
    We were cooling down.

CONJUROR.

But that wasn't what it planned on.
And it flew off its handle. But you were saying
When the telephone went?

OMORI.

Something about getting heated. . . . O yes, I was saying
Our disdainful friend here wants to send it all to blazes
His disdain can't disdain itself
Has to become a parody or antic.

Taking up slip of paper again.

Funny what a risk perdition is to taste!
Sad, isn't it, how devils do deteriorate.

CONJUROR.

Mary Nemo saw him as looking down his nose.
Looking down into that gulf he sat so near to
Sitting the nearer to make himself more giddy,
To lose more of the hold of being, narrow his front
To the volumeless, frictionless line and slip it out
Of the interplay, the entanglement, the grip of being.
Don't you Buddhists want to escape Karma?

OMORI.

Escape . . . ? Yes. But through Karma, not against it;
Not by evasion; by acquiescence
By so perfect an acceptance it can accept itself.
The comprehending, the glassy essence pure, is com-
    prehended.
Where all through all attain: there is Nirvana.

CONJUROR.

How pathetically like the perfect stew.

OMORI.

I don't say NO. It's the ultimate concoction.

CONJUROR.

You cook it up, do you?

OMORI.

Do I? What am I?

I. A. Richards

CONJUROR.
This rebel here who has such ways to tempt us. . . .

OMORI.
He aims to let all the universe abscond.

CONJUROR.
It's odd you use that word. My Nobel Prize winner,
Klaus,
He used it too.

OMORI.
He had the same feeling.
Physics is a limited, simplified Karma.

CONJUROR.
But my physicist not only hated the box
He disbelieved it.

OMORI.
Sacerdotalist! Now you and I. . . .

CONJUROR.
Can't believe or disbelieve?

OMORI.
Don't sort our thoughts that way: blacks and whites,
Aryans and non-Aryans; as though ideas had skins
Brand marks, shibboleths, criteria!
Being a yellow man myself, I notice
The politics, the salesmanship of "race."
But this conjuror's trick: "Do you believe or not?"
When it isn't at all the same as: "Will you, won't you?"
Is dirtier still. Eh! Fellow Conjuror?

CONJUROR.
I'd as lief agree. Like many another
I took up conjuring to expose mediumship.
I wanted to know *just what was being done*.
You know (only too well) where that must land you.
And then the art of seeming not to be doing it
Carried me off and left me where I am,
Specialist in the pathology of misbelievings

289

Discreditable priest to flocks of displaced believers.
Believing is a kind of plague, a smallpox;
I used to pretend that conjuring was vaccination.

OMORI.

You don't any more.

CONJUROR.

I don't dare to, and this seems to have clinched it.

OMORI.

But what do you *want* to do to our adversary?

CONJUROR.

What can I do? Hand him over to Klaus?
I think I know why I'm not going to do that.
Put him in a real safe deposit? Sink him, say,
Thirty thousand feet down in the Mindanao Deep?
Post him to the Dalai Lama, or the Nishi Hongwanji?
Present him, would you think, to the Buddhist Society,
 London?
Install him in my kitchen as a super-disposall?
Or go straight to work, take a risk and burn him?
I've thought of the last a good deal. What do *you* say?

OMORI.

It's traditional treatment for heretics.

CONJUROR.

It's that that stops me. I'm no Torquemada.
It's out of my role.

OMORI.

Why must you do anything?

CONJUROR.

Well, what with Klaus' lab a-gabble
The story will be all over the Institute already,
And that means everywhere in half an hour,
Now that Klaus hasn't his paper to hush him!
Can you blame them? I don't mind betting
My telephone would be going whole time, if I hadn't
 cut it.

And how to sit still and go on quietly working,
Or what my work from now on is I don't know.

OMORI.

You're a long way yet from being finished.
You are still on fire though this superior fiend
Has cut off some of the draft! He didn't mean to.
He planned—don't laugh—to inflame us with despair.

CONJUROR.

"Somewhere there nothing is, and there lost man
Must find what changeless vague of peace he can."

OMORI.

More of Sir Glendoveer?

CONJUROR.

No. Walter de la Mare.
"Somewhere there nothing is, and there lost man
Must find what changeless vague of peace he can."

OMORI.

That was the line and—well, it isn't working!

CONJUROR.

Just the opposite.

OMORI.

The silence deafens: the heresy's lending
Powerful aid toward the orthodox outcome.

CONJUROR.

What do *you* think I should do?

OMORI.

The thing may not really be in your hands.
The box didn't come to you, of all people, for nothing,
And what has been happening won't have been un-
remarked.

CONJUROR.

You mean that Fido here will have been drawing
conclusions?

OMORI.

Wouldn't you, in his place? Have you thought

That this box has floated down the centuries remark-
ably well.
This peculiar sheen on it comes from a thousand
Years at least of incense smoke. It has probably got
A snug enough temple somewhere to go back to.

Stroking it with his hand.

Everything suggests that it knows how to look after
itself.

CONJUROR.
So if we offered it violence . . . ?

OMORI.
It wouldn't wait.

The box vanishes.

CONJUROR.
Ha! gone!

OMORI.
Listen.

Sounds of wind off.

CONJUROR.
Conjuror!

OMORI.
Exorcist!
You look downcast. Why?

CONJUROR.
I'm going to miss it.

OMORI.
I shouldn't wonder.

CONJUROR.
You don't suppose it would come back again, do you?

OMORI.
No, no! It is much too tactful
Except when it loses its temper.
It tried it on and didn't pull it off—
It knows when it's beaten.

292

I. A. Richards

CONJUROR.

No, no! That isn't the answer! *Neti, neti!*
That wasn't why it came or why it went.

To audience.

I knew this earlier, but I forgot it.
Those voices put me off. I didn't see
The company I'd be keeping if I listened.
Now that it's gone I learn at last what it may be.
I thought it was teaching me how to vanish the cosmos,
When it was only showing me how to remember myself.
Whatever does that is due to be . . . vilified.

Yes, I'll miss it.
Giver and Ender
Returned now into the Gulf:
Shut down now on itself.

We have had our reminder.
The play is over.
Over or under? Over *and* under
What is lost but the loss?
What found but the finder?

PRODUCTION INTELLIGENCE

THE DEATH OF ODYSSEUS

by LIONEL ABEL

The Death of Odysseus was first produced by John Bernard Myers in association with The Artist's Theatre at the Amato Opera Theatre in New York on November 3, 1953 with Herbert Machiz as director and scene designer, lighting by Mildred Jackson, and costumes by Bernard Oshei.

CAST

ODYSSEUS	Jay Barney
CAPTAIN	Richard Towers
DESERTER	Joseph Raymond
TELEMACHUS	Robert Jacquin
PENELOPE	Sylvia Stone
SOLDIERS	Sam Stewart
	Guy Mayor

"A rather French play with old Odysseus in the role of *raisonneur,* very magnetic, very witty, worldly, candid and philosophical . . . (a) wonderfully intelligent and charming play."

Saul Bellow, *The Partisan Review*

"The best writing of the season so far; a more than competent production." Eric Bentley, *The New Republic*

"The quality of the writing is high throughout . . . a play which should be seen by a larger audience than the limited runs of The Artist's Theatre can accomplish."

Henry Hewes, *The Saturday Review*

LIONEL ABEL was born in New York in 1910. He attended St. John's College in Brooklyn and the University of North Carolina. He has translated, among other things, Sartre's plays, Camille Pissarro's *Letters,* and Apollinaire's *The Cubist Painters.* His poetry and criticism have appeared in *The Nation, Poetry, The Partisan Review, Spearhead, View,* and *Deucalion.* Mr. Abel's book, *Some Poems of Rimbaud,* was published by Exile's Press in 1940. His first play, in verse, *The Bow and the Gun,* appeared in *Possibilities,* in 1947, and *Absalom,* a full-length play, is being readied for production.

THE TICKLISH ACROBAT

by ROBERT HIVNOR

The Ticklish Acrobat was first produced by John Bernard Myers in association with The Artist's Theatre at the Amato Opera Theatre in New York on March 8, 1954. It was directed by Herbert Machiz; settings were by Julian Beck, costumes by Bernard Oshei, lighting by Richard Jackson; and the incidental music was contributed by Sarah Sumner. John Robertson was stage manager.

CAST

ELLIE SPROCKET	Patricia Ripley
GORJO	Peter Coury
BROTHER ZUGO	Frank Dana
MOMMA ZUGO	Jennie Lawrence
MME. HURABI	Iris O'Connor
UNCLE HENRY	Irwin Charone
BABA	Carolyn Brenner
JOE ZANELLI	Tige Andrews
BASSETT PRATT	Jack Cannon
BOMOGRICA	Joseph Brownstone
ANNA ZUGO	June Hunt
DR. SUFI	Walter Gorney
PAPA ZUGO	Robert Raymond

"Mr. Hivnor . . . is the real thing, a writer."
Saul Bellow, *The Partisan Review*

". . . a work of the deepest charm and imaginative distinction: . . . an illustrious example of what richness the specifically literary mind may yet bring to the most faded . . . of our arts.
". . . demands both publication and another representation."
Richard Hayes, *The Commonweal*

ROBERT HIVNOR was born in Zanesville, Ohio. After serving with the Army in World War II, he taught at the University of Minnesota and Reed College; he is married and the father of two children. His comedy *Too Many Thumbs* was produced at the Cherry Lane Theater in New York and the Watergate Theatre in London.

THE IMMORTAL HUSBAND
by JAMES MERRILL

The Immortal Husband was first produced by John Bernard Myers in association with The Artist's Theatre at the Theater de Lys in New York on February 14, 1955. The production was directed by Herbert Machiz; settings and costumes were designed by Richard V. Hare; lighting was by Peggy Clark; and Gene Perlowin was stage manager.

CAST

MRS. MALLOW, OLGA, NURSE	Jean Ellyn
MAID, FANYA, ENID	Mary Grace Canfield
TITHONUS	William Sheidy
GARDENER, KONSTANTIN, MARK	Scott Merrill
LAOMEDON, MEMNON	Frederick Rolf
AURORA	Anne Meacham

"Mr. Merrill's highly disciplined dialogue is replete with profound comment and quick humor."

Henry Hewes, *The Saturday Review*

"The author appears to be a playwright of major potentialities. He writes with grace, wit, and a sensitive feeling for the spoken word." John Beaufort, *The Christian Science Monitor*

"James Merrill is my favorite young American poet and he has written a play which is pure poetry plus theatre, a rare and magical combination."

Tennessee Williams

"An achieved density of experience wholly rare in the contemporary theater. It is a drama of the most faultlessly wrought texture. . . . It joins that small company of plays . . . with which . . . the American theater must come to terms."

Richard Hayes, *The Commonweal*

JAMES MERRILL was born in New York City. He has traveled extensively and for a short time lived in Rome. In 1951 Alfred Knopf published his *First Poems*, and *Short Stories*, a second book of verse, was published by Banyan Press in 1954. Mr. Merrill's works have appeared in major literary journals both here and abroad. *The Bait*, an earlier play, was produced by The Artist's Theatre in 1953 and was presented by the BBC on its Third Programme in 1955. Mr. Merrill is at present conducting a class in creative writing at Amherst College.

296

TWILIGHT CRANE

by JUNJI KINOSHITA, translated by A. C. SCOTT

JUNJI KINOSHITA was born in Tokyo in 1919. He attended Tokyo University where he received a degree in English literature in 1939.

For several years a leader in the Budo no Kai drama group, Mr. Kinoshita has written both for radio and the stage, and his works include some twenty folk plays, several of them full-length dramas. Among his more important works are *Sparks in the Darkness* (1950) and *The Ascension of a Frog* (1951); but it is especially the continued popularity and high official praise of *Twilight Crane* (*Yuzuru*) which best convey Mr. Kinoshita's importance in the modern Japanese theater.

Modestly produced for the first time in Osaka in 1949 by the Budo no Kai with Yasue Yamamoto in the role of Tsu, it received immediate critical and popular acclaim. In 1950 Mr. Kinoshita was awarded the Mainichi Press Drama Prize; and in 1952, when a major production of *Twilight Crane* was staged at the Shimbashi Embujo in Tokyo, again with Miss Yamamoto, it was received with even greater enthusiasm. *Twilight Crane* has perhaps been given more performances than any other modern Japanese play. It has been presented as an opera and as a Noh play.

Mr. Kinoshita recently visited India and Europe and is at present Professor of Drama at Meiji University in Tokyo.

~

Both a writer and artist, A. C. SCOTT was born in England in 1909.

As an officer of the British Council for Cultural Relations, Mr. Scott went to China after the war where he did research on the Classical Chinese Theater. In 1952 he went to Japan where for two years he worked with the Kabuki-za Theater in Tokyo. It was during this time that he met Junji Kinoshita and became interested in his plays.

At present Mr. Scott is living in Hong Kong where he is doing research at the Institute of Oriental Studies and continuing his English adaptations of Mr. Kinoshita's works.

His book, *The Kabuki Theatre in Japan*, was published by Allen & Unwin Ltd. in England and in the United States by Macmillan in 1955, and his study of the Classical Chinese Theater is in preparation.

A LEAK IN THE UNIVERSE

by I. A. RICHARDS

A Leak in the Universe was first presented in the home of Mr. and Mrs. William James in Cambridge, Massachusetts, on February 25, 1954, by the Poet's Theatre of Cambridge, under the direction of Edward Thommen, with the following cast:

THE CONJURER	Ivor Richards
DR. HERMANN ZOCCA	Neil Powell
DR. BALTSCHIEDER KLAUS	William Morris Hunt
MRS. NEMO	Eustacia Grandin
DR. OMORI	Whitney Haley

~

A Leak in the Universe was also presented on the BBC Third Programme on September 1, 1955. G. D. Bridson was director, and Roberto Gerhard supplied incidental music.

CAST

THE CONJURER	Stephen Murray
DR. BALTSCHIEDER KLAUS	Raymond Huntley
MRS. NEMO	Bettina Dickson
SIR GLENDOVEER PEARKS	Roger Snowdon
DR. HERMANN ZOCCA	Leslie Perrins
DR. OMORI	Carleton Hobbs

I. A. RICHARDS, author of many books about the workings of language (of which he likes *How to Read a Page* best), has spent most of his time at Cambridge University and Harvard, in China and Japan, and on the high Alps and other mountain ranges.